ROOTED2
THE BEST NEW
ARBOREAL NONFICTION

EDITED BY
JOSH MACIVOR-ANDERSEN

Outpost19 | San Francisco
outpost19.com

Published 2023 by Outpost19.

MacIvor-Andersen, Josh
        Rooted 2: The Best New Arboreal Nonfiction / Josh
MacIvor-Andersen
        ISBN 9781944853891 (pbk)

Rooted 2: The Best New Arboreal Nonfiction is the second
in an original anthology series. The initial Rooted anthology
is available in paperback editions from local and online
booksellers.

OUTPOST19

ORIGINAL PROVOCATIVE READING
SAN FRANCISCO | @OUTPOST19

ROOTED2
THE BEST NEW
ARBOREAL NONFICTION

To Kathryn, who crested a hill and
sat with me beneath the trees.

CONTENTS

Foreword | Josh MacIvor-Andersen   i

Introduction | Aimee Nezhukumatathil and
    Ross Gay   iii

Blue Atlas | Steven Church   1

I Know a Tree | Robin Foster   3

Hooters | Laura Girardeau   9

Summer Job | Scott Oglesby   13

Hitching a Ride on a Tree | Eric Sandy   15

Thinning Pines | Richard Holinger   29

Phoenix Forest | Angela Sucich   31

On Burning | Mackenzie Myers Fowler   35

Comfort on the Death of the Ancient Oak |
    Carolyn Williams-Noren   43

The Yew Without the Moon | Steven Harvey   57

Copper Beech | Judy McClure   61

The Bees | Christina Kapp   69

Catalpa Tree -*Catalpa Speciosa* |
    Aimee Nezhukumatathil   75

The Trees in the Air | Amy Boyd   81

Remembering the Wye Oak | Daniel A. Rabuzzi   91

Brief Recognizable Features | Joanna Brichetto   93

Wild Apple | Alexandria Peary   103

The Orange Tree | Kevin Richard Kaiser   123

The *Bosco Sacro* | Meg Muthupandiyan   125

Tamarack | Kit Carlson   135

Faith in a Seed | Andrea Lani   137

I Could Be a Tree | Marianne Jay Erhardt   151

A Herd of Aspen | Lyn Baldwin   155

Branch by Branch | Lydia Gwyn   175

At the Edge of Her Grasp | Brian Braganza   179

Pawpaw Grove | Ross Gay   187

Ginkgo Biloba | Richard Hackler   191

I Have Been Worrying About Space | Julie Lunde 197
To Tell Stories | Henri Bensussen 209
Apple Tree | Emma Williams 211
Oak Tree on Elm Street | Erica Trabold 213
To Grow in Spite of Poison | Kelsey Francis 225
Felled | Sophie Hall 227
Memory Vault | Lynette Vialet 237
The Fruit Will Come | Jennifer Maxon 241
Laying the Willow's Ghost | Laurie Klein 245
Branches | Emily Donaldson 249
Last One Standing | Felicity Fenton 255
Translating Trees | Courtney Amber Kilian 257
Staying with the Destruction |
        Laura M. Cotterman 263
The Power of Placement | Susan Charkes 267
Benadryl Days | Ruth Joffre 273
The Black Spruce | Corinna Cook 277
Into the Light | K Anand Gall 285
Mapping the Understory | Kimberly Willardson 289

Contributors 305
Acknowledgments 318

FOREWORD
JOSH MACIVOR-ANDERSEN

I come to this tree stuff honestly. My early desire to write for an audience beyond my mom (she reads everything!) galvanized while dangling in the humid-slick canopies of Nashville trees, dreaming up essay ideas while wielding a wicked sharp chainsaw. I used to descend to the ground, shrug off my tree gear, and head immediately home to my keyboard. To write what? Tree stories, of course.

But as I mentioned in our first anthology, I'm not that special. I've still never met a person who didn't have at least one story thematically tangled with a tree. It turns out all of us—readers and writers alike—come to this tree stuff honestly.

Some of the stories we tell are journalistic, some highly personal, and some are vehicles for immense literary success. The fact that riveting books on trees have remained readily available at your airport giftshop next to other *New York Times* bestsellers bodes well for our species, I think. And may God bless the big books on trees, the *Hidden* and *Secret Lives,* the *Overstories* and *Legacies of Luna.*

But let's not overlook the profound, often deeply personal literature that populates the pages of journals like *Willow Springs, Plant-Human Quarterly,* or *Whale Road Review,* or the fresh work by both established and emerging writers only now making its way into the world.

This is where the *Rooted* series comes in—a collective home for tree stories, a place where we can celebrate the ways our lives are framed, overlapped, and otherwise entangled with the arboreal.

The tree stories in these pages, then, are really *our* stories. Tales of birth, death, resurrection and reincarnation. Sagas of leaving and returning, of harrowing bravery and crippling fear. Lyric essays about moon trees and space debris, personal narratives braiding the assassination of JFK (on Elm Street!) with the resilience of a relationship and the suffering of surgery. Fruit, both ripe and rotted, bees and blossoms, roots and branches pruned, broken, or holding their own.

Just like us. Just like all of us.

April 2023, Terre Haute, IN

INTRODUCTION
ROSS GAY & AIMEE NEZHUKUMATATHIL

ROSS GAY: Why do you think you love trees, Aimee?

AIMEE NEZHUKUMATATHIL: Oh, this could be a whole book and I still wouldn't be able to narrow it down, right? I think we've talked about this before, when we've written tree poems together, but I feel like my answer is always sliding, changing. Today, I love trees for their verve, their moxie. Just this year (2023), a lychee tree in China—over a thousand years old—popped to life again after locals thought it was dead. And that tree was determined to have been planted in the Tang dynasty! I mean, what?! The tree is about 50 feet tall—as tall as sixteen giant pandas standing on each other's shoulders. No one knows why it erupted with fruit again, why now, but the locals are thrilled the tree is heavily dotted with lychee, offering up hundreds of red husked, ping-pong sized bounty. How about you, Ross? What is it about trees for you?

RG: There's so, so much, but part of it is exactly what you allude to here—some kind of incomprehensible wisdom, or maybe a better word is understanding, or another, *knowing* which, in this case, means the lychee tree's decision to appear dead for a while before coming back to life. For whatever reason a part of me of course wants to know, and another part of me, a part that I'm coming to trust a little bit more, doesn't want to know. That part of me just wants to witness, and wonder, and believe in this knowing of trees.

Which might also be to say that trees, in their unknowable knowing, make me feel grateful. They make *us* feel grateful. For the kindness, the compassion, the generosity and brilliance of shade, food, shelter, beauty, birdsong—how sometimes they look like they're cheering, how sometimes they moan and how sometimes they bark and how sometimes they turn into soil and how sometimes when they seem to be dead they come back to life, and how they always hold in their arms all this life, all this life, and quietly suggest, reluctant as we can be sometimes to heed the trees—who we really need to heed—how we might do the same. Don't you think?

AK: Yes! That gentle holding makes me think of *komorebi*, the Japanese word for the scatter of sunlight peeping through the overhead leaves on the forest floor, a kind of elegant, flickering script that might remind us how it is to be free in the woods. To be able to open your hand to a gift of *komorebi*. To listen for the footsteps of these mucky beauties: Salamander. Cricket. Frog. Mud puddle squelching under your toes. A warbler jumping from limb to limb. I want to talk about learning to saunter, even dawdle in the green. Come sit with me under this water oak. This sugarberry tree. This molave tree. This rainbow eucalyptus. Open your mouth and taste the air. Let your mouth be agog, even, and especially, at night. Agape. *Agape*—which, someone once told me, is the Greek word for the highest, purest form of love. Maybe let's teach ourselves the difference between red maple and sweetgum. Spicebush and sassafras. We think this book can help you with that.

BLUE ATLAS
STEVEN CHURCH

There used to be a tree in our neighbor's yard, lording over our home. A massive, blue-tinted evergreen called a Blue Atlas Cedar. Its limbs spread up and out in a wide fan almost as wide as it was tall—nearly fifty feet I would've guessed. It was a beautiful tree, my wife's favorite. Mine, too, honestly. We'd sit out in the backyard sometimes and stare at it swaying in the breeze, regal and bluish, giant and somehow still dainty, wispy, with the hint of fragility and old age. We both will admit that it was part of what initially sold us on the house. For almost three years, she was our most present neighborhood personality. Hummingbirds darted in and out of her limbs. Crows perched in the higher branches, taunting our dogs. Squirrels squirreled. When the wind blew, her limbs creaked and groaned. And Blue Atlas loomed over our swimming pool, constantly shedding thin inch-long pine-needles that whiskered the water daily. Every day I fished them out with a net attached to a pole. Every day I cared. One night during a rare windstorm in the Valley, I stepped outside and was blasted in the face by a cloud of needles, as if someone had thrown a handful of wet toothpicks at my face. I knew that, tomorrow, I'd have to clean that stuff out of our swimming pool. Still, I loved that tree. It felt like a curmudgeonly old friend, a charmingly grumpy neighbor who tossed her trash over our fence. And I've realized that owning a swimming pool has changed the way I see trees and other things. It has changed my worry meter, adding another line to the gauge, another focus. I worry about the pool and whether it's clean or not. I fuss over it and find myself thinking about my yard in ways that

1

feel new and strange. I worry about pine needles and suicidal earthworms. I worry about small things. And, if I'm being totally honest, there were some days I wished someone would come and trim the big tree back, tame it, control it more, even as I recognized this wish as a new one for me, a wish that is, frankly, contradictory to my values. I love trees. I'd hug them if I felt like they'd return the embrace. So, I'd never imagined I'd be one of those people trying to control the uncontrollable, trying to tame the natural world into something clean and clear and safe. But, Dear Blue Atlas, I know deep down inside the truth is that when that day came and a crew of men in orange shirts with saws came and tore you down, I sat on our back porch and watched them disassemble a queen and I mourned your death. I already missed your mess. I grieved the gift of your omnipresence. So, I held up a glass of beer and toasted your greatness as men with saws scrambled around your limbs, hacking and cutting, reducing you to a stump. It felt as if I was watching a particularly egregious example of misogyny. I hoisted a glass to you. Cheers to your blue. Cheers to your bark. Cheers to your resistance. It took them an entire day to kill you. Our pool has never been cleaner and I hate it because I have nothing to worry about now, nothing to worship or fear.

I KNOW A TREE
ROBIN FOSTER

I know an olive tree in Emigrant, Montana. A Russian olive tree, to be precise, which stands about thirty miles north of Yellowstone's north gate. This is not the only such tree in Paradise Valley: groves of these trees with their celadon-shaded leaves, flicking in the breeze like strips of silver ticker-tape, grow in pockets along the banks of the Yellowstone River where it passes through the valley.

But this particular tree stands alone, apart from its siblings that cluster together across the pale yellow pasture surrounding my rental cabin on two sides. This particular tree stands ten feet from my bedroom window and is the first thing on the property to alight when the sun rises over the Absaroka-Beartooth Mountains to the east, its celadon leaves now appearing white with dusted snow, strikingly offset from its near-black bark. It's not until the sun has had its way with the morning sky, rising higher towards a midday height that will create a wash of clear light across the land, when the leaves return to their greener shade of pale. Beneath the tree, grasses of pale yellow and green comingle to create a neon shade reminiscent of Mello Yello, a soda from my childhood that only ever appeared in our household when my parents packed up our Chevy van and propelled my brother and sister and me deep into the outback of northern California, or Alberta, or Nova Scotia, on the family camping trips that gave me my earliest sense of wanderlust. "Let's go check it out" was our unofficial family credo.

When I'm in the West, it's usually the cottonwood tree that I seek. Georgia O'Keefe painted a series of cottonwoods in the 1940s and '50s, trees that grew in bounty along the riverbed near her home at Ghost Ranch, New Mexico. O'Keefe painted her cottonwoods with a softer brush than we are used to seeing in her widely known florals and cityscapes. Her yellows and greens, pale in the high desert light, border on a fluorescent luminescence that drew me to these images whenever it was that I first saw them. O'Keefe painted cottonwoods in the spring, in the winter, in groves, and in solitary form that explode on the canvas before you.

It's this same luminescent shade of yellow and green that dances along the foothills of Montana before the high summer sun bleaches the hillsides to toasted almond. I am always on the lookout for the groves of cottonwoods that I expect to find along the riverbanks of any western landscape, my eyes seeking to devour the colors in real life that O'Keefe depicted on her canvas. The cottonwood is the state tree of Kansas and prospers across the plains of Wyoming and Nebraska as well. When I'm in the West, I keep my eyes peeled.

It turns out my Russian olive tree is considered a noxious weed in the state of Montana as well as several other western states, an unwelcome invasive species. I can't believe this. When I think of pests, I think of sewer rats, field mice skittering inside the walls of your house in the middle of the night, or the insidious eastern Kudzu that envelopes and suffocates every shrub and tree in its path. And yet this quiet, solitary tree shading my bedroom window from the late-day sun is on the state's eradication list. About a decade ago, the Yellowstone River Conservation District Council recommended these trees be controlled or killed, as they are charged with displacing the indigenous species in the region, including cottonwoods, quaking aspens, and willow trees.

As its name implies, the Russian olive tree is native to southern Europe and western Asia. The trees were brought to America in the early 1900s to serve as windbreaks and contain erosion along the riverbanks of the Plains and western states. They are beautifully ornamental. In what seemed like a good idea in the spirit of diversification, the introduction of a species of tree that would keep erosion in check, would serve as a windbreak against the katabatic winds, and generally enhance the native wildlife very soon became, to many, a nuisance and a pest. From what I learned during my summer in Montana, the tree is remarkably stalwart. It produces large volumes of viable seeds contained within berry-like fruit that grow in small clusters, are then eaten and dispersed by birds and mammals who make use of the bounty and then deposit the remains across the land. The tree is drought and salt tolerant, does not depend on an inordinate amount of nitrogen in the soil, and is therefore extremely hardy. It provides a habitat for predatory birds like hawks and magpies, affording these a nice home base from which to prey on duck and grouse (human hunters like to prey on duck and grouse as well). Bees and insects do not seem to favor the Russian olive tree's seeds and so do not ravage the tree as they might other woody neighbors. Beavers, too, do not seem to care for the limbs of the Russian olive trees, preferring to build their dams with cottonwoods, thus favoring the resiliency of Russian olive tree in riverbank habitats.

The Russian olive is a robust tree.

The sale of this tree is today prohibited in the state of Montana, as it seems to threaten native tree species along riverbanks and across grasslands. The U.S. Department of Agriculture has warned that native cottonwood and willows are being replaced by

Russian olive trees through *competition and succession,* although Darwinian science would applaud the tree's tenacity with gusto. Botanical appreciation is in the eye of the beholder. The Department's Integrated Pest Management Control Method recommends physical removal of the trees, as well as chemical and biological methods of eradication even though, as the Montana Audubon Society has reported, "the impact of Russian olive invasions upon [native] wildlife species is variable, site-specific, and often debated." How much of a pest is this tree? That depends on who you ask.

This particular Russian olive tree on my temporary plot of land might very well be on somebody's hit list. Park County, the county in which the hamlet of Emigrant is located, has made a concerted effort to eradicate this "horrible, nasty, invasive tree" over the past two decades. A coalition of environmental groups and landowners was organized into the Park County Cooperative Weed Management Area Group with the goal of restoring the "natural ecology" of the Yellowstone River region through the eradication of the Russian olive tree and the replanting of native cottonwoods and quaking aspens. The fecundity of the non-native species had become intolerable.

I met a ranch hand who told me of the plight of local ranchers against the Russian olive tree. The trees, he explained, clog up the gulches that mark the trickling rivulets and streams in the high prairie's undulating landscape. Cows have a hard time reaching the low water in those gulches where the tree's roots have taken hold and propagated. Driving across the state, I did notice the olive trees growing in abundance in many low-lying creeks, although cottonwoods and the proliferous sage bush eagerly spread their roots in those gulches as well. The Russian olive tree doesn't have a monopoly on seeking out the wettest places in the landscape, and you can spot a low-lying riverbed or even just the trickle of a creek from miles away, readily apparent by the sudden wall of greenery sprouting up from the otherwise dull, yellow grasses. Cottonwoods, quaking aspen, cedars, and the Russian olive tree thrive there in this otherwise dry summer climate.

*

In the spring of 2018, the Park County Cooperative Weed Management Area Group, working with American Rivers, Yellowstone River Conservation District Council, Park County Environmental Council, and landowners removed Russian olive trees from one hundred fifteen acres along the Yellowstone River as it rushes north, away from Yellowstone National Park and through the county. A report filed by the coalition acknowledges that some believe the tree provides a good habitat for birds, yet many more disagree and can find nothing of value in this "thorny, impenetrable thicket" of tree. Many landowners came together to eradicate the unwelcome invader, and in a true show of solidarity, the coalition labored to remove every Russian olive tree from the area.

Once all of the Russian olive trees had been removed, each landowner in the coalition devised a weed-control plan to ensure no wily strays take root in the future. The coalition recommends continuation of the project across the entire Yellowstone flood plain, which runs for nearly 700 miles from Yellowstone Lake across Montana to the Missouri River. The tree has been widely classified as an invader species.

My particular Russian olive tree has somehow managed to avoid the axe. Her celadon leaves of silver ticker tape all the more striking now, in light of local misgivings. Now a pale celadon, now a silvery glint of flutter, now a white dusting of snow.

What is a tree? Is a tree an indication of life, a puzzle to be solved, a signpost? Is it a metaphor? For some, a poem: I think that I shall never see, a poem lovely as a tree. For some, a scourge. My Russian olive tree abides in silence. And I wait.

HOOTERS
LAURA GIRARDEAU

They call us Hooters, but we're far from waitresses in short shorts. We're guardians of the ancient forests. We hoot endangered spotted owls down from the trees. Our uniform is lace-up boots, flannel shirts and orange vests that hold the tools of our trade: a compass, an aerial photo showing the oldest trees' rounded tops, and live mice to tempt the owls. We're perfumed with the scent of cedar and the sulfur of off-the-map hot springs. We have no use for mirrors, and we've never felt more gorgeous.

In the backwoods bars, there's a price on our heads. Loggers hang owls in effigy over the door. They think we stole their jobs, but ancient forests are like emeralds. If you mine too many, they're gone forever (owls or not), along with the jobs. They post signs that say, "I Like Spotted Owls—Fried" and "Hooters Go Home."

We're already home. We live in deep wild, where rivers are birthed.

Up the trail, the mighty McKenzie emerges from a lava tube. At Blue Hole, it spills out in turquoise surprise, playing "I Spy" on our work with its all-knowing eye. We think the river approves.

It's hard to believe we get paid for this. We're ready to risk-n-roll. The Forest Service taught us how to drive our rigs into ditches to dodge logging trucks, avoiding the cliffs. They told us to "curse our fall" if we plummet from a huge log onto the sharp jumble below. They say swearing expels air from your lungs and boosts your chances of survival. But we want to fall, into this wild life.

They taught us how to avoid getting lost. How to use a compass to escape a fortress of trees when their crowns block the sun. Our boss got lost once, called us on her radio to tell us where to pick her up. "I'm in a clear-cut," she laughed. That's all she knew. The Oregon forests are a chessboard of clear-cuts. We're pawns hopping across the board, trying to become queens.

We see the chessboard on the aerial photos we use as maps. Only a few cathedrals remain, tiny Emerald Cities. The trees stand proud like our foremothers, telling their stories in sun slants. Their skin is cinnamon and butterscotch, both rough and soft. Their canopy swallows light like a black hole, turns everything deep green. I want to get lost in Oz.

A hundred feet up these trunks is the treasure: a nested pair. The nest tree is the motherlode. If we find it, we save a mile of forest around the tree. Thanks to the Endangered Species Act, the logging trucks and bulldozers can't go there. Like green witches, we draw circles of protection around eternity. But first, we must find evidence of love. Only nested pairs are protected.

So we hoot the wild down from the treetops in its own language. We cup our hands and give four throaty barks at just the right cadence. We place a live pet-store mouse on one cinnamon trunk. Its pink candy eyes are too bright to resist. The forest holds its breath.

Then an owl flies down from its silent skyscraper, in a spotted cloak to match the dappled light. If it's a mated male, he carries the mouse to the female and gives her the gift, like a true gentleman. If they're a nested pair, she flies to the nest tree to feed the babies first.

We fly through the forest too, scaling mazes of blown-down logs to follow her. The trees take a bite out of us. Our knees and elbows bear scars, landmarks for our someday granddaughters. If we're lucky, we get there in time to see talons and tail disappear into one chosen tree. A tree that's been here since Columbus got us into this mess.

We mark the tree, and we've done it. We've saved the pair's fragile love, along with a mile of forest around it, for one more season.

More often than not, we know love is up there but can't find the nest. So we go back, off the road, off the clock. We do anything to find them. We strap on skis and hoot under the full moon at midnight. We shift our schedules to owl time, listening for nature's call-back. We lay our camping mattresses down on soft duff or hard gravel and wait.

When we get the call in deepest night, we take a compass bearing on hope. At dawn, we follow the bearing and "mouse" the owls. When they lead us to the mother tree, we mark it with an X for wild. This is the center of Nature's mile now.

This is the place your bulldozer jaws can't reach. We are the women your jaws can't reach. Your owl on a noose above the bar only stokes our fire. We've tossed out the maps and navigate with our hearts. We follow the scent of cedar to soak in secret hot springs that only Hooters know.

In a mossy cave, steam rises from the earth and dissolves our walls. Underwater, our sore muscles stand out like burnished hills. Our thighs are bronze, strong ladyhood. We've grown branches. In the hot pool, we loosen our limbs to lush. The roar of the river is all we hear.

Then, across miles and centuries, a spotted owl calls in four throaty barks. Not because we called. Just because. That's when we praise our fall into the wild.

SUMMER JOB
SCOTT OGLESBY

After graduating from high school, college was on my mind that summer of 1965, but like many Arkansas boys, a summer job was the first requirement. And because of my dad's position at International Paper, my summer job was always destined to be at the mill. What I didn't expect was to be one of seven entry-level laborers assigned to the mill's forestry division. Our main job duty was to trudge through the piney woods lugging bazooka-sized metal syringes filled with poison. The grimmest of reapers, we'd inject our toxins into the base of all the hardwoods—oaks, maples, ashes, and any other pesky tree unsuitable for pulping into paper. By definition, a rose bush in a cornfield is a weed, and by this logic we were weed killers—one-man Monsantos creating mono-agriculture with a vengeance.

At the end of our first day of stumbling through the brambled forest, my buddy who had signed up with me pulled me aside. "I don't know about you," he whispered, "but tomorrow I'm looking for another job."

Was it the sticky 104-degree heat? Or the dripping bath of sweat and industrial-strength Off, which the mosquitoes seemed to relish? Or maybe the lunchtime arm wrestling bouts, or the rude soundtrack of racist, dirty jokes from our snaggle-toothed workmates? At that point, we didn't even know about the ticks and yellow jackets. But my buddy and I never made it to the new job hunt because on our second day, it rained, which allowed our crew to loll away the entire afternoon in the back of the truck memorizing those raunchy jokes. Praying for rain, we would stick it out through the summer—all at the mighty scale of a dollar eighty-five an hour.

My intro into forestry also included controlled burns, which is where smoke first got my attention. We'd fan out around twenty-acre plots of thick brush and dig long shallow sections of connecting fire trenches. Then we'd scamper through the woods with drip torches squirting liquid flames behind us, leaving an inferno nipping at our heels. The only training we received was the straw boss's warning to get the hell out fast, and if the smoke got too thick, sprint for the trench, lie down and hold a wet rag over our noses. We did what we were told.

Company logic dictated that the only good tree was one that would soon be paper, and the PR department sloganeered brilliantly—for every tree cut down or torched, seven would be planted. They never mentioned that the new ones would all be pines— diversity was just a fantasy for some future eco-Nazi. For sure, all this forest mayhem planted the seeds for my own budding environmentalism, with an obsession for conserving paper.

If I had taken notes, I could have written a killer essay for my future sociology classes—College boys co-work summer jobs with redneck middle-school dropouts. My smugness was tempered by the fact that I had failed the paper mill's basic employment test for more appropriate indoor positions for the college-bound. My punishment for test anxiety was that instead of making paper, I was killing trees.

HITCHING A RIDE ON A TREE
ERIC SANDY

We pull into the parking lot at Tallmadge Meadows, a plot of gently rolling hills north of Akron, for our semi-regular early morning walk with the dogs, Forrest and Pierogi. A dull orange sun hangs low above the woodsy canopy. It's hazy at this hour, and the saplings stand like ghosts in the bleary-eyed morning. It's beautiful each time we arrive. As we get out of the car—tumbling cartoonishly, dogs and leashes everywhere—we see a black chicken wandering around the tree line and wonder what that's all about.

"What's *that* all about?" I ask my wife, Bridget, nodding toward the fowl. She shrugs. There's little else to say because when you're out in nature you do tend to see unexpected things. What are you supposed to do? It's the Anthropocene, they say, a new geological age, and weird feedback loops are pushing the rhythms of the natural world far out of whack. Heat domes settle over the Pacific Northwest. Dramatic scenes of flooding convey terror from places as disparate as Michigan and Germany. Strange chickens wander far from home. Even if we *think* we have control over the rest of our lives—the morning coffee, the mute button on our Zoom calls, the Fantasy Football lineup—the sense of creeping chaos is always there. Not everything is in its right place.

This is never as clear to us as in the great outdoors. Here, surprises abound.

We mostly do these early morning walks on Wednesdays, when our work-from-home routines sync. It's the summer of 2021, and the delta variant of COVID-19 is circulating across the world. This is enough of an issue that we've taken to calling it simply "delta," moving deeper into familiarity with the pandemic. It's the singular question—and the singular answer—framing so many of our conversations. The latest concerns are whether delta will disrupt an upcoming trip to Las Vegas and whether delta will cancel a bunch of concerts on our calendar. Dave Matthews Band is coming to town, and it's hard to imagine another summer without the old fellow. Why, delta, why?

So, the walks kind of help with that subtly raging uncertainty. Before we slip into the daze of staring at a computer all day and deciphering the anxieties of coworkers in chat form, it's nice to hop in the car and take a breezy adventure to a nearby park. We feel hearty doing this sort of thing. We feel active, aware of our surroundings. Today, bless her heart, it happens to be Pierogi's third birthday. We're celebrating with an extra-long walk and treats back at the house.

What I like about Tallmadge Meadows is that, as far as trails go, it's pretty much 101-level walking. The whole thing is a two-mile route—out into the forest, then back through the titular meadow. It's relatively flat. The meadow portion features a nice grassy path, which is soft beneath the shoes and makes for an easy opportunity to get your steps in. A lot of what we have around the greater Akron area, parks-wise, is steep, rocky gorges or long odysseys through the nearby national park. These trails are pleasant and arduous. They're exciting. But where an adventurous romp through craggy terrain might sound like fun to me, it gets a little complicated with Pierogi, a Treeing Walker Coonhound with the strength of three mules. She likes to tug—and I mean tug! Forrest, at a stately four years old, is more manageable on these walks. He is a boxer-hound mix who loves nothing more than strutting through a pile of leaves or thick trailside brush.

At any rate, the Meadows is low-key park life, and that's fine with us.

The point is to get out of the house every now and then. Ever since the pandemic gripped the world in a public health crisis, this has been a fairly big deal. We dance in and out of quarantine—by choice or mandate—and through it all we've got to find ways of maintaining a connection to the outside world. With delta circulating, it's fallen to us, the individuals, to manage the public health risks associated with stuff like other people and workplace culture. Truth be told, we've been out and about plenty, confirming with like-minded friends that we're double-vaxxed and ready to roll like the old days. Backyard cookouts! Baseball games! The summer has kind of whizzed by in that respect, playing catch-up on all the social activities we missed out on in 2020. And yet, there's still something sublime about retreating to a local park with only those closest to you—falling away from the masses of friends and neighbors and cousins and bosses and servers and clerks. Tallmadge Meadows satisfies that need, leaving enough time to pick up an iced coffee or a bag of bagels on the way home.

•

On the back half of the walk, rounding the bend toward the parking lot again, the vastness of the meadow is dotted with little saplings wrapped in plastic support structures. You see this sort of thing in more rugged public parks—the ones tucked into Midwest river valleys or spread out across protected wetlands. It's restoration work. It seems like the most blatant attempt to reverse course, repopulating a local ecosystem to bring back certain species (birds, insects, ecology majors). It's heartening. I like seeing fresh plantings. It reminds me that we're trying—or, rather, that *someone* is trying to maintain a grip on the natural world. I think of it like a mixing board—dialing up the gain on a particular pine tree, say.

All around the new trees, signs proclaim that this is a protected area—one meant specifically to be repopulated by various and diverse native species. Point is: Don't go wandering off-trail, absently kicking at infant roots and yanking wildflowers out of the ground for your beau.

But as we're walking, I say to Bridget, hey, what are these trees, anyway? Elms or something? It strikes me that I haven't the faintest clue what I'm really seeing when I look at the saplings. Is that even the right word, sapling? They may as well be props from the community theater. Or splotches of brown paint on a slapdash watercolor. For all my romanticization of the young trees, I'm not really sure what I'm talking about.

It strikes me, too, that this isn't the first time I've thought about this disconnect. It's not like I'm wandering haphazardly from scene to scene, but I am aware that the passing environment holds deep mysteries that— if I would only try to learn them—would enhance my relationship to my surroundings. Take the terrific clock on the University of Akron campus—one of them, at any rate. I walk by it each week on my way to class. What could be more common than a clock? It's classic American college campus background noise, but surely there's a history.

(And yes, the Martin Post Clock, at Buchtel Avenue and Union Street, was dedicated in 2010 to Paul and Dorothy Martin, late and local philanthropists and automobile magnates who met at the university in 1935. Their son, Fred, now runs a dealership in Youngstown whose cheesy television commercials have contributed to the omnipresent background noise of my life. The story of Paul and Dorothy Martin—and their clock—is part of this great ecosystem in which I'm living. Northeast Ohio, land of rivers and trees and clocks.)

Now, does this matter all that much? I'm not a historian or a taxonomist. But I admit that I'd like to be able to point to a mighty tree and say, that's a yellow buckeye! *Aesculus flava*, as we call it in the lab. And a damn fine specimen! It seems like this would be a meaningful thing to do.

I guess the reason I'd like to know some of the terminology is because things are suddenly moving very fast. The pandemic is part of this, granted, but by and large time seems to be zipping by awfully quickly. I'm either getting older (yes), or I'm beginning to see signs of the Anthropocene all around me. We're achieving a degree of escape velocity from the natural world. We're tethered to our homes, our computers, our air fryers, and meanwhile the great outdoors takes it on the chin.

Timothy Morton, a self-appointed "dark ecologist," says that the more meaningful phrase than "Anthropocene" for this current era of climate change and human-crafted destruction is the Sixth Mass Extinction. I won't get into the gritty details of the previous five, but this current one is more or less under-way, according to people far smarter than me. The Botanic Gardens Conservation International released a report this summer that insisted a full 30% of all tree species were at risk of going extinct. That seems like a lot! I'd like to know what they are—at least *some* of them—before they're gone. There's a very surreal heartache in reading these increasingly common headlines, something about a rare species that's reportedly gone extinct before scientists had ever identified it in the first place. I often think, how could they know? But that's another quirk of this moment, the fast-paced slide into climate crisis. We're moving too fast, and no one knows for sure who's at the steering wheel.

That's how it feels only when you stop to think about it, of course. Wasn't it just yesterday that I was a kid? Wandering around the woods with my pals? In reality, the Anthropocene and our human mark on the planet are moving slowly—stretched out across time.

We're just noticing these changes more and more, and it feels like the days are slipping away.

"Extinctions look like points on a timeline when you look them up on Wikipedia—but they are actually spread out over time, so that while they are happening it would be very hard to discern them," Morton writes. "They are like invisible nuclear explosions that last for thousands of years. It's our turn to be the asteroid, because the global warming that we cause is now bringing about the Sixth Mass Extinction."

It sure makes a slow morning walk at Tallmadge Meadows seem as pleasant as can be. So, before the worst comes to pass, I think—before the meadow is charred in apocalyptic doom—I'd like to understand these things the way they are now. Trees. I just want to know their story before it's too late. Grimly, I want to tell my kids what an elm tree was.

As I write this, I don't have any children—but I'd like to identify things in the future, to help explain the world around them. I get carried away thinking about this. I picture an older version of myself, somehow significantly cooler, probably at ease with most decision making, capable of managing an oil change, and I think about how I'll tell my children about the silver maple in the backyard. Too often, even, I think about this in the past tense, as though it's happened already and I'm quietly mourning the memory. I'm racing ahead of myself, eager to see things written in history and neatly categorized.

•

To solve my problem, I email Rob Curtis. He's the ecological supervisor for Summit Metro Parks. Rather, I email the kindly media relations gatekeepers at the county and work my way inward, flexing my journalistic muscles through the bureaucracy, to get to Rob. In between messages, I do a bit of my own research about the trees.

Turns out, back in 2012, the parks system acquired a batch of Virginia pine and river birch bulbs from a nursery. These two species seemed like a good fit for our damning Northeast Ohio winters, but the main reason was that a warming climate will push them northward anyway. They're southern tree species. Might as well get them used to the sights now before they're forced into new territories by the threat of climate crisis. This is called "assisted migration" in the biology world.

When I get in touch with Rob, he tells me that it usually takes about 10 years for an obvious visual change to take place in the park after a bulb or a nut is planted. The Virginia pines and river birch I was reading about are sticking out like old friends ringing the meadow. After reading that article about the 2012 planting—even just knowing *that*—this sort of detail will really dial up the attention to detail when I'm out with the family again. It's nice to be able to point to something in the natural world and have half a clue as to what it is.

After 30 years, Rob tells me, the trees will appear to us just like an extension of the densely forested parts of the park. They'll have been subsumed. By that point, that 2012 bulb planting will feel like ancient history. I'll be 54 years old, I think to myself.

There's an old chestnut worth repeating here: Something about the best time to plant a tree being 20 years ago. The second-best time to plant a tree, however, is right now.

Rob says it would be a hell of a lot easier to explain all of this in-person, so we agree to meet at the meadow, where I graciously thank him for his time and explain how my wife and our dogs, like, really love this park. Total fanboy stuff.

He walks me by the Virginia pines along the trail as I explain what I'm really trying to understand: how learning about the trees in this park might contribute in some small way to my own struggle with the dramatically shifting climate. The future is here, I say stupidly, and I'm not sure how to handle it. It feels like there's not much we can do in the face of looming disaster. Rob looks nonplussed.

"Well, planting trees—that can make a big difference," he says.

He points to the newly planted saplings around us, the young grove I've been enjoying on those morning walks. There are 1,000 new trees here, the result of an anonymous donor's goodwill; 27 different species cover a 10-acre slice of the park. These trees, Rob says, are here specifically for carbon sequestration efforts.

The carbon-sucking power of these trees—their leaves, their root systems, the interactions with the soil—will offset the carbon being belched into the air by passing traffic or by the little corner market across the street. "You can undo your personal footprint," he says.

Now, he's quick to point out that a donation of 1,000 trees is just a dent in this overarching problem of carbon capture.

Over time, urban and suburban development

has fragmented the landscape. Tallmadge Meadows, as it stands today, is just a sliver of what was once forest for as far as the eye could see. Then came farming, and, long story short, roads and houses and power lines and Uber Eats delivery drivers and rogue chickens and drainage systems. You can only wedge so much carbon sequestration into a beautiful meadow like this, so Rob is quick to point out that it falls to all of us—the residents of a given community—to plant trees and, little by little, tackle the carbon problem we've set for ourselves. One tree is better than none.

And yet, because the climate has been changing so dramatically for so long, this is a fine line we're walking. You've got to plant the *right* kind of tree for this uneven climate system. The experiment that Rob and his team began in 2012 is part of that conversation: What species will thrive here when they can no longer thrive where they're from?

But that question can be phrased any number of ways. What will thrive here which *shouldn't* thrive here? Invasive species. Rob kind of casts his arm about him, waving vaguely in the direction of the meadow and parks elsewhere in the county. "They're everywhere," he says, "and it's a real problem."

He says that nothing drives him more crazy than seeing a Norway spruce planted in some neighbor's yard in suburban Akron. A Norway spruce in Akron! That species doesn't belong here, and it will go hog-wild with seeding (as it has, Rob argues), slowly taking over the local environment and wrestling precious resources away from more helpful trees like the yellow buckeye.

I'm realizing that it really does matter whether or not you know what you're talking about when you're talking about trees.

Of those pines and birch planted back in 2012,

not all have survived. This is an experiment, Rob says, an attempt to better understand how migration will play out in the long run. He points to scraggly pines and birches, still hanging on and bracing for their tenth winter in Ohio. Migration is an imperfect process, riddled with uncertainties and the difficult work of adjusting to new terrain, new structures of feeling. The word "acclimation" itself shares some etymological DNA with the word "climate." To acclimate, to habituate, to adapt to a new climate. Not easy.

I think of climate refugees, people forced across borders by the pressures of natural disaster and escalating temperatures—drought, famine, rising sea levels. This is another tricky component of our age that's hard to pin down: It's easy to fool ourselves that "climate refugees" are a thing of dystopian fiction, but they're here. The United Nations estimated earlier this year that more than 20 million men, women and children have been displaced by climate disaster since 2010. "We need to invest now in preparedness to mitigate future protection needs and prevent further climate caused displacement," UN High Commissioner for Refugees Filippo Grandi said. "Waiting for disaster to strike is not an option."

For many, it's time to move—and fast.

In the U.S., speculation centers around the Great Lakes region and whether its cities and rural enclaves will see a considerable increase of climate refugees in the coming decades. Ohio and Michigan, in particular, are insulated in some ways from the harsher and more immediate impacts of a topsy-turvy climate system. There's plenty of fertile, flat land. We're near the largest body of freshwater in the world. We're neighborly. It all makes sense.

Even considering all of that, though, are we as

safe as we might think we are? Ohio and Michigan have played host to plenty of natural crises in recent years—flooding in greater Detroit, algal bloom poisoning in Lake Erie. So, where do we go from here?

If there are any lessons to draw from Tallmadge Meadows, one must surely grant Rob's team some foresight. It's better to prepare now because who knows how much faster this climate crisis gyre will spin? If we feel time slipping away now—and I know I do, is what I'm trying to say—then we should consider what it means to acclimate, to habituate, to adapt. If we stop short of literally becoming refugees and crossing state borders, then what might that look like?

Waiting for species to disappear is not an option. Rob underscores this along the way as we thread the pines lining the Tallmadge Meadows trail. Everyone has their own personal motivation for struggling against the weight of climate change. For him, it's straightforward.

"Personally, I just don't want to lose species," he says.

Now, is he only talking about trees?

All around us, I start to see these trees serving different purposes. This isn't how the forest originally and organically came together, long before agriculture took over Summit County and even longer before residential neighborhoods moved the farmers further south. After all of those long, slow-moving processes, we're now at the point where we really need to manage the land. Simply letting nature do its thing will no longer cut it. We've become the dominant force in the natural world—that much is clear. Now, before it's too late, as the Anthropocene speeds up, it seems like we need to use that force for something good.

Planting a tree is about as good a place to start as any.

•

After our morning walk, as we attempt to get back to the car, Bridget and I try our hardest to keep the dogs from running headlong into the wild overgrowth where the black chicken is surely nesting. Even amid the typical struggle with those two, we feel refreshed. Invigorated. And maybe we don't use those words outright, but the general Zen mindset is there after a good morning walk. We can get this in our own neighborhood—or even on a treadmill, I guess—but the extra ingredient in these moments might very well be the trees. They loom.

As we walk into the woods and then back into the meadow and finally toward the parking lot, the trees are a constant presence. They help obliterate the sights and sounds of traffic. They provide a real sense of place.

Without them, you've got little more than a yard—halfway to a commercially zoned business park.

Tallmadge Meadows is located in the city of Munroe Falls, which boasts 60% tree coverage. This is fairly staggering, as far as cities go, but then Munroe Falls is little more than a few side streets that splay outward around the park.

"Munroe Falls has reached a perfect union between the two types of conservation district and exists happily as a small part of a bigger picture, with little industry, and little space for anything other than natural areas." That's from citizen naturalist Riley Pierce's tree canopy assessment of Summit County, another fascinating document I found far down the rabbit hole of local conservation Google searches.

"Existing happily" is just a lovely way of describing a small city in Northeast Ohio.

In Akron, down the road from the meadow, just 41% of the city is covered by trees. That's nothing to sneeze at, even if it's the seasonal allergies again, but it begs the question of what could be. In between the likes of Munroe Falls and Akron is Cuyahoga Falls, my new home, which clocks a nice 54% tree coverage.

We are where we are in time. These cities very much *aren't* the forests they once were, and who would want that anyway? It might sound like I'm pining for the purity of an old-growth forest in Ohio, but that's not the era we've been given. It helps to know where we're coming from, though, to get a sense of where we're headed.

Trees are a good through-line, if we can keep them around.

Back at home, drinking coffee on the back patio before the workday begins, I pull out my phone and download an app called Leafsnap.

"Go for a walk, take a shot of a leaf," the app implores, "and this little wonder will identify its tree and give all kinds of information about it." I start to wander around the backyard, postage stamp that it is, picking up leaves from the surrounding trees and scrutinizing them through the camera in my phone.

When I've got my answers, I look up and revisit the trees I've been staring at since we moved in last year. Silver maple—two of them, tall and guardianlike. And Eastern white pine—a trio of these shorter trees, playfully squatting near the shed.

Now, with just a tilt of the eye and a handy app developed for this new millennium of ours, they took on a new sense of intimacy—like old friends. Forrest and Pierogi clearly love them. We all enjoy them in this brief moment we're sharing together. Most mornings and evenings, as I sit under our umbrella out back, I look out at these five trees in the foreground, framing my daily glimpse into a changing world. The dogs run around, barking madly at each other. We dial up the baseball broadcast from Cleveland, balls and strikes coloring the evening air. The breeze picks up just so, and the branches above us rustle in an odd and ancient rhythm. I feel acclimated, if only for the moment.

THINNING PINES
RICHARD HOLINGER

My North Woods neighbor thins white pines (*pinus stro-bus*) around his cabin. "They grow too close together. They suffocate other growth."

Like, I presume, red pines (*pinus resinosa*) or "Norways," strong, elegant, not territorial.

I object. "I love the whites. Their long, soft, furry needles." Their reach humble and thin-twigged as babies' fingers, I think, but don't say aloud. "They belong in a throng. Besides, they'll kill to survive, just as Darwin predicted the fittest would persevere." By having their frailest done in and calling it just.

Passing a copse of quaking aspen, I ask if they, too, should be reduced.

"They give," he says, and leaves it at that, as if I'm to intuit the rest, his rejoinder to my inquiry implying aspens, being aspens, defend themselves against insult and assault, vindicable by aesthete alone. Indeed, their tall, sleek, cloud-gray trunks march silently in place, spear up through thick underbrush of raspberry bushes, fiddlehead ferns, vanilla sweet grass, Pennsylvania sedge, and highbush cranberry.

Thin reasoning, but, like the aspen, stands out, trunk and limbs lit from within, burning hot enough to ignite the whole forest.

PHOENIX FOREST
ANGELA SUCICH

When we learned we were pregnant, my husband and I headed to the mountains. In a little valley town with a front door to nature, I spent mornings taking my heavy belly for walks in the clear alpine air while attempting to identify the trees. Nearly three years later, still nestled here in the Cascade Range of Washington State, I am still trying to learn my conifers.

Some come easily: the furrowed Doug fir, deep channels running between corky, crusty bark. The cheerleading Ponderosa pine, raising its needled pompoms in the wind. White pine is harder to distinguish, arrow-straight though it is. Western hemlock often stumps me, too, even with its flat-needles and droopy branches. But the spindly larch, deciduous bristle fingers waiting for autumn gold, that one I know well, like a friend encountered on the trail.

My daughter has also spent her young years among the trees. First harnessed to my chest in the front carrier, then peeking over my shoulder in the hiking backpack, always reaching out with curious eyes or a hand toward what must have seemed to her arboreal giants. Now she runs to embrace them. A tree hugger of two-and-a-half.

The other day, driving along the mountain highway that cuts through our town, I heard kissing noises from the car seat behind me. Are you giving Mama kisses? I asked my daughter. I'm kissing the trees, she said in the earnest voice of the tiny human.

Some of those trees catch fire every summer. Segments of the corridor we drive through to the west side burned for months last season. But a hundred years

31

of forest debt must be paid.

Over a century ago, in 1910, fires consumed in two days millions of acres in this state and its eastern neighbors, the impact of which would come to shape the national firefighting policy for many decades, that being total fire suppression. For the last few years, we have been breathing smoke in July, August, September, October. We live with the hum of air purifiers, with the prospect of new fires, closer ones, playing in our minds like background music.

For scores of years, a strategy of fire prevention, conceived in the image and the words of Smoky the Bear, interrupted the life cycle of forest and meadow. It led to a hundred years' worth of dry brush and debris, tinder waiting for the first lightning strike. I have an app that shows where the fires are raging in real time; this last smoke season, I gave up trying to count all those little flame icons.

But like that mythical creature, the phoenix, whose rebirth requires its immolation, a forest knows that burning is part of the game. According to medieval bestiaries, the legendary bird was believed to nest in cinnamon, to drink incense for five hundred years. But it was best known for its dying: red-gold wings fanning the flame, ever anticipating an end for its beginning, a beginning for its end.

The town where I live is on the ancestral land of the Yakama, Chinook, and Wenatchi people, who I expect knew from time immemorial how the forests worked. Long ago, they must have seen basal shoots sprouting from broken and charred snags, noticed how the cones of lodgepole pine opened in the fire's heat to release their seeds. And now I can't help thinking about that mythic bird in the same light as those serotinous cones; symbols of cyclical regeneration, renewal, hope—

signs of life rising from the scorched earth.

It's something to cling to and to use to ground myself. As a parent facing a climate-changed existence for mine and future generations, including my daughter's, I have to find my optimism where I can, without falling into the trap of magical thinking, of hoping that someone who is not us will save us. I do it by celebrating every small win: each blue-sky day pulled like magic from the smoldering air; every modest environmental victory pulled from the political smokescreen. And I try to love the way my daughter does. She is teaching me to kiss the trees.

ON BURNING
MACKENZIE MYERS FOWLER

The deeply grooved, brittle bark falls away from each log like meat from a bone. A puff of dust shoots up when I throw one on the pile, and soon the woodshed looks like it's full of smoke, though nothing's hit the furnace yet. I try not to think about what types of scat and various pathogens hang in the dust as I dump off layers of woodland detritus—pinecones, spruce needles, seed hulls, and other remnants of squirrels' feasts—before loading the pieces into my wheelbarrow.

I'm not sure how long this firewood has been here or what kind of wood it is. Maybe oak? The property is mostly conifers but has some long-standing oaks, like the big one that has become my sitting spot for outdoor meditation and coffee-sipping since we moved in. A new generation is coming in, too, like the scrappy young fellow standing sentinel in the middle of the backyard, watching over what will be the vegetable garden come spring.

My husband Jake and I can relate to the scrappy oak. We are a new generation on the land ourselves, after a recent move to this 140-year-old farmhouse in northern Michigan where I grew up. On a small plot of land in a region rapidly filling with tourists-turned-residents, it was a no-brainer. To boot, it included this corrugated steel woodshed and some firewood.

These logs, some as big as my thigh, have sat here for who knows how long. Years, probably. The house's drop ceilings, new propane furnace, and previous resident—an elderly farmer—tell us that the woodburning furnace in the basement has likely fallen out of use. The beating heart of the hearth, arrested.

•

At first, my muscles protest. These days, like millions of other Americans, I've gotten used to heat that's pumped into my house from somewhere else. A matter of weeks ago, my previous house downstate got up to temperature with the simple twist of a thermostat. I scarcely considered how my home maintained the level of comfort it offered, except for the bill that came out of my checking account each month.

Here, it's different. To pump heat in with no effort means filling a propane tank multiple times a year, to the tune of several hundred dollars a refill. We are lucky in many respects—we have nearly four acres, a private well, a quarter-acre garden plot, and my family down the road. We have old oaks and new spruces and a silver maple I'm sure will be magnificent next fall. We do not have economical, effortless heat. Staying warm means spending Sunday afternoons with the wheelbarrow and work gloves, shushing the groans of hips and shoulders and scapulae.

Fortunately for us, the old farmer's ingenuity is everywhere, from the beams of the deck that lift up to allow large items to be brought into the house, to a special door in the garage for unloading groceries at chest height. My favorite, though, is his handmade log slide that lives in the woodshed. It aligns perfectly with the basement windows so we can unload firewood from the shed right into the house, a signature of not only his handiwork but his resourcefulness and penchant for simplicity.

To keep my mind off how out of shape I am, I think of one good thing for each log that slides down the chute to land in a pile in the basement. Both list and woodpile build as I move between the wheelbarrow and shed. A log slides, and I offer a small prayer of thanks for Jake. Another log, and thanks for my job. Another log: a home in the region that feeds my soul. Another: the means to keep warm, all due to sunlight and water and photosynthesis and time. Soon, the pile reaches the top of the basement window, and my arms don't even hurt anymore. Instead, I'm flush with the warmth of work and utterly cut through with appreciation. I strip off my gloves to head inside and stack.

•

My first experience with wood heat was during 10th grade, when my parents got a woodstove to combat the unsustainable cost of a propane furnace. According to their Rutland thermometer, the optimal burn temperature is between 300 and 600 degrees Fahrenheit. So each day I went to school, I left the house with a 300-plus-degree fire burning in the living room, the room where my family said hello after coming home, said goodbye before starting the day, played board games on weekends, cuddled with our pets, watched movies together, and opened presents on Christmas. The idea of a raging flame, albeit contained, smack in the center of it all made me queasy by the time I cracked open my chemistry book in first hour. What if I came home and it was all gone?

My fears weren't entirely unfounded. As with any of the fossil fuel alternatives, there's no denying the dark side of the wood fires that heat our homes. There's the ever-present danger of creosote: the sticky, black, resinous byproduct of a less-than-optimal burn. It builds up in the chimney over time, becoming flammable at a mere 451 degrees, according to the Chimney Safety Institute of America. Just an eighth of an inch is enough to start a chimney fire; just a chimney fire is enough to ignite a whole house.

Then there are the internal health risks. When combustion destroys the chemical bonds of wood, it releases heat in the fortuitous scrambling of an equation that means wearing t-shirts inside in January. It also releases particulates that can't burn down all the way. These particulates typically come from resin, which trees use to protect themselves from damage and disease. Depending on the wood used and the efficiency of burning, each puff of smoke or ash breathed in upon opening the door could be laced with carcinogens.

My fears of a house fire fortunately haven't become a reality, at my parents' home down the road or inside my own. My fears of chronic illness due to smoke and ash may still yet crystallize into something urgent, though we are careful and mindful and hope to join the millions of people who have burned wood for thousands of years to little effect.

Depending on who you ask, burning wood is a sustainable practice, as long as trees are replanted and timber is logged responsibly. Others point to wood-burning stoves, boilers, and furnaces as complicit in climate change, since burning wood releases carbon dioxide back into the atmosphere. I'm not here to dispute the second point; surely, if every family on Earth burned wood for heat, we would blow through the trees faster than we could replace them, the air would be thick with smoke, and most of us would be sick and cold come next winter.

But we are one household on a small chunk of land in rural northern Michigan. If social media, corporations, and politicians can make individual households feel single-handedly responsible for solving environmental crises by urging us to participate in recycling, composting, growing food at home, gardening with native plants, minimizing single-use plastics, and conserving water—all of which happen actively and consciously in my home, not because of the urging but because they are fulfilling and ethical—then I am not left with guilt about burning wood. Our fuel is local, renewable, and processed mostly by human effort. For this, and for the trees that provide it, I am left with gratitude.

I patter through the house, trying to track in as little snow as possible, and make my way down the creaky basement stairs, cock my head around the low-hanging water pipe, and throw my gloves back on.

Stacking wood is not unlike a dustier, physically taxing version of Tetris. There's an optimal log for each open space below, and half-logs go on the bottom, flat side down to start a new row. It's not a serious art form, but according to my dad, there is a right way and a wrong way to do it (like so many other things). After my parents got their woodstove, weeks of my teenage summers were spent stacking wood with my brother. We learned the hard way, after a few toppled rows had to be restacked, to ensure the wood leaned backward, never forward.

Even now—especially now, with the size of the logs in my own house—I pay attention to the lean and correct it when I can. And now, like then, when a piece from the pile fits perfectly in the space waiting for it below, a little shot of dopamine runs through me.

Just as the preparation for wood heat brings an unconventional joy, the burning presents its own specific magic. After I overcame the initial fear of my parents' woodstove, I would rush out to the living room in the mornings to park myself in front of the golden fire tink-tink-tinking in its iron box, staying there until the heat on my back was unbearable and I could smell the fibers of my pajamas overheating. After a long, dark, winter day at school, coming home to the tangy smell of woodsmoke was a tonic. The woodstove was a boon in power outages or on snow days, when my mom made giant pots of soup on the hot iron top.

Of course, Jake and I don't cook on our wood furnace in the farmhouse or park ourselves in front of it to warm up in the mornings. But the heat that flows through our vents is just as comforting, and the underlying principle is the same: We can keep warm on long-term photosynthesis captured in a chopped log and depend less on fossil fuels. This means a bit more freedom, a loosening of the chain, and a greater yearning to break free altogether. It's the same satisfaction that comes with a clothesline, or a compost bin, or an organic garden—with these additions to life, we may increase our work, but we are subtracting ourselves from systems rooted in consumption without production. We are opting out in favor of something less convenient, but older and simpler and dearer.

We ask: How can we make instead of buy? How can we reuse instead of discard? What resources are around us for food, medicine, light, and heat?

What choices allow us to keep choosing?

•

Once Jake and I have lived in the house for a couple of months, winter hits in full force. Icicles take up residence on our eaves. The garden plot is tucked in under a blanket of snow, resting. But even now, the land displays its abundance. Evergreens abound: blue spruce in neat rows of five near the house, promising cover for the chickens and built-in yuletide decor when it snows. Hemlocks stand tall, providing a windbreak for the driveway. Among scattered lilacs, a maple and crabapple shade the front yard where I picture our children playing someday.

I dream of arboreal delights in the coming seasons: gnarled old apple trees laden with blush-pink petals in spring, stately deep green oaks in summer, and fiery maples in fall. But for now, we turn to the inside. Upstairs, living spaces are prepared for a season of respite with blankets and slippers and wool socks. Downstairs, there are three rows of thigh-sized logs stacked along the wall.

While I am out loading and stacking on weekends, Jake starts and ends each day with a trip to the furnace. As the sound of the metal fire door travels through thin floors on cold mornings, there's a strange comfort in its clang and creak, altogether industrial and domestic. I nestle down into the blankets, close my eyes, and smile at such tender keeping of dependable warmth.

COMFORT ON THE DEATH OF
THE ANCIENT OAK
CAROLYN WILLIAMS-NOREN

Every time I see a woman with a baby I wonder if she wants to throw down one drinking glass after another into her kitchen sink or stomp out her back door with a stack of dinner plates and hurl them, one by one, onto the concrete walk. For a long time I wondered, if she did feel this, what would allow her to say so. What would convince her that she was not the only one—that she had no reason for shame?

One time I threw Ingrid's red leather shoe in frustration—hard, cursing—and it was lost for fifteen minutes in the drifts of toddler toys on the floor. She cried the whole time I searched for it. So did her baby sister.

One time, unable to find a matching pair of mittens, I went outside and hit the side of the house with my flat hand so hard it left a dent I can still see in the siding. All the while, my husband patiently helped our daughters with their boots.

Once in the kitchen while Iris was crying in the living room and I was trying to cook dinner, I slammed my fist onto the counter so hard my arm throbbed for hours.

Most of the time, though, I behaved peacefully, softly. My body did not look, and my voice did not sound, usually, full of rage. I took good care of our baby, our babies. I'm sure now that there are no better cared for children in the world. They had my milk, my sleep, my time, my eyes, my words. All the time.

Today they are nine and seven. Ingrid is capable, wryly funny, hard to rattle. She loves to run, loves her gray and green running shoes. She loves a dozen different friends. She's learning to play the trombone. She still jumps into my arms—seventy pounds—to hug and hang and grin at me with her new big front teeth. Iris is philosophical, wondering, sensitive. Begged me last week to take her cross-country skiing in the school field on the year's first inch of snow, and I did. Our family is at ease these days. We make each other laugh. We help each other. Stretched, yes: work and house projects and school and fun. But we have contentment, a constant, filling stream of it. Nobody hits anything.

Fact: I had longed for babies.

The summer I felt whole again, the summer they were three and five, the oldest tree in our city died. I hadn't thought before about a tree dying in a given season—I'd envisioned a slow death, year after year fewer leaves, then maybe a fall in a wind storm. But this was in the newspaper: *The oldest tree in Minneapolis, an oak on a broad terrace above the river, in the sound wave of the interstate, failed to leaf out this spring.*

The tree was 300 years old, maybe 400. It had stood through the building of the city, the coming of the highway, the years of children in the field, the houses rising, other trees swelling and ebbing back. The city park department planned to cut the tree down—its trunk had rotted and was beginning to split from the weight of its branches. It was no longer safe to let stand.

I thought about the grass in the shade of the oak's canopy, how for the first summer in three hundred years the sun would be able to touch those places at every hour. How long would the shape of the roots stay—that complicated, fleshy watershed, underground, invisible?

When I tell you about my worst moments, do you want an explanation, a story? I can tell several, but how will you know which is true?

Story: We had one baby, and she needed to be held all the time. She wouldn't ride in the car without screaming. I couldn't breathe right while she screamed. Once, trying to drive to the post office, I stopped every two blocks to soothe her, which meant nurse her. It was summer; I was sweaty and too big for my clothes. I held her in the back seat, my shirt up, the door open, my legs dangling into the neighborhood avenue.

She needed to be held all the time. She needed to be held all night, to nurse all night.

Fact: I walked every morning carrying Ingrid in the sling. While I walked, I whispered stories to her, even while she slept. I wanted to show her the whole world. *The cottonwood fluff is falling. In the grass it looks like snow. You'll see snow in winter. You'll see so many beautiful things. We'll see so much together.*

Her breath smelled like butter. Her first laugh was a low, sneaky chuckle.

Facts: I was the one with the milk, the one with a long maternity leave and, after that, a part-time job. I was the one in the house, the one always nearest. My husband worked more than full time, traveled for work, and came home to our daughter's overjoyed squeals.

Fact: We did it that way on purpose. We chose it. I nursed her to sleep for every nap, for every bedtime, for many dark hours in the middle of every night. For 18 months.

The same month she began to sleep most of the night without waking, I discovered I was pregnant again.

One time I punched my own leg so hard I made a bruise. One time I tried to hit my own forehead against the wall. My husband stopped me. This was on nights when Ingrid wanted to nurse for hours.

Afternoons filled with the feeling of waiting

for my husband to come home. Waiting for him to lift something off me. The baby. The heat of the day. The guilt of wanting to set the baby down and walk away.

I developed a bump on the side of my wrist the size of a fat green pea. For two hours the afternoon I noticed it, I wept: It was cancer. I would die, and I would miss the golden privilege of seeing this beautiful child grow up.

The doctor took one look and told me it was a librarian's cyst. Benign. Caused by carrying heavy things, like books. Or babies.

Story: I couldn't handle as much as other people can. I wasn't cut out for it.

I didn't want to do us all in myself, but one night I stared out at the trees rustling in hot wind and hoped a tornado would blow all four of us away. How tragic that story would be—a promising young family, taken too soon.

Fast objects seemed faster than usual. A truck speeding beside the sidewalk was a weapon.

My mother-in-law told a story of a baby killed by a flying rock thrown by a neighbor's lawn mower. She told me this while I was sitting on our front porch cradling the baby. While the neighbor was mowing his lawn.

Lying on the bed nursing the baby to sleep, still aching where I'd torn open and been sewn back together, I wept over how perfect she was, and how much she'd already changed. Three days old.

Every time I tell a story that says "every time," my husband reminds me, "not every time."

The article about the tree had stories from neighbors—old people who'd played in the tree's shade as children. They said how tall and broad the canopy had been. People left prayers on paper, folded and tucked between ridges of bark. One said, *I don't know how to raise my daughter.*

Our children's preschool was near the oak—about four blocks' walk, just on the other side of Franklin Avenue. One day that summer, the kids and their teachers walked there, Ingrid's class, the Penguins, holding hands in pairs.

This was five years ago, and I haven't stopped thinking about a woman saying to a tree, *I don't know how to raise my daughter.*

That's the past, but it doesn't have to be the center. We're fine now. I'm fine now.

When they both started sleeping well, it all felt better.

When they were both weaned, it all felt better.

When they were both old enough to walk and talk well, it all felt better.

When I started taking a pill the doctor said would make it all feel better, it all felt better.

Rage wasn't constant, not even in the worst times. But it was inside my skin all the time, waiting.

Here's a story: Everyone is sad and miserable when her babies are young, but everybody lies about it.

Here's another: I had an illness cured by serotonin.

And another: Everybody's sad and miserable caring for babies, but only the brave admit it.

And a few more: Most people enjoy every minute of their babies. Only bad mothers feel like crawling out of their skin. Those days are so precious. Enjoy every minute.

When Ingrid was a baby I wrote a whole year's book of beautiful moments. It was a tiny journal addressed to my daughter, one page each day, each day a precious thing: *How beautiful you are—how you seem* to glow; and, *You laugh along whenever you hear someone laugh;* and, *You talked in your sleep last night: Bubbles! Bubbles! Bubbles!*

But there was no grasping any moment. Every month a new size of clothing folded up and put away. Try to catch the world's rarest butterfly without moving your feet.

Names for a baby: Fat gold watch that rearranges time. Tyrant, terrorist, bowl of applesauce. Grocery store cake with loads of white frosting. Dumpling, terrible kitten.

I've lost the chronology. From here it all seems like one time, but it was years—from one child to two—from aloneness to help to complaint to peace. Where is the right moment from which to tell the story? The moment my fist hit the counter I was without words. There were years of not knowing the story because I was too deep in it. Now are the years that fade the story. It loses its timeline, loses its sense.

But as I began to feel better, I became less ashamed of having felt miserable.

As I grew less ashamed of how unhappy I felt, I began to feel better.

It was as though an invisible third eyelid reopened. My hands, relieved of the weight of dragging myself along, were free to work—free, sometimes, to rest.

I told first close friends and then others: *This is no picnic. People say it's hard, but it is* really *hard.*

What I told them, I could say only in the past tense and only in a whisper: *Sometimes I thought if I could go back, I would. I'd have unmade them if I could.* I told about the fist on the counter, the dent in the siding, the shoe.

There needs to be a kind, fierce guardian at the gate of motherhood. Beware. It will ruin you. It's not for everyone. I was that guardian for a while.

I wanted to talk about it; to complain. More than that, I wished something, somehow had prepared me. I wished someone had said, *This is really no joke. You might hate your days.*

Story told at the natural baby store: Every object in your baby's life can be clean and soft.

Same story: Look at the garden in May, and expect it to stay neat and weedless.

All the time, I wondered why I hadn't known; I made lists, doodled cartoons of the truth wrapped in impermeable layers. We are ashamed not to like the work of motherhood. Even if we can admit unhappiness to ourselves, telling others takes more bravery. And if we say it, who will listen? Of those who listen, who will believe it's not hyperbole? Who can believe it will be the same for them?

It's not the same for everyone. Not even close.

During those years of babies and toddlers, our friends John and Kate were the outside world in our house. We went in together on a share of vegetables from a farm, and every week we met to split up the box and cook a meal. They were newly married and on the fence about children; to us, their childlessness was tonic.

The nights they came for dinner, my husband and I would chop vegetables side by side while John opened beers and Kate played a dancing game with the kids. Or I'd nurse the baby and chat with Kate while my husband and John roasted turnips and tossed a mizuna salad and grilled meat. The two of them had energy for our daughters, could see the humor and loveliness that my husband and I could only trudge through.

On regular nights I fixed our family's dinner one-armed, a baby or toddler on my hip more often than not, and we ate and cleared the table, moved on quickly through dishes and the kids' bedtime and collapse.

On the nights John and Kate came, we ate slowly, enough grownups around to keep up lively conversation while one at a time tended to a child. They stayed after the kids went to bed and brought honest interest in what to us was terribly ordinary. *How do you know how to handle this? How do you decide that? How does it feel?* They were the first friends I trusted with the rage and fatigue and shame about the rage and fatigue. They listened. Sympathetic, interested.

Imagine that woman leaving her note. *I don't know how to raise my daughter.* The paper she left behind would eventually become brittle, then soggy, disintegrate with fall's brown leather, be washed into the soil, drawn up through the roots, made part of the wood. Her unknowing, rewritten in one cylinder of fiber.

That summer it all felt better, a bag of grapes and a bottle of water, a tube of sunscreen and a stack of library books were all we needed to be out and about for hours. My girls' hair was always glowing in the sun.

The summer it all felt better, people in the news kept digging things up. In New York, in the middle of construction at the World Trade Center site, they unearthed a wooden ship a hundred years old, ruined to a skeleton but holding its shape. The image of it swinging from a crane has stayed in my mind, lodged in that summer of emerging.

As I began to be able to see and think again, I spoke more openly about the lies we tell about babies. I was sarcastic, or serious, or both. Petal pink and baby blue, flannel, tiny t-shirts embroidered with the words, *If they could just stay little.* Wherever I could, I pointed out hardness. Harder than a marathon, harder than a dissertation, harder than the flu, those months of not-sleep, of don't-know, of terror of dropping, of stepping on, of starving, of overfeeding, of failing the baby. The wail that might start any time. I ridiculed photos of babies with feathery wings, downy yellow chicks, any suggestion of purity. Babies aren't angels or little birds; they are tiny people we love to the point of pain who can't say what they need, who make noises our military—no lie—records for torture. Tiny people who wake and wake and wake, who are so fragile, who it seems could disappear by accident.

Just when I became the most vocal about this, John and Kate announced they were expecting a baby.

Throughout Kate's pregnancy, I kept up flippant talk about how hard it would be. *I'm writing a poem for you,* I told her. It's called, *Lament for a Newly Pregnant Friend.* I was thinking that I'd be the safe one to complain to. That by refusing to succumb to simple, nice celebration, I'd let Kate know she could say to me what I had been alone with.

I threw them a baby shower. I ordered a giant cake and cut up fruit and cleaned the house and put the leaf in the table, and another friend brought salads and punch. Their families and other friends filled our house. When I wasn't attending to drinks or cutting cake, I remember not knowing what to say, where to stand, which story to tell myself. Kate sat on our sofa, opening gifts, looking teary and grateful and glowing.

The tornado sirens went off that afternoon, the yellow-gray sky raining fat drops. I thought of ushering everyone into our musty basement, but that didn't seem necessary; the sirens go off for thunderstorms, real or anticipated, and so seldom do they mean real danger. We stayed in the living room, an eye on the radar. Later we learned a tornado had touched down just a couple of miles away. While we ate cake, tree upon tree was torn up at the roots.

I remember wondering, as my friend opened packages wrapped in pastel tissue and tied with light blue raffia, why is nobody saying that our friend is about to do the impossible, is heading into years of isolation and hardness, fatigue and frustration and loss of the stars?

Word of the ancient oak's demise circulated. On the neighborhood's online discussion board, people began to protest that the tree, even dead and leafless, should be left to stand. City officials countered that it was too dangerous; the weight of the limbs could easily split the hollow trunk; it might fall at any time.

Kate and John's baby was born in June, and during that summer I went to their house many times to take their dog for a run. I brought them food, cut up parsnips and turnips from their farm box so they could snack easily, one-handed.

It took me months to see how little they needed from me. One day as I arrived, I met Kate's sister on the front porch; she was just leaving, having vacuumed the stairs. My friend—during the baby's naps, I guess—was energetically contemplating a career change, making a spreadsheet of grocery prices at various stores. Every time I saw her, she said how happy and blessed she felt. She didn't seem to be lying.

Facts: Some babies sleep more than others. Some babies cry more than others. Some adults need more sleep than others. Some mothers roll with everything better than others.

Story: Motherhood transforms us, makes us large-hearted and beautiful in ways we never imagined.

Fact: No sister came over to vacuum my fucking stairs.

Fact: The word *blessed*, in this context, makes me

want to barf.

Story: Some mothers bounce back right away. It's amazing.

Another story: There's no sense comparing.

I was a beast of jealousy. I crushed myself against the difference between us like a bird at a window, trying to fly through. Was this friend hiding from me, denying me the frankness I thought we'd keep as she became a mother? Was she truly as overjoyed as she appeared? Don't we all have reasons to hide our darkest sides, even when a friend is ready to hear? Had I been a bad friend, done something to lose her trust? Was I just plain wrong about the hardness? Was it really only my own illness or weakness that made the baby years so hard for me?

I made my husband discuss it with me—this difference—over and over. These were battering, teary, bitter conversations: what happened in those years, how we each remembered them, whether it mattered that—in addition to sometimes hitting things and often feeling like I was fighting for every step through a day—I had also often smiled and laughed. The conversation seemed to have no end: was I seeing Kate clearly? Was my memory of those years right? Had I seemed, in those hard years, from the outside, as glowing and happy as Kate did now?

Light travels through air, through glass, through water, through the other side of the glass, altered by each layer. Memory is like this, and it's like this to speak across motherhood. Even one color—the baby's hair, the baby's eyes, my bruise—we can't be sure we all see the same. How strange is it, what happened to me? How bad? Who's telling the truth? Who can hear it?

And what can be compared? Who's to say what's sick and what's just unhappy? Who's to say what's a cure and what's time? Who's to warn anyone, through the butter-vision of baby?

My husband and I retold the story, rehashed the difference, until we were finished. The last conversation ended with my exhausted tears, the two of us leaning into each other: *We won't ever know what that time was. We can't know. It happened, and we didn't understand it then, and we don't now.*

I don't know how to raise my daughter. Of course the years-ago mother wrote that on paper, rolled it in a tube, left it in a fold of bark. We want to say a thing like that to someone old and quiet, someone who will hold our helplessness and not tell. We aren't asking a question or making a request. We're not quite praying; we're telling a secret. We're saying to the tree: *Hold this. Take I don't know and stretch it toward the sky, build a canopy of it.*

It's an act of faith, that telling. A wild confidence that *not knowing* knows something that we don't know. A desire to see not knowing become sheltering, enduring— no longer just confusion that flies by ungrabbed, but a monument.

The tree seems to know something, but nobody expects to hear what it knows.

The tree is *made* of the past, doesn't leave each year behind, but buries it inside itself, keeps inside what's new. Each year is thin, hidden, solid, present.

A tree is good at giving us silence and memory at once.

For months, I could hardly look at Kate and her baby. My friend's alertness, her laughter, her happy weepiness.

I stopped trying to be so close to Kate. And when I backed away, I noticed she had stepped away, too—stopped sharing, stopped asking what I thought. I deserved this distance. I'd overcompensated for the oversweet world, brought too much bitter to a time that she, like everyone, wanted to keep sweet.

I don't know how to raise my daughter. I picture this mother returning years later to the tree. Whatever mistakes she'd been afraid to make, she's made them now—or not—already. Her not knowing is no longer important. But she can still stand under the tree, the holder of that time, hollow at the center, and hear the rush of the highway, the voices of children in the field.

I'm not lying anymore when I say I'm glad that the baby year, for Kate, was golden, simple, and cherished. Now I believe her.

I have a story, too, about what my vegetable-chopping was for: to give what I thought my friends would need, yes. But more than that, I wanted to live that hard time again, but from the outside, from nearby. I wanted to be close to such an experience, to see it without being pulled down by it. I wanted—impossibly—to be with that hardness again, but from an angle where I could think, could speak.

When I see a woman with a baby now, I say very little. I'm learning to give quiet without forgetting. I try to imagine I'm meeting her under a tree—its articulate leaves—their green, spiked corners casting shadows on the grass.

Ultimately, the city sent workers to swing up and cut off the ancient oak's limbs. They left the trunk standing, open to one cut of sky, and the roots still reaching into the dark under the field. We have our monument. Not a plaque on a patch of bare ground, but a standing column, built of what we've left in its folds.

THE YEW WITHOUT THE MOON
STEVEN HARVEY

> *"the message of the Yew tree is blackness —*
> *blackness and silence"*
> Sylvia Plath, *"The Moon and the Yew Tree"*

The poet came upon her yew at night with the moon perched above its gothic shape. She longed for Mary and a face "gentled by candles" gazing down on her "in particular" but saw her mother's robe of midnight blue instead letting loose "small bats and owls" from the folds of its waxy branches.

And who can forget her "bald and wild" moon with its "O-gape of complete despair," the single detail I recalled after all these years away from her poem as I stood in the midday shadow of a yew that happened to be where I was walking. Rare where I live, it rises gloriously between the sidewalk and the asphalt of a quiet street

looking down in particular on me.

It is not silent. A breeze whispers through the leaves in an ancient language that humans no longer understand, though the sound, like a lullaby in a foreign tongue, brings comfort still.

Nor are the branches that form the conical crown black, but a dark and shimmering green made up of myriad needles spiraling on the stems

in the tangle of branches overhead.

The yew is different at night, an ebony gown, which explains why the poet saw her mother as a witch unleashing nocturnal predators, but a tree in daylight is not like Mary or a mother or a witch at all. It will not let me see faces in the lines along its shaggy hide, though a whorl in the bark holds the nub of a branch,

beckoning in a way that looks familiar.

Long ago I settled for myself the question about a deity gazing down on those who look up and, like the poet, traded saints frozen in an attitude of holiness and "floating on their delicate feet" over empty pews for "the light of the mind…cold and planetary." I too stood at the edge of my lawn on a sleepless night, scrutinizing the black beyond the dark,

and brooded,

but I have left the mind of her poem behind along with my own barefoot midnight musings. "Don't think," the philosopher admonished, "look!" Looking returns the colors that night steals away. The divine may have closed its eyes on me forever, but the world looks back, this tree posing in sunlight

teaching me how to see.

I know not to touch it, though it is inviting, the trunk like an upended stream eddying in a gnarl here at eye level asking for my hand, but Caesar in the *Gallic Wars* tells us that Cativolcus, the old and defeated chief of the Gauls, killed himself with the juice of the yew rather than surrender, and toxins seeping from any stem can sicken me.

So I just look. In sunlight the bark is several shades of brown, running from ochre in the hollows to copper at the high points where crusty flakes have peeled away. Cracked and pocked with cankers, it looks old, but tough, the bole thick and fibrous—muscular I want to say—its vascular bundles bound together like twists of rope for might,

not yearning to escape, but straining with a burden,

and even though it depends on the sun for life, I see when I step back, it is not a longing for more up above but this grappling with gravity that lifts the suicidal crown high into the sky.

Ardor, not love, keeps it alive

even at night under the O-gape of complete despair. The trunk, like a robe slowly widening toward the base and pooling on the ground, draws my eyes downward— away from the sun and moon and planets—to the earth where roots crack the asphalt, buckle the concrete, and luxuriate in the black far below.

Note: The phrase "Don't think, but look!" is from Ludwig Wittgenstein, *Philosophical Investigations* 66.

COPPER BEECH
JUDY MCCLURE

We pick up a map at the entrance to Forest Hills Cemetery, just beyond the towering red puddingstone arches. "Maybe it's over here," my wife says as we walk up a steep hill. We float along the river of meandering paths, the graves along the banks like cottages on the shoreline, but we can't find the grave we're looking for. The exquisite miniature concrete houses perched above on a steep shaded ledge distract us, labels carved into their facades—musician, poet, apothecary—designating their occupants. I climb up the hillside of this tiny town, planting my feet on the mossy rocks to get a better look, peering into the wrapped porches to see who might be sitting there, hoping someone will come out of the three-inch doors and invite me to sit a while.

Later, in front of old stone mausoleums with heavy doors, we look through small, cobwebbed windows at bedrooms for the dead with bunk beds of sarcophagi. We see stained glass windows at the back, chunks of stone that have fallen on the ground in the interior, doors with heavy padlocks. I tease my wife, "Those keep the ghosts inside."

On the way to searching for the graves of playwrights or poets, scientists or abolitionists, artists or union army soldiers, we find ourselves in other places. We circle, we make wrong turns, we move toward the center. Each time my wife and I walk in this cemetery, we start out looking for one thing and then spend most of the time finding what we don't expect.

My wife and I create memories of these dead. As we stand in front of headstones, using the scant information we find there, I calculate how old the person was when they died, often commenting on their age. Many died young, in their thirties or forties, some not until their nineties. We surmise that if you survive the flu or an infected wound or the measles, you are probably very hardy and will live a long time. Some of the stones, scrubbed of their writing by weather, leave us to write our own stories of their lives. Most of the family plots, once surrounded by wrought iron fences, are now marked only with concrete stones, a wisp of the memory of what was once there. The iron furniture for visiting family is gone.

The swirling memories of my younger sister don't always visit me when we walk in this cemetery. Her recent death still surprises me. For fifty-three years my place as the third of four siblings seemed unchangeable, until she died. She isn't buried here; her ashes fill silver lockets and bracelets worn by her children, siblings, and friends, and in two urns, one with our father and one with her husband, who all live far away. My memory, though, of the first time I saw my sister is vivid. My mom walked through the front door of our red brick house where I stood waiting for them to arrive from the hospital. Without taking her coat off, my mom handed me this smooth soft baby wrapped in a pink blanket.

Of course, this memory can't be true. I was four years old. I doubt my mother would have handed me a newborn baby. Still, the memory persists, along with my feeling that my sister had been brought home just for me. In every photo for several years, my three siblings look at the camera, but I am always looking at Katy. In later photos, our heads lean together, her red curls and pale skin filled with tan freckles rest against my cheek and short dark hair.

•

One afternoon at the cemetery, my wife and I find a tree laying on its side, a massive copper beech, recently cut down. We can see the rot inside the tree and talk about the care it must have taken to fell this giant without harming the surrounding graves. I stand on top of the six-foot-wide stump of the tree, still solidly sitting in the ground, then step down and over to the tree. I rub my hands over its bumpy bark, lean over and wrap my arms around as much of it as I can get. I rest my cheek along its rough surface, which is surprisingly soothing. We go back another day to visit the tree again, its mighty presence still apparent. I find burls on its surface and large, dark fungus growing along the stump. Ants and other bugs scurry around, hard at the work of living.

"I wonder how old it is," I say to my wife as I try counting the rings on the craggy base, but there are too many, and they are too messy. The wavy wood is surrounded by a sea of sawdust still present from its felling. Orange lichen and brown fungus, heavy concentric circles of it, line the bark in patches. Sap still oozes out of the stump. The bark reminds me of the skin of an elephant.

"A hundred and fifty years, maybe more? Probably planted the year the cemetery was created."

On the days I walk in the cemetery alone, I always make my way to the tree. I move with easy contemplative steps, careful not to disturb the sleeping residents on this town of grassy hills along curving wide paths sheltered by the canopy of arching beech, maple, oak, and gingko. My memories keep me company. Imperfect concentric circles, sometimes flaring out from a center, steady stretches of peace alternating with undulating waves expanding on one side, never realigning with the past closer to the center.

Another day, while walking, my wife says to me, "I have something I want to show you." We stray from our usual path at the back of the cemetery and instead walk straight ahead and then veer left by the pond with a shimmering kinetic sculpture. She examines the map, looks in different directions, and then finally says, "It's this way." We walk along a grass path and arrive at a small grove, a family plot surrounded by a low stone wall; in the back stands a sparkling white marble girl encased in a glass dome.

Gracie stands on a hexagon pedestal with a layer of leaves at her feet. She wears a dress with a sash, grasping the top edge in her plump hand, right above a spray of flowers. More flowers decorate the delicately embroidered bodice, all the way up to the collar. Her wavy hair, held with a bow on top of her head, flows past her shoulders, and her boots are secured with a gentle line of six buttons up the outer side of her shins. Her face is pensive, her ears tiny, and she looks beyond the glass to the trees, grass, and headstones around her. Gracie has been four years old for 140 years.

My breath is pulled from my chest at the grief of Gracie's parents at the death of their four-year-old daughter, the confusion her six-year-old brother must have felt, and the decision to hire a sculptor from Quincy to carve this tiny delicate child into a permanent memory. Then I imagine a whole cemetery of glowing white marble statues sparkling in the sunlight or incandescent under a full moon.

We have paused at many graves of children at this cemetery, some with only "baby" etched in the stone, others with no name, just small headstones with a lamb or a winged cherub on top, a symbolic memory. My wife and I contemplate the lives of the families involved. How old was the mother when the baby died?

Were there other children? How much longer does the mother live? But Gracie's memory seems alive. We stand for a long time until we walk slowly away, back towards the entrance, walking under leaves green at the upper edges of their bright red capes, engulfing the deep auburn branches, and the scattered throw rugs of brittle brown leaves crunching as we walk through them.

•

Later that fall I drive to western New York to visit my dad. On the second day of my visit, we pick up lunch, and as he puts his wallet back in his pocket and hands me our drinks and the bag of sandwiches, he says, "You might think this is weird, but what I like to do is get my lunch and then go up to a cemetery to eat it. If we get in the right spot, we can get a view of the lake." I tell him about my recent walks in the cemetery, considering our common enchantment with these peaceful, purposeful places.

The cemetery I visit with my dad sits off a wide country road on the peak of a hill. In the distance, a cerulean sky with scattered white clouds edged with silver drapes above a wash of red, ochre, and orange leaves on the outstretched arms of trees. The vast lake stretches languidly below, smooth and polished. A swath of graves surrounds us, mostly marked by flat stones embedded in the ground, all of them with upright artificial flowers in metal vases. I am already forming this afternoon into a memory, encasing it in glass.

I do think of my sister, how could I not, as I walk with my dad, who lost his youngest child less than a year earlier. But the air feels cool and dry on my skin, the trees radiate with color, and I feel easy, light, even grateful for this walk in a cemetery with my dad. Although we don't know anyone buried here, we wander the cemetery, noting the dates, ages, and wondering about names and where the people originated. I feel how grief and joy are adjacent, that pressing so closely to mortality and impermanence offers hope and spaciousness to the living.

After leaving my dad several days later, I stop, only ten minutes into my ten-hour drive. I get out of my car in a gravel parking lot on the edge of the lake, the closest portion of the shoreline to the spot where my dad poured my mom's ashes into the water from the back of a boat six years ago, softly saying, "Goodbye honey." The dead of my family are ashes now, mostly without markers attending their graves. The ethereal gauzy memories are marker enough—my mom coming home from work and setting her heavy canvas bag filled with papers to correct on top of the round white and yellow kitchen table. Her mother's swoop of styled silver hair, earlobes soft from pulling off clip-on earrings, and her pink-carpeted bathroom with carved, candy-like soaps. My other grandmother chasing down a boy who had run into me with his bicycle, the handle leaving a purplish mark across my neck, the smell of the California sun radiating from the hot concrete path. And my sister, the last time she visited Boston, arranging blue hydrangeas in my purple dining room.

•

One morning back at Forest Hills, my wife and I return to the copper beech and find that the stump of the tree has been removed, leaving an eight-foot crater of soft brown detritus. I walk on it, wanting to be where the giant originated, imagining my own roots growing deep into the fecund soil that remains. I try exhuming the memory of the stump the last time I saw it, dark and stony, like the surrounding headstones. Its memory now a crater rippling with an ocean of waves. The tree still lays on its side—I rub my hands across it, inhaling the scent of wood and crushed leaves.

I return to the cemetery again in early November, this time on my own. I visit Gracie, and then I walk along the pond, up a hill, and towards the tree. I can hear the buzz of chainsaws all around the cemetery, and I see workers with backhoes, shovels, and rakes removing debris, scraping away the physical evidence of memory. I begin bracing myself for loss. Still, when I make my way up the path and around the corner and see that the tree is gone, I am unprepared, and I start crying. I walk along the shape of the outline of the tree's remains of dry leaves and sawdust, pick up a handful of the soft tan remains, and let them slip through my fingers.

I begin mourning—the memory of my arms around the tree's vast circumference, my cheek against its comforting rough surface, and then the new memories I'll never form. I search for remains of the tree, tangible, solid memorabilia. I find a gnarled chunk, etched with wavy rings of time. The fragment fits in the palm of my hand and I close my fingers around it.

THE BEES
CHRISTINA KAPP

The flowering crab trees will bloom early, pink bursts yawning while earthen shoulders still ache with winter, but it's not time for them yet. It is still January, and students rush past the bare trees with heads bowed under hoods, backs hunched against the tug of books. Nature's paralysis is reassuring; there is still time. With the chill biting their noses, the cold permits a study of ages still unknown. In class they are told to think beyond the confines of campus. They propel their minds beyond the bone-hard earth, the steely Ohio sky, the unseen clusters of winter bees hidden away, using their collective bodies to shiver together enough warmth to survive. If the students think about honeybees at all in winter, it's likely to assume they are dead.

•

In 1986, The Talking Heads' "Road to Nowhere" was our unofficial high school graduation anthem. We rolled down our car windows to let music blare from our speakers. We blackened our lungs with cigarettes, teaching one another how to form our lips into an O and blow smoke rings. Never let them die a virgin, we said, hooking our fingers through the dissolving circles. We stoked the clouds above our heads with rage over exacting schedules: 12:04, lunch. 12:46, biology. We couldn't wait to leave high school. As long as nowhere wasn't here, it didn't matter where we were going.

•

By March, the bees bob promiscuously around the faces of students who are sprawled across benches before spring break. A buzz in the ear makes one of the girls squeal. The group of them leap up, batting the air with spiral notebooks. One of them says she's allergic, checks her backpack for her EpiPen. Once we were these students. We had come to learn things, to sit in the quad and flirt. We had not come to get stung. And we learned quickly: It is unwise to drink a Coke near a flowering crab tree.

•

On my first day of college orientation, I met a girl who had attended the same NRBQ concert I had the year before. Not that we were fans of NRBQ. The only song either of us knew was "Ridin' in My Car." We walked the halls of our dorm together, saying the names of the local bars out loud, places we had yet to locate where we would need fake IDs we didn't have. We enunciated these names carefully, as if the words themselves might be enough to intoxicate us. On the fourth floor, we found a curly-haired boy sitting in the hallway among a pile of boxes. He was snapping a vinyl record into jagged black daggers. We asked if he wanted to come with us. Where, he wanted to know. Nowhere, we shrugged.

•

A flowering crab tree lives roughly thirty to seventy years. Honeybees of the summer variety live only four to six weeks, but winter bees can live up to six months. In all things, external conditions impact lifespan. Disease, disturbances, and violence cannot be predicted. A college student ought to finish a degree in four years, but studies show that only about 55% manage to finish in six. Some drop out, some disappear. It's hard to say what happens to them.

•

The curly-haired boy lay with me on my narrow dorm bed. We kissed sloppily, like children, fully clothed. The landscape of our inexperience made us afraid to stray too far from safety in the dark. When we had had enough, we stood up and turned our backs to button the gaps in our clothes. He climbed through my second-floor window, waved farewell, and disappeared. I panicked, imagining him broken on the ground, limbs zigzagging outward, but he stood on a small portico over an entrance door one floor below. When he reached up, his hand was bleeding. Broken bottle, he said. He came back inside, and I used up all my Band Aids to cover the wound, made him promise to be more careful. I'll try, he said. Fingers crossed.

•

When I was young, my grandparents had an old apple tree in their backyard. I loved it from afar but refused to come too close. In late summer, crabapples weighed down the branches, darkening the gnarled tree trunk under a fortress of shade. The fruit fell and rotted, creating a circle on the ground. Bees hovered like smoke over the broken, browning sweetness. I had stepped on a bee before. I knew the pain of being stung. Wear shoes, my grandmother said. You'll be all right. I didn't believe her. I chose to stay away.

•

In my dorm room I listened to the Grateful Dead with *The Canterbury Tales* open in my lap. *Whan that Aprille with his shoures soote, / The droghte of March hath perced to the roote.* The curly-haired boy knocked on my door. We hadn't kissed one another in a long time. We kissed other people now. He held a six pack of Busch in bottles. So fancy, I said, pushing Chaucer away. We sat on my bed and drank the beer, peeling the labels off the damp glass. If you can peel it whole, you're sexually frustrated, he said. After the third bottle I stuck my perfect label in the back of my spiral notebook, pressing it like a flower.

•

It has been a long time since we were students. We hardly remember the bees or the flowering crab trees. (Forgetfulness is the easiest adaptation.) We are consumed with our extra decades and hazy stories. Our children are the students now, and they are different. They no longer bat the bees away; they post signs to protect them. *NO EXIT/ENTRY: Bee colony preservation outside.* We have learned new terms: Colony Collapse Disorder, sublethal effects, organophosphates, nontarget organisms. In middle age, we cluster our diminished number more tightly together, thrumming to the beats of our new worries. Bees, trees, children. The collapse of our youth.

•

Two days after the curly-haired boy and I were sexually frustrated together, a different boy came to my dorm room. He left his jacket on and dragged his feet, pacing. He told a story about a car accident. Up north, two hours away. Three boys had been in the car. Two were killed instantly, and the third, the curly-haired boy, was in the hospital. We got in my car and drove there. We didn't know how to worry properly, so we smoked cigarettes and decreed Jerry Garcia the Patron Saint of Trips. We talked about broken limbs and head injuries as if they were dinner entrees in the cafeteria, some slightly less terrible than others. When we got to the hospital, they made us stay in the lobby. We sat in vinyl seats and bought sodas from the vending machine. We watched the elevator doors slide open and closed, thinking someone might come for us, tell us we could visit our friend. No one did. We drove home. That night, the curly-haired boy died.

•

On campus, there is a memorial plaque under the flowering crab trees. It is raining and almost summer at our twenty-fifth reunion, so the blossoms have dropped, the students are gone, and the bees have moved on to summer flowers. I remember the boy on the plaque—his curly-haired stringiness, his smudgy glasses, his crooked shoulders under his tattered leather jacket—but I also remember our stories. The road to nowhere, the broken records, the narrow beds, the spiral notebooks, the beer bottle labels, and the installation of these aging trees, planted in memory of the students who had died. No one who lives here remembers them anymore. The plaque has darkened with time. It has rained and the trees drip fat splashes of memory on my shoulders and rage rises out of the fermented sweetness. The inevitable silence of branches scratches at us and we wrap our arms around our bodies. We are defensive. These trees have aged. Before I return again, these trees will be slated for replacement. Someone younger will imagine something different here. Something less high maintenance. Landscaping with better sight lines. Trees that attract fewer bees to bother the students. Then I will be the one left to do the pollinating, to tell the stories and shiver away the winters, hoping to generate enough warmth to keep our memories alive.

CATALPA TREE – *CATALPA SPECIOSA*
AIMEE NEZHUKUMATATHIL

A catalpa can give two brown girls in western Kansas a green umbrella from the sun. *Don't get too dark, too dark*, our mother would remind us as we ambled out into the relentless mid-western light. Every day after school, the bus dropped me and my younger sister off at Larned State Hospital, and every day, our classmates stared at us as the bus pulled away. I'd unlock the door to the doctor's quarters with a key tied to my yarn necklace and we'd go inside, fix ourselves snacks, and finish worksheets on fractions or spelling. We'd wait till our mom called to say we could meet her in her office, a call that meant she was about ten minutes away from being done for the day. We'd click off the TV and scramble to get our plastic jelly sandals on for the block-long walk to the hospital's administration building. Catalpa trees dotted the wide prairie grounds and watched over us as we made our way to Mom's office. My sister and I knew not to go anywhere near the fence line of the patients' residence because they sometimes were given basketball privileges outside, behind three layers of barbed wire. But occasionally I allowed myself to look at them when I rode my maroon three-speed bike, and sometimes an inmate would wave as I passed.

Catalpas stand as one of the largest deciduous trees at almost sixty feet tall and dangle long bean pods and flat seeds with wings to help them fly. These bean pods inspire some to call the catalpa *cigar tree, trumpet creeper,* or *catawba.* Catalpa trees can help you record the wind as it claps their giant heart-shaped leaves together—leaves with spit curls, not unlike a naughty boy from a fifties movie, whose first drag race ends in defeat and spilled milkshakes. But these leaves can make a right riot of applause on a particularly breezy day. A catalpa planted too close to a house is a calamity just waiting to happen, but perhaps some people think the danger isn't too menacing since catalpas also yield good tone wood for guitars. And who would challenge that song out there on the Plains?

All those songs call out to the sphinx moth, who lays about five hundred half-millimeter eggs at a time on the catalpa's leaves. These leaves are the moth's only source of food, and if left unchecked, the caterpillars can completely defoliate a single mighty tree. Kids in the Central Plains know these "worms" as good spending money. The sphinx caterpillars (also known as "catfish candy") make prized fishing bait; catfish and bluegill gobble them without seeming to get the least bit suspicious about their sudden appearance in the water.

Sometimes, before we left to pick up our mom, my sister and I gathered coins for the vending machine in the lobby of her office. In 1986, a Little Debbie brownie cost a precious thirty-five cents—precious because what little allowance we received was inconsistent, and so we couldn't count on it for gummy bracelets stacked up my arm in imitation of Madonna, or for the occasional ninety-nine-cent ice cream sandwich at Dairy Queen, or to save up for another colorful pair of jelly sandals. We were known as the daughters of the new doctor in that sleepy little county, but my mom made sure we weren't spoiled, unlike most of her coworkers' kids—children who had six or seven pairs of the latest high tops or were already talking about what luxury sports car would be their first. Extravagance, then, was the occasional afternoon when my sister and I found just enough to split a brownie between us.

After greeting the receptionist, riding the

elevator up a few stories, and walking past the patients' pool tables and lounge, we'd greet our mother with bits of chocolate in our smiles. *Cavities, cavities!* she'd cluck at us, dropping whatever she was doing to hug and kiss us hello. I only pieced it together years later—how her day was spent trying to help patients who often hurled racist taunts and violent threats against her, like *Get out of here, Chink, or I'll choke you with my own hands!*

I can't believe how she managed the microaggressions of families who told her that they couldn't understand her accent, who spoke loud and slow at her, like she—the valedictorian of her class, the first *doctora* of her tiny village in the northern Philippines— was a child who couldn't understand. But my mother always kept her calm, repeating recommendations and filing reports without losing her temper.

How did she manage to leave it all behind in that office, switching gears to listen to the ramblings of her fifth- and sixth-grade girls with their playground dramas, slights, and victories? I don't remember her talking about work while she walked home, changed out of her stylish suits, or fixed us hot meals from scratch. I only knew of what she regularly had to suffer because I'd sneak into and skim over her journals while she was in the shower or brushing her teeth. If not for those little peeks, I never would have known what she had to endure that year.

Thirty years later, I find myself underneath the largest catalpa tree in Mississippi. This tree is one of the centerpieces of the famous "tree walk" at the University of Mississippi, where I now teach. Its branches stretch horizontally to nearly the length of a bus and have to be reinforced by metal supports in several areas so the branches that are soft and starting to get mushy at the center don't fall on an unsuspecting coed.

The foot-long leaves of catalpa trees like this one, for me, always meant shade from persistent sun and shelter from unblinking eyes. When I moved to the South, I thought I'd need to make use of those wide leaves constantly, but for the first time in my life, I haven't had to. And for the first time in their young lives, my kids see brown people other than me on a daily basis. Nobody stares at me here in the South. No one stares at my parents when they visit or when they're at home now in central Florida. In their backyard, my parents spend their retirement crafting an elaborate garden, planting trees with much smaller leaves, and one of their great joys is to tend to the trees after a daily walk. To tug off any dead leaves or branches, pruning them just so, more orderly than any haircut they've ever given me. When I visit, one of my favorite things is to walk among the fruit trees with my mother while she regales me with all the tree-drama that's occurred since I was last there: *Can you believe all the flowers fell off this tree during the last hurricane? Too bad—no mangoes this year. Here is the tree where the vanda orchid grows best, remember? I told your father the birds are going to steal everything on this tree and he didn't listen, can you imagine?*

On campus, when I pass the giant catalpa tree, I think of that shy sixth grader who was so nervous when people stared. But then I remember the confident clickety-clack of my mother's heels as she walked home from work with me and my sister—when people would stare at us but my mother didn't seem to mind or notice. I remember her radiant smile when we burst through her office door, and then her laugh as she listened to our tales of the lunchroom and gym dramas of the day. I hear my own heels as I rush to meet my first class.

The campus catalpa offers up its creamy blossoms

to the morning, already sultry and humid at 9 a.m. It still stands, even through the two or three tornado warnings we've had just this first windy year in Mississippi. As I pass the enormous tree, I make note of which leaves could cover my face entirely if I ever needed them again. If I ever needed to be anonymous and shield myself from questions of *What are you?* and *Where are you from?* I keep walking. My students are waiting. My sweet southern students, who insist on calling me "Ma'am," no matter how much I gently protest. And I can't wait to see their beautiful faces.

THE TREES IN THE AIR
AMY BOYD

My nose knows trees. It remembers the pungent, twisty smell of the yellow cottonwood leaves on the ground outside my childhood home and the aroma of the tree's fallen twigs as I pulled the bark off in long strands. It knows the scent of the massive red oaks in the park where we collected acorns in plastic buckets, red hoodie zipped up, sneakers shuffling through the leaves and tossing their tannic brown smell up to my nose.

My nose remembers the slightly dusty summer scent of the rose of Sharon that grew next to the house, short and bushy. It knows the subtle, dark smell of the hemlocks surrounding the lake where I lived in New Hampshire, and how that differs from the warm rush of the aroma of white pines in a dry, sunny slope and from the rich heady perfume of the Fraser firs in the high peaks of southern Appalachia.

My nose is intimate with the smell of walnut trees that grabs you and makes you pay attention, and the smell of mesquites, slightly sweet and dry as bone. It can distinguish the leaves of sassafras from sourwood and sweetshrub from spicebush.

When I walk through the forest on a warm day, every few steps I smell something different. I know not everyone experiences the world this way; I suspect very few do. As for me, though, I'm constantly noticing a new whiff of this and hint of that. Sometimes I am able to pinpoint exactly where the strands of smell are coming from; other times I cannot, but they still register in my brain, this spot smelling different from the spot just over there. I walk through a silent olfactory symphony, melody lines from various sources weaving in and out, coming into focus and then fading away.

The smells come from lots of things: fungi decomposing the dead branches and leaves on the ground, bacteria in a particular mud puddle, the water of a nearby creek, a rotting corpse of a mouse hidden in the understory. But many, if not most, of the strands of scent come from the vast diversity of organic compounds released by all the plants around us.

•

The molecules released by plant leaves, flowers, and other tissues into the air are called biogenic volatile organic compounds (BVOCs). Inside the tissues where they are created, these chemicals can serve to protect the tree from environmental challenges such as ozone or heat stress. Once released into the air, BVOCs may do lots of things. Emitted from the flowers of a tree, they may attract pollinators, such as bees or bats, to visit the flowers and carry pollen from one to another, emissaries ensuring reproduction of these sessile giants. Similarly, BVOCs released from ripe fleshy fruits—the scent, for example, of ripe peaches—advertise to animals that will eat the soft, sweet parts and in doing so, move the seeds about, dropping them in places where they might germinate and grow.

BVOCs released when a tree's leaves are being munched by a caterpillar quickly trigger the rest of the tree to prepare to defend itself from similar marauders. Inside a tree, it can take a long time for hormonal signals to travel from one part to another, but volatile compounds released from one branch move swiftly through the air and can get the message across to distant branches much more efficiently.

These same compounds also alert predatory

insects to the fact that there are bugs eating those leaves, a fast-food advertising jingle in the form of airborne chemistry. The insect predators (wasps and such) then swoop in for the feast of caterpillars, and the tree is both restaurant and rescued damsel. This serves to help the host plant, to be sure—the enemy of its enemy is its friend. But did these BVOCs evolve for this purpose? We don't yet have evidence of that, although it's possible.

The volatiles also allow trees to communicate with each other, serving as messages to their neighbors of approaching danger. Once they receive the message, the receipient tree can suit up for a proper defense against its enemies. Biologists assume that plants are not necessarily releasing these signals purposefully with interplant communication in mind; instead, they characterize it as one plant "eavesdropping" on another by detecting the BVOCs in the air and then reacting. This can happen, though, not only between plants of the same species but also among plants of *different* species, and the physiological response that happens in the receiver of the signal can happen within seconds.

The BVOCs are certainly not—I don't think— meant to be a way of communicating with me. And yet they are doing so; I receive the signals, even if their received meaning isn't what the tree intended.

•

For a while, in the winter of 2021, COVID-19 stole my sense of being alive in the world. I was one of the lucky ones; I never actually got extremely sick, wasn't ever in the hospital or on a respirator. I didn't have months of recovery before I could walk around the block. Some did. Many died; many others will never be the same.

For me, my bout with COVID made me feel like hell for a week and then was basically over, kind of like the flu. My COVID symptoms were in some ways typical—body aching all over, total fatigue. In other ways, they were atypical: I never had a cough or respiratory symptoms, but I did develop a weird sensation that made the skin on my back and upper arms intensely sensitive, such that I wanted nothing touching me, wanted to take all my clothes off all the time, although being January, that wasn't really an option.

And then, just as my other symptoms were resolving and I was starting to feel fine, I lost all of my sense of smell. I got up in the morning and couldn't smell the coffee in my mug or the cinnamon on my oatmeal. Completely, and suddenly, my ability to smell the world was gone.

Terrified, I wandered around the house trying to find it. I would hold a bottle of vanilla just below my nose. Nothing. I would chop fresh garlic, lemon peel, *anything* I could think of that would have a powerful scent, hoping it could penetrate the wall that had suddenly become erected between me and the world. Nothing, not even the slightest hint. A completely blank slate.

I kept checking, sticking things under my nose many times a day. I read some of the research on *smell training*, showing that people who lost their sense of smell could, in some situations, recover it more fully and more quickly by basically making their sniffer practice, the olfactory system's equivalent of weightlifting.

Did it work for me? I don't really know. It was definitely worth a try. I was desperate. And yes, my sense of smell gradually, thankfully, returned. At first, I'd just get the faintest suggestions of cinnamon or grapefruit or allspice. Sometimes it was so minimal I wasn't sure if I had imagined it... but I hadn't. Slowly, it got stronger, more certain. After a few months, I was back to normal.

But that spring was hard. I was used to warm weather bringing long walks where every few steps, I would smell something new and different. I was used to spring being alive with alluring, exciting, intriguing scents all around me. Walking past a yard full of freshly spread mulch (which would normally have smelled overpowering and intense to me) and smelling *nothing* was incredibly strange. In general, I felt completely separate from the world. Without my sense of smell, I felt like a ghost, like I didn't really exist. And I wept, a lot. I wasn't at all certain I wanted to keep living if it was going to be like this, as if I wasn't actually there, as if the world wasn't real but only a two-dimensional image.

•

Once, when I was in Costa Rica as a graduate student, taking a tour of a botanic garden there, the director of the garden cut a branch from a nearby tree and held it out for us to identify by smell. I took him up on the challenge, and yes, there it was in my nose, the distinctive pungence of walnut. I knew it immediately. He smiled, pleased that I could discern its identity.

The English language has a dearth of vocabulary to describe olfaction. Wine sommeliers and tasters constantly have to refer to what wines smell or taste *like*, using nouns more often than adjectives. Most commonly, the words name fruits (orange, peach, figs, cherries, pear), but rose petals, lavender, orange peel, vanilla, and honeysuckle are also common. Odder ones include aloe vera, chocolate, heather. But it gets weirder: wine smells and tastes have been compared to beef blood, saddle leather, smoked game, brambles, charcuterie, beetroot.

But where are the adjectives? Those that are used are not particularly precise and describe more of a feel than a smell: shady, cool, sweaty, crisp. Some represent actual scents: spicy, floral, smoky, earthy. But the repertoire is limited. Words are generated in the evolution of languages for the things we value. The poverty of words to describe scents stems from our culture's emphasis on other senses, especially vision, and our lack of appreciation for our olfactory system. Vision, for example, is valued as central to our functioning, whereas smelling is just kind of a bonus, the equivalent of icing roses on a birthday cake or the chocolate on your pillow in your hotel room, something nice but not ultimately all that important.

•

Are humans impacted by BVOCs from trees? Proponents of the Japanese practice of Shinrin-yoku, otherwise known as forest bathing, think so. Nature therapy, or the idea that time in nature has benefits for human health, has ancient roots in multiple cultures, but shinrin-yoku became an official medical therapy in 1982 when the head of the Japanese Ministry of Agriculture, Forestry, and Fisheries, Tomohide Akiyama, coined the term. Akiyama wanted to promote valuing the forests in Japan for benefits other than logging and advocated for forest bathing as a way to counteract the harmful effects of overworking, depression, and urban-induced stress and anxiety. As Dr. Qing Li, a key scientist who has studied the effects of forest bathing for over 30 years, states, "Shinrin-yoku originated in Japan in the 1980s as our national health program to help...workers to reduce their stress... There are two major religions in Japan, Shinto and Buddhism. Both relate to and see forests as the realm of the divine. We even have the word *karoshi* which means death from overwork, so it makes sense for people to turn to the forests to help." Turn to the forests they did: the practice of shinrin-yoku became very popular in Japan and has spread around the world.

Science is starting to back up the acclaimed benefits of forest bathing. Studies have shown that time spent in forests, as compared to time spent in urban settings, reduces blood pressure, stress hormones, and depression, and increases natural killer (NK) cells and other immune activity that can fight cancer. It can decrease symptoms of asthma and atopic dermatitis in children. It can improve attention and memory and lower heart rates.

More research is needed, certainly, to tease apart the complex factors that might lead to these positive impacts on human health. Forests are complex places, and one's experience in a forest could potentially be influenced by all of the senses, as well as the particular activity in the forest and the person's individual health conditions and previous experiences, cultural references, and preconceived notions.

However, it's clear that BVOCs are an important part of the story. For example, research shows that terpenes, the largest class of BVOCs produced by trees, have anti-inflammatory effects on human physiology that could be beneficial in a range of conditions such as bronchitis, COPD, osteoarthritis, and skin inflammation. They also have anti-tumor effects.

One study exposed women to olfactory stimulation by a-pinene (a terpene) and found that it decreased heart rates and increased parasympathetic nervous activity, both components of enhanced physiological relaxation. Other studies have found similar results from olfactory exposure to cedrol and D-limonene, two other tree-produced terpenes. Another study showed that a stay in a hotel room including exposure to Japanese cypress oil increased NK cell activity and decreased adrenaline and noradrenaline in the urine of test subjects. These studies tell us that at least some of the health benefits of forest bathing can be traced to BVOCs.

Is their impact through our olfactory system, though, or our respiratory system? Do we need to *smell* these chemical signals to glean their benefits? We don't know yet, but one study done on genetically modified anosmic mice (i.e., mice with no sense of smell) showed that the positive effects of BVOC exposure on other mice do not show up in the anosmic mice. So at least for mice, actually smelling the forest plays a role in its impact. Whether this will hold true for humans as well has yet to be seen.

•

When I lost my sense of smell, I lost my sense of being fully alive. COVID stole it from me for a while, leaving me unable to be fully present or fully interact with what was around me. Everything felt somehow artificial. I could *see* the trees, but they couldn't really be there because I couldn't smell them. I realized that I had an unconscious habit of, every night, deliberately smelling my pillow as I lay my head down to sleep. Suddenly, when I did that, there was nothing. I didn't feel at home in my home, or even in my own *skin*, because I couldn't smell either one.

Yesterday, struggling with personal conflict and feeling ungrounded, I hiked up the mountain behind my house to a grove of white pines on the edge of a pasture. I strung my hammock between two pines just inside the grove, where I could see the sunny open hill but be shaded by the needles of the trees. There was just enough breeze to keep me from sweating and keep the flies from landing on me. I leaned back, closed my eyes, and let the wind carry a symphony of smells to me. Overriding everything was the sharp smell of the pines themselves and the thick carpet of their needles covering the ground beneath me. But as the breeze shifted directions and speeds now and then, I could get little whiffs of other things, other grace notes of scent. I couldn't name them and didn't need to; not trying to communicate with anyone else, I could let go of the world of words for a moment and just notice each olfactory strand as it wove through.

I do not know if the health benefits of terpenes and other BVOCs will play an important role in my life, will help prevent or suppress tumor growth, will blunt the effects of aging, will keep my heart steady or my nervous system happy. I do know, though, that regaining my sense of smell gave me back my sense of being alive and present in the world, that being able to smell those trees while lying in the hammock matters. My nose knows the trees; I don't ever want to lose that connection again.

REMEMBERING THE WYE OAK
DANIEL A. RABUZZI

"Maryland's Wye Oak was long recognized as the largest white oak tree in the nation. [...] On June 6, 2002 the mighty Wye Oak succumbed to time and the elements as its massive trunk collapsed during a severe thunderstorm... At its end, the tree measured 31 feet 8 inches in circumference, was 96 feet tall and had an average crown spread of 119 feet. The main bole of the tree weighed over 61,000 pounds."

— "The Quiet Giant, The Wye Oak," Maryland Department of Natural Resources, https://dnr.maryland.gov/forests/Pages/trees/giant.aspx

Size, yes of course, an immensity, but what most startled was its shape: an explosion in centuries-long slow motion, a lacework that knit itself, and unknit itself, over and over again, each time a little more unique. A shape that shaped the air and land around it, a landscape of its own making, a tree-skip that made its own region, a gentle imperium, a geography we can admire but not fully understand.

Try to coin a word for this glory: a "burstow"? a "rambullow"? I fall back on the acknowledged, the hallowed: the Wye Oak was a sprig on a branch of the World Tree, the Tree of Life, given many names by many peoples across the world. Frustration. Root for a name of my own to give it, my humble offering to this tree-as-rippling-mountain. Fail to cope my intent (also: migrating whimbrels in the distance, and the shush of

91

all those leaves, the long song of a mockingbird, the petty whispers of my stomach concerned about lunch). Resignation. No word of mine could contain, still less define, the shape of it.

Crotch, scaffold, leaders within, leaf-hoard without, yet open to all, inviting inspection, a reredos, the curtain covering the ark, hiding and revealing, hidden and hid and revealed. Swallows slide around its crown; a flycatcher darts out and back, out and back. Many congregants crowd the tabernacle, create the sermon together, green-forged lessons in homiletics.

Off-rounded, smudge-splayed, enduringly labile, self-renewing architecture, until the final terrible storm.

BRIEF, RECOGNIZABLE FEATURES
JOANNA BRICHETTO

Look up and there they are, bare and brittle against Nashville sky: skinny ribs zigzagging from a skinny spine at the end of every branch. In February, hackberry twigs are fish bones.

Leaves dropped in November, fruit was gobbled in January, so at the second month of the year, bones are their boniest. Gray-brown, slim, tapered. By the third month, secret buds will fatten into view, will swell like beads strung on wire with too much space between. Each of these buds will be a new spine by April.

The best time for bone-watching is after sunrise on a cloudy February day—not partly cloudy or mostly cloudy, but straight-up, blanket cloudy. After pinks and blues and peaches drain to white pulled tight, to an opaque scrim held just above the trees, this is when twigs are silhouetted clear and fine.

> Neighborhood playlist: interstate roar,
> a faraway train, and the whistle from
> Radnor freight yard six miles away (a
> *C-sharp*). Also crows (*caw, caw*). Also robins
> (*cuk, cuk*).

To be at home in the world, we need to learn where we are.

I look for fish bones on walks, to orient myself by hackberry. Not all hackberry twigs are straight and stiff. Some are knobby claws. Some arc and bend and droop. But the skinny zigzags are always a clue.

Another best time is a February afternoon. That's when sideways sun pulls trunks and limbs into dense relief and sculpts them into the opposite of morning's flat die-cuts. A *Celtis* chiaroscuro. Barks bloom in a frittering spectrum of grays with shadowed warts and lesions, with splats and rosettes of pale lichen that, if near enough to touch, resolve into unexpected blue.

> Afternoon playlist: interstate roar,
> but louder; street noise, leafblowers,
> chainsaws, planes, the occasional hospital
> helicopter. Also robins. Also white-throated
> sparrows and Carolina wrens, maybe a
> sapsucker; and from sidewalks, the usual
> parade of ridiculous dogs who bark at
> other ridiculous dogs.

To be at home in the world, we need to learn where we are, and when.

•

The authors of one of my favorite tree booklets invented a set of shortcuts called "Brief Recognizable Features." The initials are BRFs, pronounced *briefs*. It's a field guide for people in a hurry. The booklet teaches how to identify local oaks, so since hackberry is outside its focus, I've invented my own hackberry BRFs:

1.   Bark: gray with warts or ridges
2.   Fruit: hard, round "berries" green in spring, garnet by summer
3.   Leaves: entire, with a lopsided base, and partly toothed (sometimes toothless) with three main veins
4.   Twigs: gray fishbones

These BRFs cover both northern and southern hackberry but are too brief to key one from the other. We'd need to be less hurried for that. What matters is that we know it's a hackberry, and that hackberry belongs.

•

One of my husband's colleagues bought property farther from town, and when Michael told him I write about hackberries, the man groaned, "Oh, *hackberries*." Predictably, he'd cut all his down. They were "in the way." He was glad to cut them down "before they fell down," as per their reputation as city trees too near a driveway and for having "soft" wood and "weak crotches."

But did he replace the lost biomass with native trees that could fill the ecological gap? Hackberry trees co-evolved with wildlife here: they make new butterflies, feed migrating warblers, keep winter robins and waxwings alive, and support our local foodwebs with root, wood, bark, bud, twig, gall, leaf, flower, and fruit.

No. He replaced them with Exotic Landscaping and a Sculpture Garden which will demand weekly maintenance and toxic sprays. He fashioned what had been habitat into his own image: into features that wildlife will find unrecognizable.

•

My fishbone opener was meant to be poetic and calendrical and to point a reader toward twigs, but the quickest brief recognizable feature year-round is bark. Bark with warts. Hackberries are famous for warts. What other tree has so awkward a dermatological condition?

Even textbook descriptions are awkward: "clusters of warty growth protruding from the smooth surface at random." "Twisted looking. . . warty singles to warty rows."

But the three hackberry trees in my yard—typical, warty—are not awkward in the least.

> 1.   Bark on the driveway tree is dove gray with charcoal accents, confettied with lichen in chartreuse and palest blue. Both trunks of this forked tree wear thick, curling crisps of blackened cork that beg to be picked like scabs. Here and there are "warty singles."
> 2.   The next tree over has fewer crisps, but more warts.
> 3.   The tree next to that is combed in vertical ridges. And all these crisps, warts, and ridges are made of the same stuff: layer upon layer of cork.

This corky wart right here—I wish I could show you—I can count thirty layers, some as thin as a sheet of paper, some as thick as the cardboard of a cereal box. How long does it take a tree to build these squiggly, successive piles?

They look so much like sedimentary strata, I'm tempted to think they've been laid down, not grown up. Each bump is a landform, a butte, as if material had been deposited in periodic doses, and then, over eons, eroded, marooned.

Sometimes, the buttes and warts are scattershot. Sometimes they align in rough columns, with valleys so deep and tight they can squeeze a coin and keep it there. And sometimes, especially when seen from a moving car, a hackberry trunk is as smooth as beech. But should the car slow down, there will be warts.

To be at home in the world, we need to learn where we are, and how.

•

Hackberries are the first trees I look for, but I look for all the trees. On walks, at parking lots, in woods, by roads. I can't help it. It's a habit.

Another kind of habit is another kind of brief recognizable feature: the *tree's* habit as seen from a distance. Habit in the botanical sense; of shape, form, silhouette, garments, *gestalt*: a tree's accustomed habit.

This was one lesson from a tree class at Warner Park. Deb taught it every winter. First, we'd spend the morning indoors staring at twigs, testing ourselves to "key out" species by features neither brief nor recognizable, and too small to see without a hand-lens: leaf scars, vascular bundles, terminal buds, false terminal buds. After lunch, Deb walked us toward the meadow, which by that point felt enormous.

And while we stood together under a big, cold sky, Deb would point at distant blobs and *name them*. Elms were vase-shaped; cedars were green ovals and pyramids; sweetgums were bare pyramids. Rustling, silver-copper blobs were beech. Sycamore skeletons were white, buckeyes were deer antlers, hackberries were vases but sort of crooked. We were in the presence of a superpower: Deb could see the forest and the trees at the same time. And simply by showing this superpower to us, she passed it to us.

To be at home in the world, we need to learn where we are, and who we are with.

What are the trees in my yard? What are the

trees in my neighbor's yard, the interstate easement, the parking lot? Are they native? Are they in the right place? Do they need help? Do I need help?

•

Once upon a time, I was dead. Long story, but what helped make me less dead, were trees.

Dead is the wrong word, but I have yet to find the right one. A phrase from Sonya Huber's *Pain Woman Takes Your Keys* comes close: "dog-paddling in private dunk tanks of terror." I paddled every minute for days and nights of weeks and months that took a year to scrabble clear from.

When life began flickering back—life being a three-dimensional solid, a body, a weight, any heavy thing that did not spin or fly—one of the flickers was this: *Here is a tree. Here are trees. I knew trees, once. This tree at my door is a sugar maple.*

Being dead, I couldn't drive, of course, but sometimes I could ride in a car. The highlight of a day was to go with Michael as he drove the kids to school, so I could watch our boy and girl walk hand-in-hand toward the building. This was what I'd envisioned when the little one was born: that my kids would be Kindergartener and Senior the same year at the same school, and so I needed to see it, to be there, to not be dead, and if I saw it I might be able to remember it later and feel not just the grasping pain but the happiness, too, like taking a photograph with the hope that you'll appreciate it later. I did take a photograph. I did appreciate it later. I still do.

In the car, to keep my brain from spinning out of my scalp, I tried to anchor it to things that mattered. As trees passed, I named them, *identified* them, which meant I had to remember species from far back before I died, but luckily, so many were hackberries because Nashville is the unofficial hackberry capital of the world, and I concentrated as best I could, brought my mind to bear as I aimed at each one: hackberry, elm, hackberry, dogwood, Osage orange, sweetgum, hackberry out the window. Trees lined every road, and they helped me. I thanked them. Thanking them helped me. Thank you *catalpa*, thank you *willow oak*, thank you *hackberry, hackberry, hackberry*.

To be at home in the world, we need to learn where we are, and why.

Everyone says Nature heals, and I say, *Yes, it can, but*—there is always a but—*to heal us is not what nature is for.*

Years ago, on another tree hike at Warner, some well-meaning walker mentioned casually, *Trees give us oxygen!* Heather, our leader, heard this and paused. She announced in her East-Tennessee Teacher Voice: "Trees don't give us oxygen." Even the birds got quiet. "Trees *produce* oxygen, but they do not make it for *us*."

When I checked with Heather recently, she said "Guess it's more like we *take* oxygen, isn't it?"

If you find healing in Nature, take it.

Take it.

And then, when you feel better, give it back?

To be at home in the world, we need to have a world.

•

I walked the neighborhood at dawn today, when it dawned on me that I've overlooked an additional BRF. It's a variation on habit—part of that at-a-glance superpower—and by showing it to you, I hope to pass it to you.

Naked hackberries dance. One trunk or two or three, it doesn't matter, but the bigger the tree, the bigger the dance.

It was the pale sky again that backdropped the dancers so well. At first I noticed that the oldest hackberries looked planned, sculpted, as if they were bonsai specimens, but huge. Trunks were frozen in motion. Primary limbs climbed and curved in counterpoise, in a balanced give-and-take, in magnificent *contrapposto*. Yes, secondary branches and twigs were all juts and fishbones, but the fatter limbs were like *limbs*—human arms and legs proportionally sized at the joints—meaty and startlingly graceful.

This was a look peculiar to hackberries. Not the long, slow arc of elm. Not the skinny arms of sugar maple. Not the forthright reach of oak. *Dancing*.

When I got home, Michael was leaving for his first walk, so I joined him, and after a half-block of me feigning interest in his day, I got to the point.

"Look at the hackberries."

He looked at the big trees on both sides of the street that were giving and taking as if choreographed, and how they surged just shy of each other's crowns.

"See those lines? I'm desperate for the right description. I've been thinking all morning. Can you help? What's a good adjective? It has to be brief."

The good adjective came with no hesitation. "Sinuous," he said.

Sinuous it is. From the word where we get sinus: "curve, fold, or hollow." Related to insinuate: "to impart or suggest in an artful or indirect way."

Hackberry habit is curved, artful, indirect. It is sinuous. Warts and all.

•

The easiest way to find February fishbones is not to look for them. Simply listen for the robins. When snow covers grass, and when there is no chance of a chance invertebrate, and when the only food for a robin is berries, and when the only berries are exotics that local birds avoid unless starving, robins will flock to hackberry trees for the lingering fruit.

> Snow playlist: *cuks* and *pips* and *squawks* so
> raucous, even normal passersby look up.

And when you look up—you who are lucky to have heard the commotion and to wonder what it's about—note how the snow looks like thick, buttercream icing slathered on cake, and how it highlights every insinuating branch, how it fills those famous crotches, and how every wart on the trunk's windward side wears a coin of white.

This is the world, and you are at home in it.

And when you look up, note that the breast of a "robin red-breast" is not red, but a spicy, rusty apricot. It is the same apricot on the smaller breast of its cousin the bluebird, who also strips hackberry trees in February, and who might be eating on the same twig as the robin, but who flits faster and with less to say, and with miraculous wings that out-blue any sky, and are, in fact, a feature that no one needs to teach you: instantly recognizable, and achingly brief.

WILD APPLE
ALEXANDRIA PEARY

It seems the life of an apple tree in an orchard means living under constant stress from humans. We're a source of stress for our friends, colleagues, family, employees, and ourselves, and it turns out we bother trees. Apple trees are prevented from their natural inclination to manspread, grow in all directions toward the sun, and produce smaller, less edible fruit that is open to entertaining diseases like apple scab, bitter rot, and bitter pit. By nature, apple trees want to swell too large for harvest ladders; they want to produce at their own pace and timing, not scheduled around the best weekends for U-Pick. Apple trees need to be cajoled, pinned, bound, twisted, to produce revenue to sustain a business and satisfy customers. If an apple grower stresses an apple tree properly through chemically thinning, the weaker fruit in the next generation will drop off, letting the king blossom thrive. This king bloom will yield the biggest apple of the group. Like us, the apple is crop dusted with other people's expectations. The apple has long been burdened with symbolic meaning and opinions about how an individual or a nation should conduct itself— in the Bible; in Thoreau's 1862 *Atlantic Monthly* essay, "Wild Apples"; in mythology, Mediterranean or Johnny Appleseed; in clichés like the "apple doesn't fall far from the tree"; and as a bluish icon on laptops. An apple tree is decorated with symbols and morals, not just red fruit, making it as over-determined as a Christmas tree.

Anyone else caught driving their vehicle inside Valley Cemetery, established in 1793 in Londonderry, New Hampshire, excepting municipality workers, would find themselves in big, big trouble. In late

November 2019, we drive roughshod through the cemetery, Andy Mack's minivan plunging up and down on frost-heaved ground like a sailing vessel on rough seas. A fallen branch and overgrown scrub trees scrape the undercarriage and passenger side, as though Puritanical wilderness was trying for a comeback. He points to the mound of winterized grass over the crypt where a few years ago the groundhogs hosted their Day of the Dead, rummaging a human skull and leaving it squarely on top of the crypt like a cantaloupe rind on a compost heap. Briefly, Andy had deliberated carrying the skull to the town offices but decided to make a call on his flip phone to the town grave diggers. He suggested that they fix the situation, pronto.

Like all the graveyards we tour this pre-pandemic afternoon, Valley Cemetery is in proximity to an apple orchard. Another smaller graveyard is on site in the orchard. There's a good chance Andy's family donated the land for Valley Cemetery or was involved in its establishment, as the Mack's were for the town's Presbyterian church, the town's first elementary school, and the town's high school. Andy Mack is the 84-year-old owner of Mack's Apples, a heritage business his family has run for eight generations, since 1732, with employees, the Searles and Crosses, also in it for the long-haul for two or three generations. By mid-afternoon, although he's escorted me to several cemeteries, Andy Mack hasn't shown me the graves of close family members— his wife who predeceased him four decades ago from complications from diabetes, or his infant daughter, or his parents, or his cousin who favored bright lipstick and was a descendant of a Colonel Pillsbury from the Battle of Antietam. Where are the Pinkertons, Leaches, Pillsburys, and Thorntons now, other than names on the sides of buildings? Henry David Thoreau asked, "Who is most dead, –a hero by whose monument you stand, or his descendants of whom you have never heard?"

Until a few months ago, our next cemetery stop abutted a competitor's orchard, bulldozed for a new shopping plaza. Old Hill Graveyard comes with a higher proportion of those tooth-worn, lichen-covered markers and carved skulls with wings at cheekbone level expected of a Halloween graveyard. It's a graveyard of settlers, whereas Valley Cemetery is a depository of early civic leaders. Andy escorts me to the first grave of a relative, John Mack, who came with his wife Isabella from Ireland in 1732 and Who Left This Life in 1753. His ancestor is the only Mack in a crowd of other Scots-Irish, including the McCleary, Wallace, Boyd, Thompson, and Campbell clans. The Scots-Irish first arrived in Boston in 1717. After being rebuffed by the Puritans, the Scots-Irish settled in Nutfield (Londonderry's maiden name) where they planted the first potato in North America, according to the New England Historical Society, and fended off a land grab from neighboring Haverhill, Massachusetts. Andy once stretched out on John Mack's grave and found the length between head and footstone an exact match to his body size. Andy is a fairly small man, probably one hundred fifty pounds and five foot eight when not curved over from back surgery. He favors lined windbreakers and baseball caps and looks like a widowed grandfather on a family outing to the lake, except for the collarless linen shirt he wears when photographed with United States presidential candidates, a soul patch, and the enigmatic tattoo on his left calf.

After an afternoon of graveyard tours, I wait with Andy Mack outside the farm store in his minivan. Instead of passenger seats, a homemade billboard about climate crisis fills the back. Several half-eaten apples of the Jonagold variety, a whiffle-ball sized apple sold as a dessert fruit, perch of the dashboard, a nibbled core in the cup holder. Andy crushes my poet laureate business card into a homemade wooden cellphone holder. Business is robust at Mack's Apples even late on a weekend late in the year, though no one realizes this next round of holidays will be our last family gatherings for two years. The combination of New Hampshire and Massachusetts license plates in the parking lot is refreshed every minute like a busy arrival-departure board. Wooden crates the size of a small car are filled with pumpkins, with children's wagons instead of shopping carts for pulling purchases to cash registers. A barefoot statue of Johnny Appleseed, his hands painted pollen yellow as though he's participating in a Hindu ceremony, and an inverted sauce pot on his head, stands near an entrance to the farm store.

A few of Andy's signature 4-foot by 8-foot Howard-Finster-meets-Jenny-Holzer signs are visible on the curb, more posted in the pick-your-own: *We Fiddle The World Burns. It's Time It's Time It's Time. Doubt Science? To Heck with the Planet. 9 Years Old? 11 Years Old? / A Good Time / To Start Thinking: / Who Will You Want / To Run Your Country? Questions? Disagree? Let's Talk Andy Mack, SR.* Andy Mack is an outspoken Democrat in a predominantly Republican town. Andy's political signs are his large-scale calling card. He inserts these calling cards into the landscape—in the orchards across from the Matthew Thornton Elementary School, near the Presbyterian and Methodist churches and Masonic Hall, around his business. The signage functions as branding, keeping Andy Mack on the town's mind, important during his extended absences from New England, like a loyal assistant covering for an out-of-office boss. He's written all over the rolling fields of Londonderry.

Politics doesn't always mix well with the apple business, however. Drakew27 on Instagram: "Get your grubby, sticky socialist hands off my fruit."

We sit in silence as he peers over the steering wheel at the family farmhouse. It's a structure that stares back without cordiality in a New England RBF, painted cold white and lacking adornment of shutters or porch decorations. He needs to knock on that front door soon and have difficult conversations with his oldest son, also named Andrew, who as of that autumn is in line to buy the farm business. Pastor Karla Dias, minister of the Presbyterian church, the oldest of its denomination in the Northeast, interrupts his pondering and approaches Andy to hold-shake his hand through the driver's side window. She thanks Andy for hosting recent visitors from Londonderry, Ireland, at the church, adding, "God put me in this church to be the first female minister." The vote to build the Presbyterian church was held in the kitchen in the Mack farmhouse in 1837.

Nowadays, a visit to Mack's Apples is a must-have public relations opportunity for attracting votes from this first-in-the-nation state in American presidential politics, a status up for debate since the demographics of New Hampshire don't align with the rest of the country. A short list of politicians to stump speech at Mack's Apples during the last eight presidential elections includes both Bushes, Newt Gingrich, Bob Dole, the Obamas (clocking in three visits with the Secret Service directing sharp shooters to set up in the orchard), Joe Biden, Kamala Harris, and Bernie Sanders. The make-up crew took so long styling John Edwards' hair that the light became too dim for photographs by the pond. Pete Buttigieg's handlers declined a visit because the open-air apple market is under-heated. Kamala Harris' September 2019 Instagram post is standard fare for how politicians leverage the business: "Picking out apples in New Hampshire at Mack's Apple Stand. The Mack Family has farmed the land since 1732, making it the oldest single family-run farm in the Granite State." It turns out that behind that glossy rendition of tradition and social acceptance is a man facing a Shakespearean level of conflict—and the fate of the farm is uncertain.

From the parking lot, the wizened remnants of an apple tree are visible in the closest picking area, a Gravenstein, a descendant of trees from the original farm. The ancient Gravenstein is propped by a board. All but one attempt to graft the tree onto a new generation has failed. The only surviving part of the nineteenth-century tree is an index finger-sized twig on a nondescript host sapling. Normally, the success rate on tree grafts is 100%. Andy Mack's longtime general manager, Mike Cross, doesn't have high hopes for the viability of the graft. It's possibly the end of the line. He explains that "Apple trees, if they think they're on their way out, put up a big crop, and that usually kills them. They spend all their energy." The Gravenstein generated a bumper crop two years ago, a final fireworks display of productivity, then nothing.

After two and a half centuries of Andrews, Johns, and Wallaces, Andy Mack has produced three grown sons, only one of whom lives in the area, a younger son who resided for long stretches in India and Japan, and a middle son who seems to have also fallen far from the tree, and between them, two grandchildren. Andy Mack is reluctant to hand the reigns of the family farm to any of these descendants. The three sons haven't spent their adult lives working side-by-side with their father, learning the ropes. Instead, Andy's farmed with the father and sons of another family, the Crosses, and the father and daughters of the Searles, families that are not Mack biologically but are grafted onto the business.

Until recently, Mack's Apples' competitor for longevity had been Tuttle's Red Barn, in Dover, New Hampshire, begun in 1632 with a land grant from Charles II of England and continued through eleven generations. In 2013 William Penn Tuttle III and his sister Lucy sold the business, citing exhaustion and age, compounded by a lack of interest in maintaining the Red Barn in the younger Tuttle generation. How do families like the Macks, with a publicly known lineage of 287 years, manage expectations, their own and outsiders, that they'll continue? What's it like growing up knowing that either you or a sibling will be picked to remain in place like a tree, committed to the family profession, living and possibly dying in the family's ancestral home?

After an aborted attempt to transfer Mack's Apples from father to oldest son in 2015, Andy Mack Jr., a radio DJ and the only son remaining in New Hampshire, is interviewed in a local paper saying, "It's one of the toughest things about this business—the fact that you have that long history, and you don't really want to be the person that breaks it." As Andy Mack Sr. quipped during our autumn of conversations, it's nothing like selling a gas station, a potshot at my parents' convenience store in Maine. Andy Mack's customers, many of whom are out-of-staters, buy a ye ol' New England experience and apple-scented nostalgia, not a pack of Marlboros and a Diet Pepsi. Londonderry residents, encouraged to treat the orchards like a public park, seem to believe they're co-owners in the orchard tradition without the physical and emotional burdens of legacy farming. While the rest of us mortals sign mortgage papers in the company of the loan officer of the local bank, the Mack's bought a portion of their property from a signer of the Declaration of Independence. A laminated copy of the original deed hangs lopsidedly from a thick nail over the seconds bins in the shop: *Matthew Thornton to John Mack, February 3, 1779, For and in consideration of the sum of five shillings.*

•

In his 1862 essay, "Wild Apples," Thoreau heaped projections and personifications on apple trees to instruct his fellow nineteenth-century citizens how to live. One should avoid becoming like the cultivated, grafted apple tree, which only leads to a mushy character. Simply by coming indoors, a wild apple and a human lose their natural vitality. Thoreau was an anti-orchard man. Thoreau preferred that cultivated trees wander off into the wilderness to join oaks, pines, and maples and be pruned by grazing beasts, not people. During his lifetime, Andy Mack has been responsible for the production of at least two million bushels of orchard apples, at 120 apples per bushel, so around 240 million apples. In this regard, Andy Mack is the antithesis of Thoreau, though in other ways, he's Thoreau's soul mate.

Andy would be comfortable living in a yurt or tree house and has slept as a millionaire in his van on a beach. Andy Mack resides in a studio apartment in the Bunkhouse, a weathered and shingled three-story cross between a ski chalet and a barn situated a few yards behind the main store and a minute's walk to the 1750 farmhouse. During harvest season, as many as eighty Jamaican fruit pickers are housed in the rest of the Bunkhouse where at least one birth and one death has happened. I would have guessed that Andy had dwelled a few months in the Bunkhouse; the answer is thirty years. He woke up one morning in the 1990s and realized he couldn't hear the songbirds, just traffic from busy Mammoth Road, so he vacated the family farmhouse, leaving it to his oldest son and daughter-in-law, and moved to the Bunkhouse. Andy Mack lives more like a nineteen-year-old college student in his parents' drafty barn than an octogenarian at the head of a million-dollar business.

In Andy Mack's living quarters, you won't find a coffee table or dresser, matching dishware or cutlery, clothes hangers, photographs of his grandchildren (when I mention that omission, his sons' school photo from the 1980s is tacked onto a wall), typical travel souvenirs, a pet of any species, Tupperware, a Mon-Tues-Wed-Thurs-Fri-Sat-Sun pill dispenser, shoehorns, certainly no dry cleaning bags, houseplants, wine rack, golf clubs, walk-in closets, washer and dryer, cuff links, dishwasher, dining room table, vacuum cleaner, golf clubs, hair dryer, decaf coffee, floor rugs or throw pillows, coasters, anything cute, teeth whitening toothpaste, scented candles, a cookbook, a smart home device, guest towels, religious iconography, air conditioning, hand lotion, a bread basket, bookends or indeed bookshelves, table lamps. It would require an hour's brisk effort to move Andy out of his home of thirty years. Like remainders from a yard sale, his belongings would be declined as a donation to Goodwill. Left outside in a cardboard box, his material possessions would sink into the earth within a few seasons or become like the shards of old bottles near abandoned rock walls in New England. His furniture consists of a drafting table made from particle board, the type of shelving you might expect in a garage, a homemade bed, and a lawn and desk chair. Carved into his desk is a wish for Londonderry, *Make*

This Town a Happy(ier) Place, a miniature of his outdoor political signage. On a window ledge over his mattress, several cereal bowls with spoons suggest he eats meals in bed, with a view of the orchard and bird feeders. The wood floors are painted Granny Smith green. His grandfather walked across the same floor, so to Andy it's "soul to soul and sole to sole," and he can "reach his grandfather, picture the soul part of the man" through the floorboards.

In a set-up reminiscent of a Naples' street altar, Andy displays a photo of President Obama. His other possessions are a photo of his second son's wife, a 9/11 first responder holding a walkie-talkie at the World Trade Towers, a Norman Rockwell print of parade attendees including Andy's uncle, and a time-faded color photograph of Andy windsurfing thirty years ago. Stacks of books sit on the floor and include new editions of *The Iliad* and *The Odyssey.* His prized possession is a plastic-wrapped set of first edition *Lonely Planet Biking Guides* to the Mediterranean.

Andy Mack left the business for long stretches at a time, starting in 1989, when he was fifty-two, not an outrageous retirement age for a successful businessman. His extended absences are cloaked by the political signage and by his employees who run the business. Mid-life he disappeared to the Mediterranean and Caribbean, his happiest times teaching windsurfing and sleeping on beaches in his van or in a hammock, far away from New Hampshire.

He'd been responsible for the farm since graduating from the University of New Hampshire. One morning in the 1950s, Andy woke to discover that his older brother Wallace had absconded with his motorcycle, parked outside their fraternity house. The presumptive heir to the family farm, his brother left a note and drove off to pursue an engineering opportunity outside the state. Meanwhile, Andy had been offered a job after graduation with the United Fruit Company. The job would have sent him to Central America, an early chance to depart that Andy decided to forfeit. His fiancée was diabetic, and he thought Sandy wouldn't receive the same medical care overseas. His mother called Andy and said, "Your father would really like it if you came back home to the farm." So Andy worked his adult life at the farm, including a stretch alongside his father until his mother's death in 1965, when Andy remembers "Dad said, 'I'm out of here.' My father said he wanted to go see how they picked apples in Washington State." Andy's mother died from a self-inflicted gunshot wound to her abdomen, Andy at her side, helpless to do anything as she bled out in the farmhouse. His newborn daughter, Jennifer, was born premature with a heart defect and after seven weeks of life died in a Boston hospital in 1967. His wife Sandy passed away at age forty-five in 1980 during surgery for a pacemaker. Andy Mack's middle son once remarked to his father that the orchard wasn't good for the Mack women. I thought of apple trees in early May, covered in hundreds of white flounces of blossoms, visited by bees—planted women staying put to produce. When he made his first departure, business was not the best, and Andy was recognizing that he was sensitive to cold and lack of light of New England winters. "Okay, Mack," he told himself, "You've got to go where it's warm." Andy says, "If I hadn't had the gumption to leave, I'd be dead or better still…" and trails off. He explains, "I had to go off by myself."

Far from New Hampshire and apple trees, he crafts a new identity as a farmer who's teaching windsurfing to the beautiful young people, a millionaire businessman who sleeps in his van on beaches. In Aruba he teaches for a year until local officials noticed that they had an illegal immigrant working and told him to leave "or we'll send you to an island of our choice." Andy decided to tour the Caribbean, ending up in Barbados, where he found a job managing a hotel's sailing area and making buoys out of tires filled with concrete. A self-described employed beach bum, Andy Mack sought anonymity in another culture and continent, just a maintenance worker for another man's business enterprise. His longest time away from the farm was seven months. Barbados was followed by the Curaçao Islands, Maui, the Columbia River Gorge, and Tarifa, on the southern tip of Spain. He follows his passions, windsurfing and biking; he behaves like a much younger man. He focuses on hardcore athletic accomplishment like an ancient Greek. In his mid-fifties, Andy takes up serious biking. He ascends the Alpe de Huez in the French high Alps, the route of the Tour de France, building up strength to the point where he could complete five climbs in nine days, totaling 90–100 climbs, including a dozen climbs in the Canazei in the Dolomites. He was seventy-two years old. From his desk chair in the Bunkhouse, he tells me that "Achieving some level of skill was important to me. It's easy to stay healthy in your seventies. I was at my peak. I was doing more than I had in my sixties, and I was still gaining strength, as far as I was concerned, and I went on to windsurf for quite a few more years."

During the past seven years, so into his eighties and well past traditional retirement age, Andy's been back on the farm. He stopped traveling seven years ago because of back problems from lugging around a windsurfing board and two knee surgeries. His advanced age has made discussion about the farm's future unavoidable. For any kind of family business, succession between generations is a time of maximum vulnerability. Andy follows the monarch model of family business continuity—the king does not relinquish control but dies on the job—or possibly the model of a general—officially retiring but returning to cut in when there's a perceived problem in the younger generation's management. He's not an ambassador—a retired owner who reappears only at key moments to lend credibility—or a governor—someone who permanently leaves and at a fixed date—or an inventor, retiring but contributing insights as requested. Andy Mack is the king blossom.

His back-and-forth feuding with his oldest son has been hitting the local newspapers during those seven years. When Andy Mack Jr. resigned from running the farm after two years in 2012, Andy Mack Sr. said his suspicions were confirmed: "I said a long time ago, we'd never be able to work together, and this proved it." Andy Mack then changed the plans for the business by making Mike Cross, his long-term manager, a partner, displacing his oldest son. A series of headlines in local newspapers tells a turbulent story about the farm's future, apple gossip tabloid-style: "Father, Son Part Ways in the Orchard" (January 2012); "Mack's Apples Moves on to the Next Generation" (August 2015); "The Future of Mack's Apples is Up in the Air" (February 2020). He spends Thanksgiving 2019 with a buddy rather than the son and daughter-in-law who live a few yards up the lane. In February 2020, a few weeks before the pandemic, Andy announces in the *Union Leader* that he has "reversed his previous decision to pass the historic orchard to his son Andy Mack Jr. and is looking for other family members to take the reins." He's considering Wallace Mack IV, the son of his older brother, or possibly donating the farm to a university.

Andy vents, "My son, he would like to own the farm, but he has not the slightest passion for farming," and his son responds, "Out of respect for my dad, I'm just not going to comment."

Even without high-stake legacy issues, it can be easier spending time with people who are not family. Over the past four months, I have spent more one-on-one time listening to Andy Mack than I have my whole adult life with my father, and this is happening as my father receives a prognosis of prostate cancer and begins radiation treatments. The last occasion my parents and my brother, his wife, and their children—relatives who live only an hour away in Massachusetts—visited my house in Londonderry was in 2014, and when they did visit, after Sunday lunch, we actually took the kids to Mack's U-Pick. I try to imagine this failure in my family life broadcasted in newspaper headlines, "Parents Go to NH to Buy Tax Free Furniture Without Stopping By to See Grandchildren," "Adult Daughter Has Regrets," or "Three Thanksgiving Invites in a Row, Declined." All of us are crop dusted with other people's expectations; it's just part of living with everyone else. People judge, judge, judge—weighing in with their opinions about keeping a business running, maintaining tradition, or lifestyle choices. It's hard to stay family patriarch while behaving like a proverbial beach bum; it's hard to find validation for one's athletic prowess at an advanced age when many people have signed away physical maintenance. For decades, Andy Mack has taken measures to untangle himself from the bindings of domesticity, family, and a heritage business. When he gives me his youngest son's confessional college thesis to read, it makes me uncomfortable. The boy's longing for a father after the early loss of his mother is in plain sight. The Mack family isn't interested in the hundred pounds of rocks he's brought from Spanish beaches or the bell from a temple in India, and they don't want to hear about his travels. Would it have been more or less acceptable if Andy vacationed conventionally, say, on a Viking Cruise or in a rented villa? Would there have been more or less discord if he invited his sons to join him?

•

About a mile away from Mack's Apples, piles of fill and crushed rock, excavation equipment and toppled apple trees scar the landscape: a dozen symbolic trees are left standing, looking like driftwood, or amputated to stumps. Backhoes, graders, dump truck, bulldozer, and a Porta Potty, crushed gravel, and pavement because they've paved paradise and put up a parking lot. A manmade pond that looks like a giant tarp held down by tires compensates for the wetlands taken by the development. Apple processing buildings have been requisitioned and resemble a D.O.T. headquarters, with an ominous sign out front, "Firewood for Sale."

In 2017, after a decade of debate, the developer Pillsbury Realty began demolishing Woodmont Orchards, one of Londonderry's four apple orchards, to make way for an after-the-fact New England-style town commons, 2020 style, with Market Basket, TJ Max, Sports Authority, a state liquor store, a beer hall, a Hallmark gift shop, with more to come for its 600 planned acres, twenty-four acres of which Andy Mack sold to them. A headline reads, "Can You Build a Downtown from Scratch? Londonderry is About to Find Out." Despite its history as the second-largest settled area in New Hampshire after Portsmouth during the signing of the Constitution, a territory once encompassing neighboring towns including what's now the city of Manchester, even parts of Massachusetts, Londonderry recognizes that it lacks a core. The town split from Derry in 1827 in a divorce that left Derry with an old-fashioned downtown and Londonderry its rocky soil.

Everyone these days has an opinion about the demolition of Woodmont Orchards, especially people who have never grown anything more than a patio tomato plant. "I think it's a shame what they've done to the apple orchards," my daughter's twelve-year old playmate proclaims from the back seat as we drive past another flattened swath that a month ago had been covered with rows of apple trees. Among residents, there's concern that this "mixed-use urban village" will backfire, so that "if the architecture and landscaping fall flat, Woodmont could have all the appeal of living in an outlet mall." The tendency is to think the town's identity is linked with apples, but that signature trait may go the way of the Lithia waters Londonderry was famous for in the nineteenth century. Residents release tension around these changes in their landscape by playing "Londonderry-monopoly," a fundraising event sponsored by the Rotary in which players can buy Mack's Apples (both its land and business) for $200 and "scoop up some surrounding properties and corner the residential development market." For April Fools' Day in 2011, Andy Mack Jr.'s practical joke meant hosting a two-hour press conference on Twitter announcing the fake news that his family business had been purchased by neighboring Sunnycrest Farm.

People like what the orchards symbolize; it's apple trees for the sake of having apple trees, but cultivated apple trees are finicky prima donnas. It's not as simple as planting petunia beds around a municipal area: apple trees are not easily made ornamental. They'll quickly slip into producing the hard, knotty, spotted fruit that Thoreau favored, and without steady pruning, a formerly tame tree will become a spinning branch turbine of new growth. In August 2013, the organization calling itself Save Woodmont Apple Trees, otherwise known as SWAT, held a rally for locals "to say goodbye to 10,000 trees," seeking to save 609 trees for a new public park. "The attendees will form a 'group hug' by holding hands around the apple trees" though "attendees are free to hug any particular apples trees they like."

Three hundred acres of Mack's Apples' four hundred acres are protected from development under a conservation easement. People already treat Mack's Apples as public land, something the Mack family has encouraged. The orchards have become a kind of town park where locals walk dogs, jog on hiking trails, have their engagement photos taken, and bring their kids sledding in a Grandma Moses style tableau. If Londonderry possessed a town center during the past forty years, it has been Mack's Apples. This is partly because of a business choice made by the Mack's years ago to move from wholesale to retail. Mack's also started one of the first pick-your-own operations in the area around 1968. Mack's interfaces with the community. It has held a green business showcase, 5-K cross country races, a popular pie baking contest, an annual Democratic BBQ, various arts events, a military appreciation day, a senior citizens' bake sale, an annual Boy Scouts Christmas tree bonfire, and sponsored the Mack Plaque, a popular athletic competition each fall between the public high school and its rival, Pinkerton Academy.

When they sold 280 acres for nearly $7 million to a Massachusetts-based real estate developer with ties to the DeMoulas family of the Market Basket franchise fame, Bob and Steve Lievens, co-owners of Woodmont Orchards, "quietly chose not to actively farm the land" and equally quietly slipped away. Of the Lievens' decision, Andy Mack commented in the local newspaper, "They will be missed, not just for the sight of their agriculture, but by their fraternity of fellow farmers." It would be a different departure altogether if Mack's Apples left town.

•

For several weeks in January 2020, two signs in the orchard stay face planted into the ground, knocked over by human or weather forces and not returned to an upright position. A sign the dimensions of a king-sized mattress on the outside of the apple shop functions like a Rorschach test. It reads: "Londonderry 2050?: Planet Earth Our Only Home," with an apple tree in the lower left and tellingly a palm tree bending in the wind on a doormat-sized island in the upper right.

Andy Mack is reversing the Sphinx riddle. First, he walks stooped with a cane from spinal implant surgery but then begins to straighten. He's rejuvenating. During our last conversation in his apartment in the Bunkhouse before everything in the world changes, Andy elevates both legs on a stool several feet above the floor, like a yoga pose. The bright foil of a Dorito's bag is mostly covered by bedding. Evening is happening fast and cold in the window behind Andy. Another New England winter has commenced, although its awfulness will soon become not one that any almanac could predict, and the father and little boy who'd been sledding during the afternoon—hats with earmuffs, I half expect to see old fashioned Flexible Flyer sleds—have packed it up and headed home. It's time for Andy to depart. He's hoping to leave soon, initially staying in the country with a trip to Florida, but later he's been invited to a vineyard in France where he might help with the next harvest. He's working out at the local gym to regain strength for windsurfing. Two of his vans still wait for him, parked at an airport in Toulouse, France, and in storage in Maui, and are said to have rotting tires but otherwise are road worthy. A red carry-on-sized suitcase waits near his bed, his name and address on the suitcase fabric.

"I will probably bug out sometime soon," he says, after his last doctor's appointment on February 3, a few days before it becomes clear that COVID-19 might result in global tragedy. It's time for Andy Mack to depart from New Hampshire because, as he says looking past his bed with its thin sleeping bag and out the window at the orchard, "I think I've been dissolving into a person that I'm not."

Postscript

During my last phone conversation with Andy Mack, I hang up when he questions my parenting abilities. Did I think I was harming my children by working so much? I block his calls.

After holding the town and his sons hostage for years with his decision, he scorches any chance at reconciliation. In 2021, Andy Mack finally does it. In a cruel joke, he sells the family farm to the owner of a paving company—Joni Mitchell lyrics be damned. The new owner assures the community that he has only the best of non-condominium construction intentions. In the end, Andy Mack abandons us to who we really are at heart—a citizenry with a Panera built on top of a demolished eighteenth-century tavern, three different pharmacies located at the same intersection, our franchised soul walking toward a Hallmark Greeting Card shop. The local art society hosts an exhibition of his political signs. Two seasons later, the newspaper announces that the town seeks to hire someone with expertise in managing the snarl of apple trees. The trees seem to have happily, full-throatedly, and very quickly returned to the wild.

Crisp air, press of ladder run on instep,
tree sway and dappled light, then stem twist
and the weight of apple in hand—

reaching through that leafy green, did we ask
what else we were after?

— Betsy Sholl

Note: Family succession terms borrowed from Jeffrey A.

THE ORANGE TREE
KEVIN RICHARD KAISER

The orange tree is rooted in damp black soil, shaded by its own shape. One orange, fallen to this soil, has been bitten by some nocturnal critter who left the peel mostly intact except for what seems a diagonal slice. From another grounded orange, a seafoam green mold fringed in white spreads across a patch of peel.

We have buried dead and pieces of the dead under the surface where these oranges decompose. In one year alone, we scratched, on three occasions, shallow graves into the dense soil: once for a cat-slain bird and twice for the fragments of human embryos: the "products of conception," the young male ER doctor called the latter, pushing gloved fingers inside you as the female nurse's eyes rolled helplessly in the skull.

Here, as a child, I buried other beings, whole beings—a dog, two birds, lizards, frogs—but never conceived of burying embryos. That is, the shards we salvaged.

What I saw him withdraw as you lie on your back—knees up, legs wide, pelvis tilted by a bedpan for the benefit of his inspection—were neither products of conception nor fragments of embryo lost amidst handfuls of placenta: they were the hearts of deer, held in the hands of the hunter. When we finally feel ready to bury the products of our child, they are putrefying.

The orange tree is so fragrant when bearing fruit.

There was a third that only you knew about, too tiny to salvage.

Above, the orange tree's branches are weighted by fruits as the leaves maintain a constant green that has, in the past, been whitened by ash flies—but a couple of these branches are barren. I had thought of cutting them until I noticed they were in use. On the thin twigs that twist from these branches, hummingbirds perch in the sun, the ruby throats of the males shining in the light.

Next year, the oranges will have been nourished by the flesh and blood of what was buried here. We won't be here to eat the fruit. We won't be here to bury any more in this soil, to dig with our fingers and wear the black beneath our nails, to scrub the blood from our palms with the sticky, dark earth. We won't be here, but we will still be, as they are, somewhere else, somehow else.

THE *BOSCO SACRO*
MEG MUTHUPANDIYAN

Where the southern wall of the *Sanctuario di San Francisco* is intersected by a brace of short walls we slowly pass through, my gait John Wayne weary, his feet calloused and crying for rest. It is nearly night in Umbria, but night announces itself to the region's mountains and valleys differently. Down below, Spoleto's light-bath has been slowly draining for hours—its urban sky and surfaces falling cool blue as the city empties of day. Here, among the ancient oaks of the *Bosco Sacro*, the sun wields an exacting scalpel, carving up the deep, umber shadows of the forest with short, meticulous incisions of firelight.

It would require three adults holding hands to encircle the bulbous bases of some of these holm oaks. There are only two of us; we take simple pleasure from feeling so young within their presence. Twisted and knotted, gilt with lime green lichen and jade moss, the root systems grip the humus-rich earth with an almost violent insistence, like the rheumatic fingers by which an aged Nonna sits in her doorway at the end of the day, gripping her cane. Two of the trunks are split open, revealing the tree's fibrous heartwood. Still, they remain, miraculously, alive.

Last year's foliage has only lately fallen to the graven earth. While brown, the leaves barely make a sound as we step on their slender spines; they are still waxy, still in possession of that armor that enabled them to defend these evergreen oaks from water loss. Above us in the canopy, small copses of deep green oak leaves, each subtly toothed and thick as a bay leaf, protrude stiffly from their branches, a new crop of sentinels unperturbed.

There's a stillness in this late stage of life, this late stage of day; the community of the *Bosco Sacro* bears no exception. Only a parliament of fowls newly returned from Africa are restless with discourse. The chatter is incessant, almost aggressive in its insistence. We can't identify them by sight or by call... high among the upper most branches of the bower they remain hidden, invisible to the pilgrims' scanning eyes below.

Some eight hundred years ago, Francesco and his companions took refuge in some of the natural limestone caves that are to be found in this sacred forest. Time is an extraordinary construct when we resist reducing it to a human scale; only two generations of trees have passed since he stepped over these deeply intertwined roots, brushed his palms across these armored trunks, and looked up into the apse of the coppery bower that now holds our attention. Only two generations of trees ago, he took communion with creation in this solemn, lovely place, as we now do.

And then, an opening. The light softens. Like a sculpture in a Japanese garden, two limestone stele stand, set on top of one another. They are inscribed in light and lichen—reproductions of the *Lux Spoletina*, a five-thousand-year-old law dictating the consequences of violating this wood.

Honce loucum – nequis violatod – neque
ex vehito neque – exferto quod louci –
siet nequet cedito – nesei quo die res deiai
atuna fiet eod die – quod reisdinai cau[s]a
[f]iat sine dolo cedere – [l]icedot seiquis

Violasit iove bovid – piaclum datod
seiquies scies – violasit dolo malo –
iovei bovid piaclum – datod et a CCC –

126

moltai suntod – eius piacli
moltaique dicator – exactio est –

> This sacred forest let nobody profane or carry
> away on carts or by hand that which belongs
> to the forest, or cut wood, except on the day of
> the annual sacrifice. On that day thanks to the
> sacrifice it will be allowed to cut without fraud.
> If anyone... profanes it, they will pay atonement
> to Jupiter with an ox; if anyone knowingly and
> with ill-intention profanes it, to Jupiter they will
> pay atonement with an ox and 300 asses will
> be the fine. The atonement and the fine will be
> exacted by the dictator.

For centuries, the original stele, now housed in the Civic Archaeological Museum of Spoleto, were two of many encircling this Sacred Forest, marking its boundaries and its interdictions. Perhaps in an interesting play on words, the law inscribed on them is not known as the *lex locus*, or law of the place, but as *lex luci*, the law of the light. The sharp blade of the blood orange sun rays slice through the darkness held by the trees. One, almost completely illuminated in hues of carnelian and amber, provokes thoughts of Moses's burning bush—the holy fire that burned but did not consume.

I feel myself in near perfect communion with the ancients who made this edict; though their reverence for the sacred grove was perhaps a bit more deeply motivated by fear than awe. Centuries and languages removed, our sympathies are ignited here, among the forest's prisms.

•

What, indeed, is in a word? Ask any student of a language which is second to their native tongue. They are particularly well equipped with second sight, to know and speak of a civilization's particularities, for language is both a civilization's mirror and its compass.

Take for example Latin, whose four distinct classifications for groves—*silva, nemus, saltus, lucus*—reveal much about what the ancient Romans valued about the forests within their land communities and how they performed their values. A *silva* is perhaps the most familiar and yet non-specific of the terms, meaning simply a wooded grove. A *nemus* is a large woodland with particular aesthetic virtues which invites one to wander and let the poetic juices flow. A *saltus*, like the silva, is less characterized by its effect on the wanderer-through than its physical attributes—a woodland that clings to the side of a mountain or some such uneven terrain. And the *lucus*, as we know, which is a sacred grove. Like a *nemus*, it is a grove which demanded protection and invited ritual offerings. As the Platonist author Apuleius notes of such groves in the ancient text *Florida*,

Vt ferme religiosis uiantium moris est, cum aliqui lucus aut aliqui locus sanctus in uia oblatus est, uotum po stulare, pomum adponere, paulisper adsidere (1.1)

It is the usual practice of wayfarers with a religious disposition, when they come upon a sacred grove
or holy place by the roadside, to utter a prayer, to offer an apple, and pause for a moment from their journeying.

The *luci* were not merely sites protected from

deforestation, hunting, or misuse by religious edict or the sites wherein travelers-through and pilgrims performed small acts of devotion. They were, as historian Ken Dowden notes, also the land communities for which annual festivals were held and akin to which small communities formed and grew.[1] The sacred groves were not merely a fulcrum of human life and ritual but provided human lives with eschatological meaning.

They also, notably, preserved the lives of these forests through countless generations. In the context of a discussion on ancient Roman environmental laws, scholar Andreas Wacke notes "The effectiveness of the religious tabus [sic] as a non-legal restraint mechanism is not to be underestimated."[2] That which was holy remained unsullied, untouched.

•

Thousands of years later, the *Bosco Sacro* was no longer the domain of Jupiter, but of the God of Francisco. It was here among these trees in 1218 that he gathered fallen holm oak branches and wove them with pliant young willow, here upon this stony path where he and his fellows ground the abundant limestone to paste their simple wicker walls with lime, and here within this deep and abiding grove where his ceaseless spiritual wandering seeded a permanent sanctuary that others would maintain in his memory. Over the centuries that followed, the simple grottos and chapel he constructed in the *Bosco Sacro* would welcome pilgrims such as Saint Bernardino da Siena, Michelangelo de Buonarroti, and,

---

1   See *European Paganism.*

2   Wacke, Andreas. "Protection of the Environment in Ancient Roman Law?" *Roman Legal Tradition.* Vol. 1. 2002. 1-24.

less notably, ourselves.

Although he wrote the Canticle of the Creatures during his stay in another forest some seven years later, the *Bosco Sacro*, and the spirit governing its centuries-long protection as a place sanctified by and in perpetual glory to god, were surely muses. Consider the evolution of this beloved hymn. According to accounts from his companions, he shared his intentions before penning the poem of praise. "I wish to compose a new hymn about the Lord's creatures, of which we make daily use, without which we cannot live," they recounted, "and with which the human race greatly offends its Creator."[3] In the wake of this desire to remind us that the whole of the earth and the universe bears the mark of divinity and is thus the subject of praise and honor, he wrote stanzas one through nine in his native Umbrian dialect:

Altissimu, onnipotente, bon Signore,
tue so' le laude, la gloria e l'honore et onne benedictione.

Ad te solo, Altissimo, se konfano,
et nullu homo ène dignu te mentovare.

Laudato si', mi' Signore, cum tucte le tue creature,
spetialmente messor lo frate sole,
lo qual è iorno, et allumini noi per lui.

Et ellu è bellu e radiante cum grande splendore:
de te, Altissimo, porta significatione.

Laudato si', mi' Signore, per sora luna e le stelle:
in celu l'ài formate clarite et pretiose et belle.

---

3   Francis of Assisi: *Early Documents, Vol 1, The Saint.* 113.

Laudato si', mi' Signore, per frate vento
et per aere et nubilo et sereno et onne tempo,
per lo quale a le tue creature dài sustentamento.

Laudato si', mi' Signore, per sor'aqua,
la quale è multo utile et humile et pretiosa et casta.

Laudato si', mi' Signore, per frate focu,
per lo quale ennallumini la nocte:
ed ello è bello et iocundo et robustoso et forte.

Laudato si', mi' Signore, per sora nostra matre terra,
la quale ne sustenta et governa,
et produce diversi fructi con coloriti flori et herba.

> Most High, all-powerful, good Lord,
> Yours are the praises, the glory, and the
> honour, and all blessing.

> To You alone, Most High, do they belong,
> and no human is worthy to mention Your
> name.

> Praised be You, my Lord, with all Your
> creatures,
> especially Sir Brother Sun,
> Who is the day and through whom You give
> us light.

> And he is beautiful and radiant with great
> splendour;
> and bears a likeness of You, Most High One.

> Praised be You, my Lord, through Sister
> Moon and the stars,

in heaven You formed them clear and
precious and beautiful.

Praised be You, my Lord, through Brother
Wind,
and through the air, cloudy and serene, and
every kind of weather,
through whom You give sustenance to Your
creatures.

Praised be You, my Lord, through Sister
Water,
who is very useful and humble and precious
and chaste.

Praised be You, my Lord, through Brother
Fire,
through whom You light the night,
and he is beautiful and playful and robust
and strong.

Praised be You, my Lord, through our Sister
Mother Earth,
who sustains and governs us,
and who produces various fruit with
coloured flowers and herbs.[4]

It was only later, during two separate moments
in the year of life that remained for him, that he
would add the final lines of the poem. Lines ten and
eleven would be added in response to news he was
given that a conflict had broken out between Assisi's

---

4   Both the Umbrian and the English translation
were taken from the Franciscan Seculars website. http://
franciscanseculars.com/the-canticle-of-the-creatures/

secular and religious authorities. The final stanzas, his contemporaries recount, were authored by the saint on his deathbed.

•

Today the *Bosco Sacro* lies within lands besotted with Francesco's life and enterprise. It is a forest within a chain of forests, caves, springs, sanctuaries, and other geographical features strung together as the *Via Francisco*—a way which bears a trace of the evolution of his spirit, from the Perugia of his imprisonment as a young nobleman and soldier, to the Assisi of his renouncement of his birthright and worldly goods, on through the emergence of his theological vision and religious rule in Rieti and Rome.

Where we stand on that path, the sun has re-sheathed its last blade of light, and the caucus of birds has adjourned. In the dusk the trees loom large above us, making plenary that what is deemed sacred in one generation can be sustained through transmutation in the next. We are standing soft-footed on soft ground. The feeling that this grove is holy, worthy of protection and praise as one beloved by a creator—it is more than a mere residue of the re-sanctification of this space over the past 2200 years. As it breathes in the night air, the forest truly whispers of its sanctity. Its exhale into the darkness draws a sort of prayer from my lips: *may the Bosco Sacro ever remain an impetus for human reverence, poetic feeling, and the creation of mythic memory.*

TAMARACK
KIT CARLSON

Larix laricina. No Latin-speaking Roman ever saw you, rising up out of North American swamps and bogs in October, golden in the autumn sun, every single needle a shot of joy. But there you are, scientifically named— genus and species, as though to say "larch-like larch" will make more sense in Latin. Larch. American larch. Eastern larch. Larch is what they called you, something like a European deciduous cone-bearing tree, but nothing like those trees, really.

Thousands of years ago, Gauls living in the Alps said *larihha*, and there it was—a tree named and claimed by language. Coming to this continent, Europeans looked at you and said, "ah, like at home. Larch." As though you were like anything back home. Tamarack. Hackamatack. Natives named you too. The Algonquins called you *ahmentak*, "wood used for snowshoes." As though all you were good for was your supple wood, bent and bound to bear humans across the winter drifts. As though you existed only for this function.

Isn't that how we feel we have to do it? We are the creatures who name and name and name, who wrap the world with words. You need no name. It is enough to plant your roots in the sandy shore. It is enough to drink the lake all day. It is enough to fling your needles into the October wind, gilt confetti against blue, blue, infinitely blue sky.

FAITH IN A SEED
ANDREA LANI

Deep within the arboretum across the street from my office, along the edge of a field of raggedy wildflowers, sixty American chestnut trees grow in four neat rows. The trees were planted fourteen years ago, on a sunny but cool morning in June. My husband, Curry, worked at the arboretum at the time and had invited teams of draft horses to plow the furrows into which he planted the knee-high whippets just dug from their nursery beds. I took our infant son, Milo, to the arboretum to watch the enormous horses draw plows that peeled back wide strips of sod, to see his father lower tiny trees into the ground. Milo, two weeks old at the time, was snuggled deep in a front pack, his still-wobbly head asleep against my chest. Neither horse nor tree made an impression on his newborn mind. I might have forgotten the day myself, if not for the momentousness of it being our first big outing after his birth, the connection of his father to the event, and the proximity of the arboretum to my workplace, allowing me to return and visit the chestnuts years later.

Here in Maine, we sit at the northern fringe of the American chestnut's former range, which in the 1800s spread south to Georgia and west to Ohio. Chestnuts made up one quarter of the timber in eastern hardwood forests; that is, one in four trees—or, more precisely, one in four potential boards of wood—in the forest was a chestnut. The chestnut grew fast, flowered late enough to avoid frost, and produced abundant crops of nuts that fed wildlife, livestock, and humans alike. Its wood was light, strong, straight-grained, and rot-resistant, good for everything from railroad ties to dulcimers. As a tree, it was almost too good to be true. Until tragedy struck.

In the late 1800s, nurseries began importing Chinese and Japanese chestnut trees, species more compact and suitable to cultivation than their big, wild, American cousin. Along with these trees came an invader—a fungus for which the Asian species had defense mechanisms but which devastated the American chestnut. It infected the trees through wounds in their bark and cut off the flow of water and nutrients within the tree. At first, foresters tried a scattershot of strategies to slow the spread of the fungus. Once they realized there was no stopping the blight, they encouraged landowners to cut down the remaining trees to salvage the wood, eliminating any possibility of naturally blight-resistant individuals surviving and spreading their genes. Within half a century from the time the blight was first discovered in 1904, the fungus and concomitant logging operations had obliterated more than four billion trees.

The loss of the chestnut completely altered the character of the eastern forests, from which plants made up the understory to the species of wildlife that foraged there. The demise of the American chestnut likely contributed to the demise of the passenger pigeon. But unlike that ill-fated bird, whose last known member died in 1914, the American chestnut lived on in isolated individuals, stump sprouts, and research groves. After numerous failed attempts to hybridize American and Asian chestnuts to create a blight-resistant tree, scientists began a program of "back-crossing" in the 1980s, with the goal of creating a tree that had the stature of an American chestnut and the vigor of a Chinese chestnut. The process entailed the careful crossing of the two species, with each generation possessing a little more American genetics than the one before, while retaining the Chinese tree's resistance. Offspring of each stage in the crossing were planted in groves, inoculated with chestnut blight, and examined for resistance. Some pollen or seeds might be collected for further cultivation, but none of the trees in the early back-crossing generations were meant, or expected, to survive, let alone grow to one hundred feet tall.

•

I grew up in Colorado, far from the chestnut's natural range, decades after that tree had faded from the landscape. I had probably heard the phrase "chestnut blight" at some time or other. I imagine it occupied the same part of my brain as "Dutch elm disease" and "gypsy moth"—bad things that happened to trees in faraway times and places. Otherwise, my associations with the tree were limited to "chestnuts roasting on an open fire" and the taste of an actual roasted chestnut from an aluminum foil packet my dad bought at a street fair one winter. The nut, likely from an Italian chestnut, had a waxy texture and a sweet but moldy flavor—more of a smell than a taste, settling in the back of the throat rather than the tongue. Though an adventurous eater, I declined a second bite.

Twenty years later, as I watched Curry lower chestnut seedlings into the ground at the arboretum, our baby nestled against my chest, I didn't know much more about the chestnut's plight than I had when I bit into that warm, funky-tasting nut. I had only a vague awareness that the seedlings had something to do with the American Chestnut Foundation's efforts to restore the tree. It would be a few months before I read *Prodigal Summer*, Barbara Kingsolver's novel about love, fecundity, and the American chestnut. The book helped me begin to understand a bit about what we lost when we unwittingly unleashed a deadly pathogen on our forests and then willfully harvested what remained of the trees, but it would be years before I would truly feel in my own heart the loss of a tree I had never known.

•

The drafty old red-brick building where I work is one of several functionally and aesthetically similar structures built over a period of a hundred years or so to house the state's mentally ill patients. Over the last few decades, as the inpatient population dropped, many of the buildings on the euphemistically termed "campus" were either abandoned or converted into state office buildings, such as the one I work in. Even after the last of the patients moved to a shiny, modern hospital in 2004, state workers remained in the old buildings, and on hot, humid days the blond interior brick walls of my office exude the mingled smells of urine and despair of the hospital it once was. It is necessary to escape those walls, and in fine weather, I make weekly, if not daily, pilgrimages to the arboretum across the street.

The arboretum spans 224 acres of woods, fields, and wetlands, with trees—both cultivated and wild-born—scattered throughout. The property served as the farm for the mental hospital, providing not only food for the patients, but also horticultural therapy, before that was a thing, until the state eliminated unpaid labor by patients in the 1970s. The property became an arboretum in 1981. Since I moved to central Maine in 1997, I've regularly walked, snow-shoed, and cross-country skied its trails. My usual route takes me through a hay meadow, past six species of oak, along a dilapidated boardwalk that crosses a man-made wetland, through a stand of white pines, by a shallow pond, and up and down a hillside trail bordered by carefully tended hosta plants and shaded by gracefully arching paper birch trees. This loop takes me about 30 minutes, my lunch break, if I don't stop and dawdle over the turtles in the wetland or the dragonflies near the pond. When I really need to get out—for my mental or physical health—I venture farther afield to the deep woods, the rhododendron garden, the green ash and larch plantations, and the nut tree collection.

It is near the nut trees—butternut, hickory, black walnut—that the chestnut trees march in their four straight rows. I probably ambled by the trees over the years as they grew from saplings, but they did not make an impression on me until one late-summer day three years ago, just over eleven years after we watched them go into the ground. I don't remember if I headed with purpose toward the chestnut grove that day or happened upon it on my wanderings, but once among the trees, I sat beneath number C-13, my back firm against a trunk as stout as an elephant's leg, and marveled at how much they had grown. Those spindly whippets reached up into the sky at least twenty feet. Most of the trees were still healthy then, their limbs dense with foliage. The ends of the branches bore clusters of spiny burrs the size and color of tennis balls, each one housing a nut, the seed of another generation. At eleven years old, the trees were reproducing.

Eleven is an in-between year, a pupal phase, the age everything changes. At ten, Milo's cheeks still held their soft baby roundness, his feet pattered across our wood floors, his voice, though never high-pitched, still rolled like marbles. By twelve, his face had sharpened into its adult contours, he thudded as he walked, his voice dropped into a baritone I didn't recognize over the phone. These physical changes crept in during eleven, unnoticed by me until they had taken firm, irrevocable hold. Eleven also brought about a rending of the fabric of our relationship marked by aversion to physical affection, small rebellions against homework and school, and a know-it-all attitude, all played against a soundtrack of heavy sarcasm. By twelve, he had returned to the fold of my arms, reengaged in schoolwork, and ratcheted down the smart-aleck tone to humorous irony. But I didn't realize on that day, beneath the bright green branches of the eleven-year-old chestnut trees, that Milo was in the midst of a year of transition, of distancing himself from me, from childhood, as he made his first major leap toward becoming a man, and that the chestnuts, too, balanced at a hinge-point.

•

American chestnut trees, in their heyday, were not the tallest trees in the forest, growing to a height of only one hundred feet. (The eastern white pine, Maine's state tree, is said to have reached 230 feet prior to European settlement.) But the chestnut was glorious in the horizontal dimension, with a one-hundred-foot crown spread and a diameter of ten to twelve feet. Had Milo and I known an American chestnut tree in its full glory, we'd have been able to lie down head-to-head behind a tree, our toes not poking out past the edges of the trunk. We could camp in the shade of its massive crown with six-hundred or so of our closest friends. But we never knew the chestnut, nor did we witness the eastern hardwood forest before the blight, dominated by trees of such majestic breadth and prolific food production. We don't, in effect, know what we are missing.

But we do have a forest we know well. Outside

our front door, a little to the left, grows a stand of eastern hemlock trees. Though they fall far short of the chestnut's height and girth, they are great shaggy beasts. Lacking the regular, conical form we expect of trees in the pine family, their limbs and branches, bristly with short, uneven needles, careen every which way, like a field-grown pine crossed with a fir and badly in need of a shave and a haircut. For a few days each winter, a porcupine takes up residence in one of the trees nearest the house. From the living room window, we can watch as it clips and drops feathery branches onto the snow below.

If we push aside the lower branches of one of the hemlocks and wade through the prickly wild raspberry canes that border the yard, we drop down a short hill onto a trail that follows a ridge of glacial till before making a U-turn downhill to the west branch of the Eastern River. The trail passes through two more hemlock groves, one farther along the ridge and another lining both banks of the river. We moved into our house when Milo was a year old. At the beginning of that winter, he wanted me to carry him over the "snow-wadee"—or "snow-water," his word for the wet, slushy stuff of November. By February, freezing and thawing had packed the accumulation of many snowstorms firm enough to support even my weight. Milo would run through the woods over this crust, with no regard for the trail, heading in whatever direction took his fancy, disappearing beneath curtains of the hemlocks' enveloping branches.

The ash trees are less noticeable than the hemlocks. They grow tall and straight, their crowns fading into the sky, high above eye level. You don't notice them until you look for them, and then you see them everywhere, the neat bark of their trunks ridged in narrow, even plates like the spines of books on library shelves, their compound leaves attached opposite each other to twigs high above your head. White ash, along with white pine, American beech, paper and yellow birch, red oak, and red maple, fill in the stretches of woods between the hemlock groves, and black ash grow with wet feet down in the swampy area we cross on wobbly, rotten logs.

Both of these trees, the hemlocks and the ashes, may stand on the brink of the same fate as the chestnuts. Both face foes that, like the chestnut blight, were unwittingly introduced from Asia and to which the trees have shown almost no resistance. The hemlock wooly adelgid is an aphid-like insect whose larva inserts a feeding tube into the base of a hemlock needle and extracts nutrients, causing the needles to dry out and fall from the tree. Unable to grow and photosynthesize, limbs and branches begin to die back, and within four years the tree may die. A US Forest Service bulletin on hemlock wooly adelgid states, "This non-native pest has impacts comparable to those of the gypsy moth, Dutch Elm disease, and chestnut blight." The larva of the emerald ash borer, a beetle also imported from Asia, burrows through the inner bark of an ash tree. Its tunnels cut off the flow of water and nutrients within the tree, in much the same way that the chestnut blight fungus strangles its host. Trees die within two to four years of infestation. In a review of the insect, authors Daniel A. Herms and Deborah G. McCullough write, "As [emerald ash borer] continues to spread, its ecological and economic impacts in North America are expected to rival or exceed those of chestnut blight and Dutch elm disease, invasive pathogens that devastated natural and urban forests in the twentieth century." How many more chestnut blights can our forests withstand?

Scientists have been scrambling to understand the biology and behavior of these insect invaders, their efforts eerily mirroring those of the chestnut's champions. Quarantines and control strategies have been tested and discarded. Landowners have been advised to salvage their standing trees. Genetics have been mapped and cross-breeding programs begun. Pests-of-the-pests have been tested and released. The process appears to be moving at a faster clip than when the chestnut blight was first discovered, in the early days of forest pathology, which gives me hope that we've learned something since then, if not the most vital lesson of all: don't create the problem in the first place.

If efforts to control hemlock wooly adelgid and emerald ash borer prove successful before these pests reach our own backyard here in Maine, that does not necessarily mean our forest is safe. Nearly every tree in our woods has a foe with its name on it: white pine blister rust, beech bark disease, spruce budworm. The Asian longhorn beetle has more catholic tastes and would happily dine on most of the hardwood trees in our woods. The biggest unknown is what will happen to our trees, their pests, the other plants and animals in our little kingdom as the climate continues to shift to milder winters, hotter summers, and more extreme and unpredictable storms. Regardless of the outcome of insect infestations and climate change, I think it's safe to say that if Milo wanders these woods as an old man, he will walk through a changed forest. Perhaps we can attribute such change to the natural flux that has characterized our wild world since the beginning of time, or perhaps the landscape will be diminished in diversity and ecological value due to the insatiable hungers of mankind. I expect that, if nothing else, a forest of some kind will still cover these acres. *Trees can't not grow here*, as the stone walls that meander through our woods, once the boundaries of open farm fields, can attest. Curry bush-hogs our two meadows twice a year to keep woody vegetation from taking over the grass and milkweed and goldenrod.

If the forest does change—catastrophically or gradually—over the next fifty years, will Milo even notice? At fourteen, he is more given to playing the guitar than running through the woods, though he will walk with me to the river if I ask him. He has never complained about our rural existence, but I don't know how much the woods outside our front door mean to him. I don't know if even he knows. I'm fairly confident he can tell the difference between a hemlock and a pine and a fir, but I don't know whether he could pick an ash out of a lineup of hardwoods. I had meant to teach him the names of all of the trees and birds and flowers on our land when he was little, but it turned out that being in the woods mattered more to us than naming them. This may have been an error on my part. "The beginning of wisdom is to call things by their right names," goes a Chinese proverb. Studies have shown that children today can recognize hundreds of corporate logos but can't name the trees in their own yard, while another study found that the more plants and animals children could name, the more appreciation they had for nature. If, one hundred years ago, people had not known the name of the huge tree that littered the forest floor with nuts every fall and filled the air with an odd, pungent fragrance each spring, would they have gone to such great, though largely futile, lengths to save the American chestnut? Would they have mourned the tree deeply enough to devote decades to bringing it back from death? Will anyone mourn the hemlocks and ashes with such intensity? Will my sons?

•

Since rediscovering the chestnut grove three years ago, I have made a point of returning to it at least once each year, in August or September. I like to sit at the base of a tree, leaning against a trunk no thicker than my waist, and try to imagine its giant ancestors. The tallest of the trees reaches maybe twenty-five or thirty feet, and I can see how a tree that has grown that much in fourteen years could shoot up to a hundred feet, unimpeded by disease. At that time of year, the chestnuts bear fruit—burrs that cling to the ends of branches, shrouding the trees' seeds within their spiky armor. The leaves, which have not yet begun to turn autumn brown, resemble beech leaves—wide in the middle and pointed at both ends, with deep, furrowed veins and serrated edges—but chestnut leaves are longer and darker green with sharper teeth than beech leaves.

Milo just started high school. He will be taller than me by his next birthday. Much of what goes on in his days—and in his head—is a mystery to me. My son is growing up, and the chestnuts his dad planted when he was a baby are dying. All but a handful are bare for the top ten or fifteen feet; many have withered back to bundles of branches that sprout from the roots of the sickly parent tree—mighty giants reduced to shrubs. The bark of the dead and dying chestnuts is brittle and brown, peppered with tiny orange dots of fungus.

This year I make a second pilgrimage to the grove, in late October. The leaves have turned russet, their scalloped edges curling back on themselves like fossils of ancient sea creatures. The burrs, too, have turned brown, a rich, chocolatey color, their spines dried and splintered. They have split open, blooming outward in four lobes. The inside surface is the exact opposite of the outside, soft and velvety, a gentle cradle for the growing seed. I search the ground for ripe nuts but find nothing. I wonder if squirrels or deer have taken them away or if the burrs were sterile, hollow husks all along.

A few days later we come to the arboretum as a family for a volunteer breakfast. After my children stuff themselves with sausages and French toast, I drag them out onto the trails. As we walk, I quiz them on the trees. Beech. Birch. Pine. Cedar. Aspen. Maple. Fir. Oak. They get them all correct, and though we pass no hemlock or ash I am relieved that I have taught them this much at least. We wander the trails, making turns at random, and I don't realize we're approaching the chestnuts until I see in the distance their barren limbs held aloft, graceful as dancers' arms. My chest tightens. What will I say to Milo when we step into the grove? Will I tell him about that day more than fourteen years ago when his dad planted these trees while he slept, cradled to my chest? Will I tell him about the forests of giants that once spanned the eastern states, and how human mistakes felled the entire species? Before we reach the grove, however, Curry turns down a trail that takes us in another direction. I feel relief and a pang of guilt. Why do I dread talking to my son about the chestnut trees? Am I afraid that the knowledge will hurt him too much, or that he won't care at all?

If I had thought about it at the time, I might have chosen a more auspicious first outing for my first baby than to go watch the planting of doomed trees. But on that day, I could no more imagine fourteen years in the future than I could fourteen thousand years. In the throes of new-motherhood, the prospect of my sweet baby becoming a teenager was as unforeseeable as the destruction of the keystone tree species of the eastern forests must have been to the early nurserymen who inadvertently invited the chestnut blight fungus onto our shores. Since becoming a mother, I have held something akin to a chestnut burr in my heart—the tender, velvety inside holds hope for my children's future; on the brittle, spiny outside is skewered despair about what that future might hold. The saga of the American chestnut manifests that burr. On the outside is a tragedy, both ecological and economic, representing the worst side of humanity—hubris, an insatiable desire for control over nature, a refusal to consider the consequences of our actions. Cradled within is a story that highlights our best selves—the ability to recognize mistakes, the desire to right wrongs, the tenacity to persevere in the face of terrible odds. After all, the history of the American chestnut's demise and rebirth might be the most auspicious first story to introduce to a child.

Henry David Thoreau wrote, "Though I do not believe that a plant will spring up where no seed has been, I have great faith in a seed. Convince me that you have a seed there, and I am prepared to expect wonders." This philosophy applies not only to the blight-resistant chestnut seeds that so many dedicated souls have worked to create over the years, but also to our children. We plant the seeds of love and kindness, time in nature, a healthy start at life, and stand back, prepared to expect wonders. To bring a species back from extinction—for the American chestnut is functionally extinct—is an act of faith, of peering fate directly in the eye and declaring that you will not be undone, on par with only one other human act that I can think of: bringing an infant into this world, raising him through the trials of each stage of childhood, and launching him into an uncertain world when he becomes an adult.

I can't say whether my son absorbed the seeds of the noble traits expressed by the American chestnut's champions as he snoozed through the planting of the saplings, or if those traits have taken root inside him over the last fourteen years. He's still too young to have made great mistakes that require righting. I do know that I imagine him growing up to be like an American chestnut—tall and strong and bountiful with his gifts—crossed with the love and persistence of those who wish to restore this iconic tree to its former glory. I have a vision in my mind: a tree one hundred feet tall, and beneath it the child I gave birth to, gray-haired, a little stooped, his blue eyes nestled in wrinkles, resting against the broad trunk, in the vast shade cast by the spreading crown, a tree driven to extinction long before his birth and reborn during his lifetime.

I COULD BE A TREE
MARIANNE JAY ERHARDT

> "And the tree was happy."
> — *The Giving Tree* by Shel Silverstein

My friend Kristen says the book should be called *The Taking Boy*, a story of using mothers up. A story of hollow children, taking our apples to sell, our branches to build, our trunks to carve into boats that will float them away. A story that grows a boy into a bitter old man, leaves a mother stumped. Kristen and I have two kids apiece, and they have climbed our trunks and whispered wishes into our hair and demanded impossible gifts with no shame. We're power walking at work, past the quad, behind the practice fields. Late fall. I have nineteen minutes until my next meeting. She is three thousand steps behind where her FitBit wants her to be. We've talked tantrums and grant applications, committee work and gifted education, and she asks me, "Do you think we're missing the point?" It's the kind of question that should stop us in our tracks, invite us to take an extra breath of cold, bright air. But we don't have time to stop. That's what the walk is for. A stop that's not a stop. "Probably," I answer, moving, staying warm, missing lots of things.

The book—its sketches and sadness—means little to me, a mere shower gift years back. But it makes me cry, and my boys like that. And the man is stupid, they like that, too. A single crop of apples won't get you that much money, they say. What kind of house can he build with those branches? What kind of boat? And they say you, tree, are equally dumb. A mother should know to stop giving. This boy will keep taking until there is nothing left. It's how boys are built.

You must, therefore, be a bad mother. Blame me for this idea. I was explaining some consequence for rude behavior. *If I let you (talk to me that way/ leave crumbs all over the floor / pee on your brother), I wouldn't be a very good mama, would I?* They were quiet for a moment. Their faces flushed with realization. I don't think it had ever occurred to them that mothers could be good or bad. That parents could be better or worse. And now it will never un-occur to them. *No,* they said. *If you let us (decapitate the stuffed animals / have candy for breakfast / wear these stained pants on picture day), you would be a bad mama. A bad one.*

My older child has recently heard that a mother might be bad not only through neglect or overindulgence, but through outright abuse. He knows that some parents harm their children. That some grown-ups have mean ideas, wild hands, ways to hurt that are hard to imagine. He wants these grown-ups dead, he says. And in prison. He wants to gun them with a knife and kick all of their horrible arms together until the glue dries and they have to stop. Until the pain they make is contained and returned, a gift in a box. I want him in a tree, away from all of that.

But a bad mother is not the same as a sad mother. You are sad, despite the book's refrain that the boy makes you happy, eating your fruit. Makes you happy, weaving crowns out of your leaves, happy, carving initials into your bark, cutting, chopping until your branches fall from their space in the sky and crash to the earth, that ragged sketch.

Here is more of me, mothers say. Mothers smile. I know the risk. I know what it is to tell my boys how pleased I am with their rendition of childhood. I encourage them to like art and vegetables and climbing, to roll their eyes at "Tough Guy" t-shirts and yogurt tubes decorated with cartoon characters. *Mom, It's not like Spiderman is in that yogurt, right? The yogurt companies just want kids to whine to their moms until they buy junk.* And I hug them close as if they are the most brilliant children on the planet. There are times I have made them feel that my happiness is the difficult work of their lives.

And apples fall, but not far. Of course, I have been the child of an unhappy mother. Unhappy despite the fact that not one of her seven children was using drugs, failing school, running away, leaving the church, or coming out of the closet. Yet. We slouched, spoke with the wrong voices, insisted on catching our death with damp hair and bare legs though the weather demanded tights. But it's not that we didn't try to make her happy; I went a decade without a haircut. I prayed to St. Theresa on my knees every night of third grade. I volunteered to go grocery shopping with her, arranged fake flowers—tulips, carnations—on the bathroom counter, hand-copied choreography for her Adult Tap students, countless index cards with the perfect words —shuffle, hop, step, slap, dig, stamp, triplet, around the world, drawbacks, scuff, and Maxie Ford.

It wasn't until I was seventeen that I realized I had no business making her happy. It happened all at once. Her eyes were on the news—fires, kidnappings, events she blamed on those taken—and I was leaving the living room, exasperated. And suddenly, I wasn't. *Good night*, I said. *I love you*, I said, meaning it for once. It was as if a seed I never saw planted now sprouted, flourished, found itself radiating years of sunlight it had been secretly hoarding. Let me be clear. This wasn't understanding or forgiveness. This wasn't some generous bouquet gripped in a fist. She knew; she didn't meet my eyes when I said it. This was a gift to myself alone. I could be a tree and be alive. I could be a tree and not be locked in place, in wanting. She was my mother. She was only my mother.

I am sad from time to time. The Taking Boy is sad, too. He never gets his money, his house, his wife and children. Or if he does he loses them somehow. Maybe he is bad to them like he was bad to you. Maybe they give him away. Maybe his sons say, *We're the boy, now. You have to be the tree!* and he isn't able to feed them or hide them or hold them to the brilliant sky. I don't blame the boy. And I don't blame you, tree. When I was pregnant with my first, my mother's womb held cancer. When I visited, she was sick from chemo, the news was on mute. And I told her, a baby. To make her happy. But also because I wanted her like the old days. I wanted her to tell me that I could be good at this lonely give and take. That I could be good. Who else could make me believe a thing like that?

A HERD OF ASPEN
LYN BALDWIN

On Day Five, my demented mother exclaims, "Oh, look at the herd of trees."

The view out my mother's hospital window—five floors above the traffic of Vancouver's West 12th Avenue—looks mostly onto the adjacent medical tower. But to the southwest, trees shade one corner of lawn.

"They're keeping that herd well," she says excitedly. "They need a lot of water to stay green in this heat."

As it has so often before, paying attention to plants—those incandescent beings that link visible sky with subterranean soil—serves as common language with my mother. Sitting next to her, neither my stepfather nor I correct my mother's use of *herd*. As a collective noun, it might not be the one I would use to describe a gathering of trees, but unlike most of what has occupied my mother's attention for the last five days, I can see this herd of trees.

•

Five days ago, my stepfather called the paramedics when he found my mother crumpled against their kitchen wall, unable to talk or stand. Four days ago, a helicopter flew my mother southeast across the rocky knolls of British Columbia's Sunshine Coast towards Vancouver. By the time my sister, Laurie, found her on a gurney in Vancouver General Hospital's emergency room, my mother was, in my sister's words, "completely off her rocker." Displaced from home, separated from her husband, my mother was tearing the IV from her

155

arm, ripping the catheter from her urethra, spilling blood across her gurney. When my sister suggested they call for a nurse, my mother growled, "Don't you fucking dare."

In an act that still stuns me with its raw courage, my sister had defied our mother and summoned help with the push of a red button.

On the afternoon of Day 2 with my stepfather still en route, nurses secured my mother's torso to her gurney with blue webbing, tied her hands to its silver bars with cotton straps.

On the evening of Day 2 when my stepfather finally arrived, he took one look at my mother's lips thinned with rage, her bruised arms and fidgety fingers and snapped at the intern, "Just drug her."

On the morning of Day 3, when my stepfather and I returned, my mother was still in the ER, still restrained, but her fingers crept less often towards her IV. Emergency surgery, we were told, was less and less likely. The doctors thought that a brain seizure, not a stroke, had caused the paralysis leading to her hospitalization. But they wanted more tests to determine if her ongoing hallucinations stemmed from something other than her vascular dementia. Both of my mother's carotid arteries are severely clogged: one more than 90% and one only 50%. Surgery, they say, will kill her, but day-by-day, her clogged arteries starve her brain of oxygen. Minute-by-minute, neurons die, leaving lacunae in both my mother's memory and coherence.

By late afternoon, my mother had been transferred five floors up to what I would learn to call the Neuro Ward.

On Day 4, the blue netting was gone, the white straps piled on the windowsill. But my mother's fury, never very distant, was only marginally restrained by her pleasure to see us. As the day wore on, our inability to see what she did—the penguins flying by, the white bird sitting on the windowsill, the bugs on the ceiling—drained her patience. My attempts to translate what she was seeing—penguins into pigeons, the white bird into cotton straps, bugs into holes in the ceiling tiles—irritated her. She wanted confirmation, not explanation. All day my mother was short with me and barely civil with my sister. Laurie, after all, was the betrayer—the one who'd pushed the red button. On Day 4, my sister, my stepfather and I may not have shared my mother's visual reality, but all four of us understood that there was vengeance to be wreaked.

•

But on this morning, Day 5, when my stepfather and I reached her doorway, my mother was sitting up, dressed in her own clothes in a chair next to the window, her long white hair swept up into a French braid. Best of all, when we joined her, I saw them.

A herd of trees.

Now, when she turns from the trees to ask, "Well, now what are we going to do?" I am encouraged enough to wonder if she's up for a game of crib.

My suggestion feels wildly optimistic. This is a woman who couldn't talk five days ago, who's already pointed to the Sharp's container hanging on the wall and told us, as if confessing a secret, "That man climbed into my bed last night."

But I'll do anything to avoid another day of failed translation.

Somehow, it works. Mom has no trouble holding her cards, no trouble counting 15-2, 15-4, relying on my stepdad only to track what cards are in the crib and whose turn it is to deal. She doesn't remember all the rules, but none of us do. I Google if a run must be of the same suit, and collectively, we ignore the subtleties of jacks. The cards, just bought from the gift shop, are too slick, and we don't have a cribbage board, but somehow the game contains us.

For the next three days, cribbage becomes part of our routine. I drive my stepdad to the hospital, drop him off, park, go get Mom a cup of "good" coffee, and take the elevator five floors up for a morning round of crib. At noon, I leave—both to give my parents some privacy and to buy my stepdad lunch—before returning to sit in my mother's room until it's time to drive my stepdad back through rush hour traffic to my sister's house.

But it is on Day 5—the day of my mother's herd of trees and our first cribbage game—that I think to walk east into the Mount Pleasant neighborhood. My mother divorced her parents shortly after I was born, but her grandfather—a man who she adored, who first taught her to play cribbage, who she spoke of often even if we never visited—lived not far from here. Beneath the oppression of this July's heat wave, the houses are gracious, the tree trunks are broad, the canopy abundant.

Looking up, I guess: oak and elm, locust and hornbeam? All plants gather stories, but those of trees extend across decades, even centuries. My mother will turn 78 this October. Standing in a street whose houses I can't afford, I'm in the company of trees that might have heard my mother's voice as a young girl, that shaded her as she learned to ride a bike, that could remember her long after I am gone. Here in Vancouver, all three of us—my mother, my stepfather and me—are displaced from the plants we now live alongside. My parents' flora roots on a small farm at the end of a coastal highway, two hundred kilometers northwest of where I stand. Mine grows in a rolling grassland three hundred kilometers to the northeast. But the botany of the lower Fraser River, from my sister's house 30 kilometers distant in the suburbs of Port Coquitlam to the urbane streets of Mount Pleasant, is woven into my mother's history, even if it's a history she rarely shared.

When I return with a strawberry smoothie for my stepdad—the only food he can stomach at lunch—my mother is fast asleep, mouth agape. In the silence, confronted with my mother's aging body, I long for the indeterminacy of trees. I spend each fall teaching university students that trees, unlike humans, constantly reimagine themselves. From the tip of each branch, in a sheath beneath their bark, trees grow eternally through the division of meristem cells. Year after year, hundreds of thousands of cells quietly splitting in two, forming new stem, leaf, wood and root. Older branches, diseased leaves or spent flowers fall; meristems build anew. Over and over again.

But there are few trees inside this hospital. This is a sparse botany, solitary and contained. From my chair inside my mother's room, I see only two plants: a pot of pink blooms atop a monitor in the hallway and the tea rose my sister brought yesterday. When my mother wakes, she needs to be reminded who brought the rose, but she knows more of its buds have opened. This is, after all, a woman who supplemented her bartender's wage arranging flowers for local restaurants, who once replaced my bedroom wall with grow lights and plant shelving when she ran out of room in her greenhouse and whose over-sized garden grew local long before the phrase became slogan.

As we stand to leave, my stepdad looking more exhausted than usual, I ask him if he knows the name of the pink-flowered plant on the hospital monitor.

It is in his careful consideration of the plant's pink petals, its ovate leaves, that I begin to consider how deeply plants run in my family.

In my car, negotiating the bunched-up traffic adjacent to the enormous excavation for the new Mount Pleasant subway station, I ask my stepdad—this man born in the sparse sage of eastern Montana, now cleaved to the coastal forests of BC—if he thinks there's room for the roots of Vancouver's urban forest. Trained as a city planner, married to my mother, my stepdad spent nearly forty years with one foot mired in development blueprints and one foot dug into the garden. After days spent in hospital towers, I've been trying to imagine the sheer volume of infrastructure—the sewers and electric, water and gas, and soon subways—that run belowground. Doesn't all of this interrupt the web of connections needed for this city's aboveground forest? Is there soil enough for one root to find another, for mycorrhizal connections to link tree with tree?

My stepdad's not worried. You'd be surprised, he says, on how little you need to get by.

•

Day 8. My sister, off-work, drives our stepfather into the hospital. For the first time in a week, I can breathe. I can form thoughts beyond the need to change lanes, find a parking spot, a nurse, or to wait for the next test. In my sister's garden, I call my husband and daughter, sort through email, check-in with students, reschedule meetings, sign contracts. Mid-morning, I stand beneath a rich canopy of bigleaf maple and Douglas-fir and red alder in a forested park just up the road from my sister's house. The descending call of Swainson's thrush fills the clear air. A few steps down the trail, a flycatcher feeds four hatchlings huddled together on a red alder branch. With each step I take, each name I list, tension seeps from my body. This may not be my botany, but it is one I learned as a first-year doctoral student: May lily, corydalis, vine maple, *Claytonia sibirica*, red elderberry.

On the far side of the marsh, I find my favorite huckleberry, *Vaccinium parviflorum*: its red berries tart on my tongue. My mother's parents—like so many in the 1950s—left Vancouver for a brand-new suburb in Port Coquitlam. I think my mother went to high school not far from here, but I know little of my grandparent's house.

In this tiny park just above the floodplain of the Fraser River, surrounded by urban sprawl, I inhale as deep as I can. All around me, birds sing.

Mountains erode, trees topple. Nothing is forever. But in the face of my mother's growing dementia, my stepdad's increasing frailty, the presence of this scrap of intact forest feels nothing less than miraculous.

•

Day 9. I am returned to chauffeur duty. But when I leave the hospital at lunch, I'm no longer aimless. I've got a map of Vancouver's trees on my phone. I've practised scrolling through its grey street grid for the bright red pins labelling each tree rooted on city property. I have notes in my field journal on how to separate European hornbeam from American elm, sycamore maple from Norway maple. The map counts more maples than any other genera, but few of them are this landscape's native bigleaf maple.

Even so, I want to know more about my mother's herd of trees: the forest she learned as a young girl; the one she returned to as a young mother. My sister was born in this hospital, maybe even my mother, although she says she's not sure. I turn right on Laurel Street and start a list, using whatever name—scientific or common—that comes first: wisteria, *fagus*, ginkgo, elm. Every forest, urban or not, has an understory. I stop at the covey of lavender plants guarding the parking garage that's been lifting $18.75 from my bank account each day. Three different bumblebee species collect from its flowers, and a few feet away, a strappy thallose liverwort, *Marchantia polymorpha*, colonizes bare ground. *Latuca muralis* blooms yellow beside a row of yew shrubs in the deep shade outside the ER entrance. Quinacridone gold and sap green mosses climb up the trunks of maples. From the tree map I learn that the enormous tree nearly straight across from the ER is an American elm. Further on sits a European hornbean, a Japanese katsura. I walk east along 10th Avenue, headed back towards the neighborhood once populated by my mother's relatives. The next block opens to a green space.

And there, unexpectedly, row upon row of blueberry bushes—members of the same genus as the red huckleberries I found yesterday. An elderly Asian gentleman works methodically to fill two Starbucks cups with plump blueberries. A dogwalker exclaims, "Oh they're ripe," ties her Labradoodle in the shade of an elm and sets to serious picking. A toddler, not yet walking by himself but clad in a bright orange t-shirt emblazoned with the words "Hear Me Roar," pulls his father toward the bushes.

Five floors up, my mother sleeps beneath a sign emblazoned with her last name and a warning that she needs hand-holding. As the "Hear Me Roar" toddler stuffs his first berry into his mouth, I think that whoever wrote "Needs Hand-Holding" does not understand the fierce independence of my mother's mind, perforated or not. My mother has already fallen several times yet still refuses to use a walker or ring for a nurse. But even so, watching the movements of a small body suspended between desire and support, I think that who we are, both figuratively and literally, always depends on others. Biologically, the growing body of this small human will be built with the carbon that once lived in other bodies, other plants. When the toddler in orange is the same age as my mother, some of the carbon molecules from these blueberries will linger in his teeth; his bones, continuously remodelled, will reflect the meals he ate only in the last five to ten years.

Above me, my mother's body is failing. In fits and starts, in seizures and clogged carotid arteries. She has, a doctor told me today, a frail brain. But even here, displaced from her normal flora, it's clear that she finds some sense of herself in the nurses' growing recognition that her husband will arrive each morning, that shortly after, one of her daughters will arrive with a cup of "good" coffee. In her room, my parents still flare at one another—my mother's lips thinning in irritation; my stepfather's voice rising when my mother has contradicted him for the umpteenth time—but my mother reaches often for my stepfather's hand, worrying about how cold it is. Each time, they hold hands longer than I anticipate.

I empty my own mug and fill it with blueberries— gifts from these plants that belong more to bog and mountain forest than to city street. I taste a few and pick as many as my mug will hold to bring back to my mother.

But when I return to her room, she's not interested in the blueberries. This might be my mother's original forest, but today its botany is distraction more

163

for me than for her. Sitting in her chair by the window, my mother says, "See, your dad has already left."

But when my stepdad, who is right beside me, says, "No I'm right here," molecules leap lacunae, and she says, "Of course you are."

•

On Day 10, my mother is adrift. Caught in the logistics of patient transfer between hospitals—from Vancouver General back to the one closest to their farm. Later when asked, she won't know if she made the trip lying on a gurney or sitting in a wheelchair. My stepdad and I take the first ferry of the morning, driving the coastal highway northwest until it ends near their farm, only to speed back into town when the hospital calls to tell us she's arrived.

We find my mother, dressed in her own clothes, lying atop a bed, head turned away from the window. Enraged.

I'm grateful when, sitting up, she comments on the trees in the greenspace across the road, but it's clear that she's less rooted than she's been in days.

"Look," she says, "there's horses, cows, out there. Whose farm is this?"

Along with my mother's coherence, her tea roses are gone, lost in the transfer.

Three hours later, when my stepfather is exhausted and I say it's time to leave, my mother's agitation gets worse.

"You can't leave me with that man"—she's already taken an intense dislike to her roommate, a seemingly gentle man with thick glasses and a strong accent.

"He's crazy," she says. "And that nurse is just stupid."

For one moment, I forget who I'm talking to.

"Be nice," I say, as I bend to kiss her cheek.

The fury in her eyes could ignite forests into flame.

•

As I drive my stepfather home through the slanted light of a summer evening, I think about the subterranean connections that translate trees into forest. My mother and stepfather have created an island built for two. Their mycorrhizal net has been pruned, trimmed, hacked back by my mother's willingness to take offence. And my stepdad—well, he's beyond tired.

•

Day 11. My stepdad and I arrive early to meet my mother's doctor on his rounds. He is lean and trim and tan. He knows my parents and for this, I am nearly weak with relief. He seems to respect my stepfather's quiet fortitude, even as he worries how long my stepfather can manage as the primary caretaker. He also knows how quickly my mother's surliness disappears when you make her laugh. This is my mother's second hospital stay in less than a month, and he teases her that she has to stay long enough this time so that she doesn't bounce right back. She's making too much work for him. And, he really hates hospitals.

This my mother can understand, even respect.

But when he takes my stepfather and me down the hall to talk, all levity has left this man's words. My mother, he says, either goes home with my stepdad or into complex care, likely on a locked ward. Her dementia is too advanced for assisted living. He warns

165

us that he's seen cases like my mother's decline rapidly. He won't release my mother to us, unless they promise to get her community nursing help.

Back in my mother's hospital room, I worry about the connectivity, or lack thereof, implied by this doctor's use of *they*—an unexplained network of health care workers who appear to have the capacity to decide how much help my islanded parents will receive. This is not a world whose forms I can identify or name. Through it all, my mother sleeps.

•

Day 12. I'm in a horrible meeting with my stepfather and the community care coordinator. Hers is, I know, a difficult job, but within minutes, I'm antagonized. She has yet to meet my mother, but she doesn't, she says, rapidly scanning her notes, really see the need for home care, contradicting the referral that my mother's doctor just made. And my stepdad—well, he's lying. Or at the very least, minimizing.

The woman tells us that my mom has a "violence and aggression" warning attached to her file from the Vancouver ER. Immediately I am a child again, needing to translate my mother's outrageousness into acceptable norms. When the nurse asks if she's ever been aggressive with us, I bite my tongue as my stepfather denies. Neither of us mention the torrent of words that can fall so easily from her enraged mouth.

Back beside my mother's sleeping form, I text my sister the community care coordinator's number. Still en route, still out of our stepdad's hearing, my sister won't minimize.

From my mother's hospital room window, I play the tree identification game. Across the street:

Douglas fir and western hemlock, red alder and maybe big-leaf maple. Closer, on the grounds of the complex care unit where my mother is likely to end up: a poplar and maybe one of the trees I learned in Vancouver, a Japanese katsura.

In bed, my mother's skin sags even as it grows flushed. I wonder if sleep is her new ally; a chance to escape the chaos of a web interrupted.

I go back to tree watching. A red cedar, a European beech, pruned shrubs.

Do the trees on this side of the road, in the shadow of this hospital, catch the tension of those who come and go; do they remember those who never leave? Do they wonder about our limits, our inability to breathe in oxygen across our epidermis, to layer and spread and root anew from leg or arm, to grow forever? Do they sense, in the drift of chemicals on windswept air, the lives ending?

My mother, the doctor said yesterday, doesn't remember from one moment to the next. We are back, he said, to "her essential nature."

But that's the point. My mother's essence, for as long as I can remember, has been this subterranean rage ready to erupt.

I've never understood its origin. For years I've assumed that it germinated first in those stark years when she divorced her parents, but she's never said, and neither my sister nor I were ever bold enough to ask. Certainly, it's not my stepdad. He's the only one who can divert her rage.

But when my sister finally arrives, having driven my stepdad's van from her house, my stepdad stands up and declares, "You girls wait for your mom to get discharged. I'll go get dinner started."

For the first time in two weeks, my stepdad has

his own vehicle to drive on a road he knows well. He's going home.

As soon as my stepdad leaves, my mother's irritability spikes. The reality she has worried about for years—all independence lost to her daughters—has come true, if only for a few hours.

•

I am in my car, fan on full, doors open, trying to vent some of the heat that has built up throughout this hot day. The discharge papers have come through. We have a promise that a case manager will assess my mother before the end of the week.

My phone bings. A text from my sister.

I think I need help.

By the time I run, heart pounding, up four flights of stairs, my mother is a solid lump of wretchedness, refusing to leave her hospital room.

When I try to cajole her, "Come on Mom, let's blow this popsicle joint," she flings her fist, hard and fast, at my face. Her flesh misses mine; her rage, as always, flies true.

I step back and call my stepdad.

Through the speaker of my phone, my stepdad says, "Honey, talk to me. Why won't you come home? This is what you've been waiting for."

For five agonizing minutes he pleads with her. But my mother's anger cannot be placated by something so trivial as a phone call.

Do we know—my stepdad, my sister and me—that this is the vengeance, her piece of flesh, for that moment nearly two weeks ago when Laurie pushed the red call button?

When I go out to the nurses' station to tell them

that my mom won't leave with my sister and me, a kind nurse tells me, "It's not your mother, dear; it's the dementia."

•

For thirty minutes, Laurie and I sit vigil, just out of reach.

When my stepdad finally arrives in the doorway, I walk out of the room and my sister follows. I go as far as I can without losing sight of my mother's door, but Laurie lingers within earshot.

Later I will learn the details. Later I will learn that even my stepdad grew frustrated before declaring, "Alright, you decide: either get back into bed or leave with me." But in the hall, it's only a few minutes before I see my mother and stepfather, hand in hand, fast-walking towards the elevator.

Laurie, I say, let's take the stairs. I can't imagine standing next to our mother in a confined space right now.

We reach the bottom floor just in time to see my mom and stepdad walk out into the brutal heat, my mother's hand still clutching my stepfather's.

I drive northwest, my sister beside me, knowing that this day might not end soon. My mother might rage, might throw my suitcase out of the house, or insist that my stepfather do it.

Or it might settle down.

In the half hour drive, I'm tempted, as I always am when my mother's anger erupts, to sort the day for cause and effect. But maybe no drive is long enough to understand the unfathomable. Instead, as Laurie and I follow in the wake of my stepfather's van, I silently list the plants we drive past: Douglas fir, big-leaf maple, *Plagiomnium*, *Populus* in the clear-cut, goat's beard, ocean spray.

•

Day 13. If my mother's anger rages up from below, the visible botany of her farm tames it far better than any blue webbing or cotton straps. Even her dementia stabilizes.

This morning, waking at home, her transformation is nothing less than miraculous. She still shifts localities and decades; she still flares at being corrected, but slipping into consciousness on the farm, walking onto the deck that my stepdad built, seeing green apples turning red in the orchard, roots her in a way I feared was no longer possible. Apple and pear, meadow grass and red alder, linden tree and sword fern, big-leaf maple and Douglas fir—I've never been more grateful for any flora than the one that populates my parent's farm.

Yet, for the next two days, Laurie and I battle its excess. This botany is a meadow and orchard claimed from a creek-side forest, enriched by millennia of intermittent floods. Everything here grows fast. My parents might be plant people, but their bones and muscle no longer have the capacity to restrain the meristematic growth of their farm. A maple tree has sprouted in the vegetable beds, a pin cherry blocks the gate to the satellite dish, and orchard grass barricades the greenhouse door. For my sister and me, these five acres have become more burden than refuge. Yet neither of us begrudge this farm's botany. Both Laurie and I understand that if our mother is forced to permanently leave this flora, her demented mind will have to be drugged into compliance. We know that we are only one slip, one broken hip away from permanently losing our mother.

Is it any wonder that Laurie and I mow and

weed whack grass, clip endless canes of Himalayan blackberry, clear the limited paths my stepfather now walks—out to the satellite dish, between the back door and his van? Is it any wonder that when my parents fill out the necessary forms for the case manager who comes to visit, but then refuse any ongoing help, that both my sister and I lose our tempers? That as we sit listening to our parents minimize their daily challenges to this funny middle-aged woman, we vibrate with unspoken rage? That when the case manager leaves, my sister and I follow? That, in the small village at the end of a highway, we sit and drink cold pear cider— sometimes laughing, sometimes crying—in the shade of an enormous cedar until it's nearly too dark to see?

•

Day 15.   Lawns mowed, carpets vacuumed, wood stacked, house as clean as we can get it. My sister and I don't leave early, but early enough. Behind the wheel of my car, I am a stranger to myself. After two weeks in the company of my demented mother, any minor dissatisfaction translates instantly into irritation. I don't trust myself with my own daughter, my husband, my home. I take my sister to the ferry terminal and turn back.

Daughters of demented mothers. It's not just me and my sister. We are an ever-growing club. Two of whom live on this coastline; two of whom who will provide refuge and ask nothing in return. I've already called.

•

Day 16.   My friends are night owls and on the first

morning, I wake into a welcome silence, free to linger alone on their wide porch, free to watch their blonde cat, Lexie, stalk ineffectually through tall grass. In an overgrown garden inherited from a previous owner, an apple tree leans, rosemary sprawls, fennel drifts. My friends, I realize, are cat people, book people, music people, but not plant people.

I am nearly weak with relief.

On the second morning, I walk a narrow park that stretches from bog to seashore, from cedar and *sphagnum* to beach grass and salal. By the time I navigate back to my friends' overgrown yard for lunch, I am returned.

•

Day 18. I am in my car before first light. East of the mountains, my home lies at nearly the same latitude as my parents' farm. But getting there from here requires traversing a great V of interlocked ferries and highways. First southeast along the coast, curving around one headland and then another; carried by ferry across fjord; driving more tortuous curves; another ferry and then a fast-moving urban highway, sweeping my car into the lowlands of the Fraser River. Navigating through the botany of my mother's history, past the exit to my sister's house.

My sister is, like me, another plant person. Laurie never graduated high school, but she learned enough about growing plants from our mother to lie her way into a job in a Home Depot greenhouse. Now, after twenty years of working for Home Depot, her garden blooms with the abundance of potted plants never sold. Hers is a frugal, if resplendent, botany. Yet if my sister and parents marked their lives with domesticated plants, I carved a small measure of independence by first learning the Latin names of native species and then learning the names of plants—mosses and liverworts—too small to identify with the naked eye. It is this botany that gave me a profession, that let me find a home in the grasslands where the aspen cluster in stands as tidy as any herd of cows.

Not far from my sister's exit, just above the 49th parallel, the highway I'm following bends abruptly northeast. The second leg of my V-route home. Climbing out of the Fraser River floodplain, I'm grateful for the coastal botany that still mostly roots my mother's frail brain in family, if not always time or place. But as I swoop northeast across the high plateau that will take me home, I wonder if I ever truly understood the consolation of trees before now.

Isn't it only when we risk the loss of those bodies closest to us that we can comprehend the grace of trees' persistent growth? Isn't it only in the strained silences of words left unspoken that we can imagine the comfort of those who gossip without lips or tongue? Isn't it only when we lose the stories of our elders that we can remember to consult the archives embedded in trees' ringed trunks?

I'm not sure. I'm not even sure how long I'll be home before the next emergency calls me back across the mountains. But if no botany escapes what lies beneath, no botany comforts more than the familiar.

There, just on the horizon.

A herd of aspen, grazing in the mid-day light.

BRANCH BY BRANCH
LYDIA GWYN

It's spring and the green tongues of bulbs slip through the blouses of their earth. I can see the hyacinths I planted last fall, their new tips peeking out of the bed by our back porch. I survey the yard from the kitchen window. The crocuses have already come, like grasses at first and then like tiny cotton swabs on the ground. Our hill is full of them, and once they open our backyard will be a stroke of purple.

Last night's dreams brought a parade of soft sofas and more buildings with hidden rooms and a ghost unlocking and opening my front door. I was in college again. I had an apartment with silhouette paintings on the walls and a friend who would come over for wine and snacks. She kept telling me about her boyfriend's premature ejaculation. The ghost turned out to be a janitor trying to contact his still-living wife. Her name was Margaret.

I wish I could have one of my flying dreams again.

For breakfast, I sneak into my daughter's bake sale items and steal a couple chocolate chip cookies. I dip them in my coffee and admire her work, perfect in texture, perfect in flavor. I slip three dollars into her money bag.

Today there is so much outdoor work to be done. Paths to clear, gutters to clean, fences to repair. I've promised my husband I'd help him remove the elephant ear in our easement, which is dangerously close to the power lines. And then there are the ailanthus trees to contend with.

My husband is sick of dealing with the

ailanthus. They're taking over everything, pushing out the native elms and sourwood, growing in our flower beds and in the foundation of our home. He's tried killing them by stripping a ring of their bark away, a technique called girdling, but it only kills the one ailanthus, not the million others that spring up from their rhizome-like root system.

Girdling is essentially what the ash beetles do to our ash trees, leaving behind brittle gold and gray skeletons that fall branch by branch to the forest floor.

The ailanthus is the same Tree of Heaven from *A Tree Grows in Brooklyn,* a book I read late in life and loved. When we bought our home and started ridding our acreage of all the ailanthus, I was pained at first, thinking of Francie and her resilience. Now, I'm ripping them by the roots out of my vegetable gardens.

I would love to turn the page and start all over with a new home, new land.

My husband would love to wave a wand and replace all the ailanthus with the trees from his wish list. Elms and persimmons, hollies and magnolias, more pawpaws to replace the ones that didn't make it last year.

He's never read *A Tree Grows in Brooklyn.*

By the end of the day, I know I'll be exhausted, as I am on so many days of lawn work. A drowsiness will settle into my bones and brain, and by dinner time, I'll be ready to reach for the lamp chain and lie down in my bed.

It's cool today, but the kind of cool I welcome on manual labor days. I watched the news before bed last night and saw the weather everywhere, a nor'easter churning in one part of the country and a thundersnow in another. I've never seen lightning and snow at the same time.

I imagine the muffled thunder, the flash of electricity in the clouds, and think about a fun experiment I tried as a kid, when my friends and I would buy a bag of Wintergreen Lifesavers and take them into a closet. We knew the Lifesavers would spark when broken apart, and so we'd close the closet door, turn out the lights and chew handfuls of mints. We'd peer into each other's open mouths, and sparks blue as stars would illuminate our faces.

AT THE EDGE OF HER GRASP
BRIAN BRAGANZA

I first found this stand, *Juglans nigra*, black walnut trees, when they were just a few inches in diameter. The eastern white pines, equally young, were lavish and untrained. This mingling of pine and black walnut is a specialized plantation technique: rows of black walnuts neatly knitted with rows of white pines. As the bushy pines age, they coax the walnut stems to grasp for sunlight, growing a clear straight grain to someday make a fine table, turn a bowl, fashion a guitar neck.

More than two decades later, snow squawks beneath my feet and the CN train's icy howl hangs in the air. A memory of these trees unfurls and I find the rail-side trail and return to this place. The Juglans trees' straight stems are now forty feet high and twelve inches in diameter. Some of the pines that coached them to grow are standing deadwood, whorls of barkless branches; tracks along their trunks are the typewritten testament of the yellow-bellied sapsucker. Other fallen pines are snow-covered hummocks. The black walnut trees accumulate biomass in the abundant sunlight, feeding off the nutrients from the decaying pines, and breathing into the spaciousness between trees. Their deep taproots steeped in the rich, alkaline soil above the limestone bedrock of this country. The black walnut roots produce Juglone, a natural herbicide. As the trees mature, stretching to the light, this toxin disperses, saturating the soil surrounding the shallow rooted pines. Poisoned, they die.

This plantation replicates an ecological principle: elements in the natural system are in constant conversation and utilize each other; they feed and succeed. I wonder about this forester who invested seeds into the earth not for their own capital gain, nor for their children's. I envision a grandchild, grown into an adult, screwing tight a vice while curls of chocolate brown shavings tumble over the blade of the plane to litter the floor; a jointer, carpenter's glue and clamps, legs turned on a lathe. A harvest table holding a family dinner two generations in the future.

•

Growing up brown in a white town, I hid my bruises from my parent's view. Amidst the shame of my skin color and never feeling I matched up to the faces and bodies around me, I detached myself from my parents and their Indian-ness. I hid in my room on Sunday mornings as my mother cooked my favorite chicken curry so the scent wouldn't infuse my clothing before we left for church. I'd convinced myself that I could blend into these white places I inhabited, while simultaneously disassociating from those who shared my brownness, internalizing that which separated me.

I fooled myself for a long time, and yet my parents' essence was lodged in the rings of my becoming. Over time I recognized that I could not escape my parents' lineage, nor would I want to. Over time I recognized that their seeds thrived at my core. Seeds of pain and perseverance weathering their childhood familial loss: the death of my mother's parents and abuses by her older brothers; my paternal grandfather abandoned my father while priests trespassed against him in his altar boy's gown. Seeds of fear and courage as, just married, they left Bombay in their twenties, venturing with bags packed and a child in her belly, the only brown family in a small town in postwar Germany. Even though I grew up far from our ancestral land, I fed off the nutrients of these decaying generational legacies that shaped me. As a child and young man, my

180

own reach for the sun was often eclipsed by my struggle for identity and belonging. Despite my estrangement, my parents consistently encouraged my potential to stretch towards the sky. Claiming their rightful place in a white time, they encouraged me to follow my path; to seek my own light, oblivious of the unstable ancestral soil that left me quaking.

•

As my father lies dying in the hospital, my mother and I crouch on her lawn digging weeds—this her meditation and her perseveration. In between visits to the hospital and confounding negotiations with doctors, we sit on the grass, heads bowed beneath a July sun. She shares stories about her courtship with my father, how they'd meet in the dance halls of Bombay or walk along the beaches of Goa. A secret between them. I share memories of our early years in Canada, my father's fumbles using Kentucky Fried Chicken as bait on the line and blowing up the heavy air mattresses with a foot pump under the weakly stretched canvas tent, the water pooled and dripping as we slept; or later towing the pop-up camper behind his green '69 LeMans. He worked hard as we tried to fit in. At times, my mother and I shift over the lawn of my childhood in silence, the steel weeding tools diving in, our fingers selecting and vanquishing dandelion or couch grass roots. She wonders aloud about the next garbage and recycling pick up. The mundane and profound.

Since my father's death, I've watched my mother's memory slowly unravel. Perhaps this too was a secret kept between them, or a secret beyond their knowing. Perhaps they buoyed each other with their enduring love. Six months later we visit my father's columbarium; returning through town, my mother drifts to another time, "It's good to be back," she says with affirmation. "Where are we right now?" I ask. She responds with images of their life in Rehau, Germany, in the 1960s, how welcome they felt, the good friends they had. I grasp for the mother I once knew, finger-like shadows of hardwoods on a wintery afternoon.

•

White-breasted nuthatches wait at the forest's edge, dive with a headlong undulation to land at the feeder, peck a seed and within seconds, flick back under cover. As my mother's frontal lobe recedes and the blood vessels in her brain constrict, her clutch on the recent and distant past slips from her grasp like seeds to snow. In order to track the immediate moment and what might come next, she makes meticulous lists in her fine cursive, a remnant of her legal secretary's shorthand:

> Take out garbage and recycling
> Buy oranges
> Brian arrives
> Lobster for dinner
> Have breakfast

The mundane and profound. Completing each task, she excises it with scissors, so by end of day her list is a jigsaw of all that remains undone, while jobs completed are litter in the trash.

It has become difficult for my mother to plan in advance. In the days before Christmas, I ask what we'll have for our family dinner; she brushes me off saying she can't think that far ahead. The narrowing of her memory of *what was*, and the struggle for foresight of *what might come*, means her life circulates into an ever-tightening spiral of repetitive steps and patterns of *what is*.

While my mother's memory declines, her body has not forgotten how to dance. Any time Elvis or Hank Williams strikes up on the radio, she reaches for whoever's hand is closest, leads them through foxtrot, jive, and swing, maneuvers of my parent's courting on the Bombay dance floors. She recalls their wedding, a soft waltz glide across the hardwood floor, my father at the edge of her grasp.

•

A friend once gave me a bushel basket of black walnut seeds he'd collected from his family property in the Annapolis Valley. Their shape and colour like limes, the outer husk a sweet citrus smell. Picking them out and rolling them on the gravel laneway to break open the husk, a black dye slips across my hands like gloves. The hard shell inside, tougher than store-bought English walnuts, I take a hammer to break them open on the stone wall, dig out the dense meat with a metal skewer.

Twenty-eight hundred years ago, ancient Greeks intuitively understood the benefits of consuming walnuts due to their striking resemblance to the human brain. Cracked open, there are distinct left and right hemispheres, wrinkles and folds not unlike the cortex of our brain, all contained in a protective hard skull of a shell.

We now know that walnuts contain high concentrations of DHA, a type of Omega-3 fatty acid which supports an increase in mental performance and prevents age-related cognitive decline. These active ingredients cross our blood barrier and stimulate the production of neurotransmitters, including serotonin, for optimal brain function. The oil in walnuts is also known to help break down plaque build-up in our brain. Walnuts don't just look like brains, they provide nutrients such as healthy fatty acids, which specifically nourish our brain, memory, and mental function.[1]

I plant sixty of the black walnut seeds along the north facing slope of my drumlin farm in Nova Scotia, amongst the aspen, sweet fern, and alder. The fraying hem of the forest creeps out into the meadow. Twenty germinate pushing up through matted pasture grass. In the fall I wrap a wire mesh around the stems to keep the mice-gnawing at bay. Over ten years, a few have grown three feet tall, while many still struggle in the dense clay soil. I attempt to utilize the poplar stand in the same way the pines were used in the plantation. I imagine the walnuts reaching toward the sun filtering through the large tooth aspen leaves; as the Juglans grow, the toxin prevents the continued spread of poplars into the meadow.

Like the forester, I now understand that I've not only planted these trees for the generations to come, but that this act is also an investment in myself and an acknowledgement of the debit to my ancestry. Though I may not reap any timber or turn bowls, I harvest gratitude and delight as I observe the trees' climb to the sky and growing shadow over time. In planting and nurturing, there is familial healing as I root down in the lineage of identities that inhabit me.

•

---

1   https://www.dailypioneer.com/2013/sunday-edition/what-links-walnuts-to-brain.html   https://www.brainhq.com/brain-resources/brain-healthy-foods-nutrition/nuts-brain-health

Along the south slope of the pasture, I'd planted three English walnut seedlings, *Juglans regia*. With minimal attention they've grown through the unkempt grass. Struggling, dying back numerous times, they have coppiced again and again from their roots, a tenacity to thrive. One has now surpassed my height with its pale zigzag trunk and tangled branches. I'm not growing these for clear grain furniture wood, rather for the brain-like, nutrient-fortified meat of the seeds.

PAWPAW GROVE
ROSS GAY

Yesterday I left my building on campus and was biking along the Jordan River—truly, it's called the Jordan River, and unlike its more famous cousin, was named for David Starr Jordan, one-time president of Indiana University, eventual president of Stanford University, and pioneer in the field of eugenics—to investigate what I suspected, zooming by a few days back, might be a pawpaw grove. It is a sweet correction this computer keeps making, turning pawpaw into papaw, which means, for those of you not from this neck of the woods, papa or grandpa, which a pawpaw grove can feel like, especially standing inside of it midday, when the light limns the big leaves like stained glass and suddenly you're inside something ancient and protective.

It only now occurs to me that not every reader will know the pawpaw, which doubles my delight, for I am introducing you to the largest fruit native to the States. Its custardy meat surrounds a handful of large black seeds. It tastes like a blend of banana and mango, in that tropical ballpark, shocking here in the Midwest, and as a consequence of its flavor profile it has been called the Indiana or Hoosier banana, the Michigan banana, the Kentucky banana, the Ohio banana, the West Virginia banana, and probably the Pennsylvania banana. And maybe the Virginia banana. And most likely the Illinois banana. Alabama banana for sure. And the banana of Kansas. The leaves seem to be insecticidal and smell that way. The flowers are so labial they will warm your heart.

Telling where this grove is—between Ballantine Hall and the President's House, right along the river, which is actually a creek—is not, evidently, the kind of thing you always do, which I learned when I asked my friend Julie where the pawpaw grove was that she was raving about the previous year. "I'm not telling!" she laughed, incredulous, though she doesn't remember this interaction, or her pawpaw grove, conveniently. I admire her pawpaw covetousness. It reminds me of the dreams I still sometimes have—sleeping dreams—of treasure of one kind or another. As a kid it used to be money, especially silver coins, often in big old chests, something I imagine was informed at least somewhat by the movie *Goonies*.

But as I get older, the treasure in my dreams seems to shift. Now it's a veggie burger and French fries up the hill and around the bend that I can't remember how to get to. Or one final football game, granted thanks to some kind of athletic eligibility snafu, at which, when I arrive for it, usually late, my teammates either don't recognize me or would rather I didn't play. Or, less miserably: last night I left an event in celebration of my Uncle Roy, who was also Barack Obama, because I was underdressed [a theme]. I found some beautiful green pants that fit me well in a chest of drawers in my childhood apartment, though I lost track of the festivities, so enamored was I of these pants. My mother stepped out from the hall, shouting disapprovingly that the first speaker had already finished, turning quickly on her heel to return to her seat.

The delight of a pawpaw grove, in addition to the groveness, which is also a kind of naveness, is in learning how to spot the fruit, which hangs in clusters, often, and somewhat high in the tree. This encourages pointing, especially if you are not alone, a human faculty that deserves at least a little celebration, something I realized when I pointed toward a grape I had tossed in the direction of a dog to no effect, and then a few days later pointing at a bird for a baby to notice, same result. The pointing skill, pointing and following the point, is acquired (I wonder if there is a pointing stage), and a miracle of cognition. A miracle to know there is an invisible line between the index finger and that barely discernible trio of fruit swaying way up in the canopy, blending into the leaves until they twist barely into the light, and out of it. There's one, you whisper, lest they fly away.

GINGKO BILOBA
RICHARD HACKLER

The ginkgo biloba tree has been around, in something like its current form, for over 200 million years. Its natural range once spanned forests around the globe, but contemporary ginkgos are a tame species: they live in cities, mostly, in parks and arboretums and wherever else we've decided to put them. And it makes sense that we'd keep them around: ginkgos are a hearty, endlessly adaptable tree, able to thrive in the cramped spaces and depleted soils of, say, the strip of land between the sidewalk and street in front of my apartment, in a deindustrialized stretch of Northeast Minneapolis.

Plus, they're beautiful trees, with fan-shaped leaves that turn a shocked yellow in October and shimmer over my house like a constellation of tiny suns. This is what my neighborhood is like in the fall: the sunlight sifting through the ginkgos, filling the air with a pale, insistent light as lovely as a hymn. But then in November—after the skies have grayed and the winds picked up—the leaves fall, all at once, and collect on our sidewalks in big florescent clumps that I kick apart while I wait for the bus, blowing into my hands beneath the stricken ginkgos, their limbs mute as extinguished candles.

At this point, while the ginkgos are leafless, they aren't yet naked: they still have their seeds. Ginkgo biloba seeds are the size and color of apricots, and they hang almost luridly from their branches, making the trees look like a band of knobby, leering ghosts. The seeds dangle for a week or two—poised, almost, beneath the steely skies—until it starts to get cold for real, around mid-November, and the seeds begin dropping, at first one by one (you'll hear a thud on your roof and think: maybe a squirrel?), and then faster, and then, for a day or two, it's a torrent—they land like hail on our houses and cars and heads, collect in mounds in our yards and gardens, splatter and rot and ruin paint jobs, grind into a paste that slicks the sidewalk, sticks to our shoes, and follows us inside. And, famously, they release a stench when they fall that reminds some people of vomit but to me smells like rotting flesh or dogshit. The smell hangs over the neighborhood like a mood, an expression of the sullenness most of us feel here in mid-November in this cold, gray city.

My neighbors get so angry about this, every year, when the wind is sharp and smells like dogshit. My neighbors stand at their stoops, frown into the breeze, drink their coffee and say, *Why do we have these trees? The city should do something. Someone should cut those things down!*

And I stand there on the sidewalk and nod and say, *Yes, yes, they sure do smell, they sure are messy, someone should get a chainsaw, ha ha!* And then I say goodbye and continue on my walk.

I say this to be polite because, really, I love our ginkgo trees. For their beauty, sure, for the way they transform my neighborhood's October into an elegy for summer; and for their adaptability, for the line I can draw from the gingko in front of my house to one whose seeds fed dinosaurs during the Jurassic. But I love them most for the way they mess with us, every year, raining their seeds on our heads like a mock plague, a sly rebuke and gleeful giving away of the lies that animate our worst ideas: that we are separate from the natural world, that we are rightly in control and can act on nature however we like.

Most cities have taken to planting only male

ginkgo trees, which don't develop seeds, but even this isn't foolproof: it's difficult to identify the sex of a young gingko and, hilariously, the branches of a male gingko can change sex and begin producing the seeds anyway. They do this when they sense there aren't enough female trees around to continue reproducing. They do this so they can survive.

We plant ginkgo trees in our cities because we want it all: we want the beauty of the natural world and the ease and sterility of the industrial one. We want wide roads and short commutes and parks full of picturesque trees beneath which we can do yoga. We want 99 cent hamburgers and direct flights to London, and when we think of "nature," we think of it first as a sort of psychic resource, a retreat we can drive to on summer weekends when we need to "recharge." We want the giddy freedom of infinite, consequenceless choice, we comfortable people in leafy neighborhoods whose factories have been converted, charmingly, into food halls. And we want the nightmares this culture has helped unleash—the mass die-offs, the depleted aquifers, the burning hillsides and smoke-dimmed skies—to stay outside our field of vision.

But the ginkgo tree—with its fleshy and smelly and inconvenient aliveness—is an ambassador from that exiled natural world, and one that's here, maybe, to remind us that we can't exile nature. Not really. *You are a part of nature*, say the ginkgo trees, say the coyotes that stalk our suburban dogs, the raccoons that overturn our trash cans, the squirrels that thump around our attics, and all the other emissaries of mild chaos that might work to check our sense of control—if we wanted our sense of control checked. The truth, of course, is that we can understand the gingko however we like: as a gentle reprimand from the natural world, or as an exception to the rule of our dominance, an inconvenience we can either indulge or, when we've had enough, exterminate.

"We have no recourse at this point," said Terry Robinson, the superintendent of Iowa City's Forestry Division, in an interview with CBS News shortly before the city removed one of its last ginkgo trees. "It creates a sanitation problem for us because we have to be down there cleaning it up as often as possible."

The natural world, as so many indigenous, radical, and mystical traditions have been demonstrating for millennia, can be understood any number of ways. It can be a place apart from us, a place we mournfully plunder, sighing and shrugging at humanity's propensity to blow the tops off mountains and poison watersheds, or it can be everything, the entire world, including us and the gingko bilobas lining our streets. A limitless natural world is one in which we relinquish our dominance and the sense of alienation that makes plunder possible and instead embrace our role as part of a complex, varied whole. Such a shift would require an overhaul of our metaphors and narrative conventions—no more "nature" as separate, unpeopled and "unspoiled"; no more limitless growth as an economic imperative; no more nonhuman world as a discrete collection of resources for us to exploit. Instead, our approach would necessarily be humbler, more vulnerable and receptive to criticism, even when that criticism comes from a tree.

Whatever hope left for a future that isn't an escalating nightmare rests in this shift, I think, this willingness to be checked and humbled by all of our neighbors, human and nonhuman alike, and to appreciate, love, and learn from the places we live.

And the ginkgo isn't only a smelly nuisance—

scrape away the flesh of the seed and you're left with the nut, which one writer describes as the "camembert of nuts... complex and utterly good to eat." Humans have been cultivating ginkgos for food for at least 1,000 years, and we may have even rescued them from extinction, as the trees had become rare, living only in isolated clumps in a few small pockets of China. Over the past millennium, though, ginkgos have retaken their former range, spreading throughout China into Korea and Japan and back into the Americas, where they hadn't lived since before the last ice age. This story—one in which people grow with and give to a fellow creature, each working to ensure the other's survival—could be lifted from a more hopeful history than we're used to reading, one in which people are something more, something better, than spoilers of the natural world. There are stories like this throughout human history—stories of cooperation, of living within limits, of people using their gifts to give to the world's abundance and diversity. These stories are told today by water protectors chaining themselves to excavating equipment, by neighborhood groups fighting to turn superfund sites into urban farms, by nuns climbing over fences to pray outside of missile silos, and by every person whose sense of self and solidarity extends radically, remarkably, to the land itself. These are stories we can all begin to tell, and strive to live by, though it requires the sort of sustained attention our wider culture was built to wring out of us.

But let's try anyway: to reject the mournful platitudes of the plunderers, to refuse the nightmares delegated to us, and to recognize and nurture, instead, our ties to each other and the places we live, the places here to sustain us, just as we are here—this is true, I'm sure of it—to sustain them.

I HAVE BEEN WORRYING ABOUT SPACE
JULIE LUNDE

. . . .
. . . .
. . . and what crowds it. Space junk; space debris. When last I was able to check the public count, the Space Surveillance Networks were actively tracking 30,810 debris objects in space. I go cold in the face of large numbers like this one, am unable to envision the problem. Even if I could, even when I try, paralytic stasis hits me, hits most of us confronting a too-big fear. But I cannot stop thinking about this count . . . .
. . . .
. . . .
. . . .
. . . . . I love this Danish saying I learned from my father: *hear the flea bark like a dog.* You say it when someone talks a big game, makes threats you're not intimidated by. It's something similar to saying *their bark is worse than their bite*, shrugging off an opponent, *you don't scare me* . . . . . .
. . . .
. . . .
. . . . it is something else when this saying is reversed: a silent, open jaw ready to clench. A threat cloaked in a soft wingbeat. Even this reversal is a quiet one, unsaid. The earth's darkest perils love the game of surprise, but it is not so common for us to say to each other that someone's bite is worse than their bark, nor that the dog barks just like a flea. I haven't been able to check the count for six months now because the URL to the count site no longer works . . . .
. . . .

. . . .
. . . . Lily and I visit our moon
tree at least once a week. We trek to campus sweat-heavy
through hundred-degree heat and press our palms to
the bark like we're packing snow. I hug and feel the
tree's pressure against my heart. Its cracks and patterns
feel like elephant skin. A nearby sign announces the
tree's origin: . . . .
. . . .
. . . . Bicentennial Moon Tree . . . .
. . . .
. . . . . This seedling was grown from the very seeds . . . .
. . . . . journeyed to the moon and back on board Apollo
. . . . . 14. It symbolizes the major role forests played . . . .
. . . . . in developing our American Heritage and the . . . .
. . . . . role forests have in our future. This planting . . . . .
. . . . .was made possible by: State Forester of Arizona, . .
. . . . . U.S. Forest Service and NASA . . . .
. . . . *April 30th 1976*
. . . .
. . . . .To my ear, it sounds like the language of a family
bumper sticker, *SEEDLING ON BOARD* . . . .
. . . .
. . . .
. . . . and I love this story often retold about my
mother and aunt, twins, as children. One night, home
alone, they heard a loud bang on the stairs and hid
inside their bedroom closet. My aunt whispered: *I'm
sacred, are you?* and my mother replied, *I'm sacred, too.*
Seven years old, they knew even then that the creaks of
an empty house are more ominous at night than in
daylight, that saying something aloud makes it real, that
acknowledgement always strengthens its object. Better
to claim a divine anagram, they must have thought,
than to admit to *scared* and strengthen fear . . . .

. . . .
. . . .
. . . .
. . . Eleven years after Apollo 14 (the moon tree's seed's flight), theaters filled for the following opening scene . .

. . . .
. . . .
. . . . . *EXT: FOREST: NIGHT* . . . .
. . . .
. . . .*A small fern grows on the forest floor. An alien hand, with*
. . . .*two fingers protruding,reaches out for the fern. The alien*
. . . .*groans. A rabbit turns and listens. The fingers dig up the*
. . .*plant as the rabbit watches. The alien then carefully*
. . .*uproots the plant. A small wayward alien walks alone*
. . . .*among the gigantic redwood trees* . . . .

. . . .
. . . . That E.T. is a botanist goes mostly unmentioned outside of the movie's promotional materials; within the movie it is referenced only here, in this opening scene, and in E.T.'s special connection to a pot of dahlias. Why bother at all with botany, then? Except that a botanist is one who comes in peace, a scientist whose desires seem benign, or in line with the bullshit traditions of our "American Heritage": to tend the land, allegedly, to spread our seeds. In the thick of spaceflight giddiness, an era when civilian space travel seemed nearly imaginable, Spielberg was wise to cast his shipwrecked alien in the botanist's unassuming pose

. . . .
. . . .
. . . .
. . . .
. . . . To get to our moon tree, Lily and I must walk past the tree ring laboratory, up the campus mall, past the student union, past the library, across the street and

towards the Kuiper Space Sciences building, near which our moon tree sits tucked on its small grassy plot. Ours is a sycamore, but there are others: loblollys, redwoods, sweetgums, and firs. 500 seeds were sent to space. After the seeds returned from their flight, they were planted across the U.S. haphazardly, their locations still being tracked down now. At present there are 85 known moon trees, of which University of Arizona's is only one . . . . .
. . . .
. . . .
. . . .
. . . . .When my dog is afraid, she hides somewhere enclosed: curled up behind the bathroom door or beneath the kitchen table, head pressed to a leg. When she is stressed, she yawns or licks her lips. Rarely does she bark out of fear; she only barks when she has something to say, like *it's time for my dinner* or *I see a cat!* When we have a monsoon, her fear's biggest foe, I play meditation music loud enough to drown out the rain's sound until she falls asleep . . . .
. . . .
. . . .
. . . .
. . . . Fear is a part of what drives me to the moon tree. It is a strong, sun-warmed body I can lean on for comfort on days I feel anxious, that slow burn of fear. What scares me? Spiders. Heartache. Failure. I am afraid I am boring or sometimes a bad friend. I am afraid I cannot match up to my students' huge needs. I am afraid of so many small, personal things. I'm made terrified by some fewer, but larger, concerns. Palm pressed to the bark, I quiet . . . .
. . . .
. . . .
. . . . briefly.

The tree has become my *sacred* symbol. It both calms and stokes my agonies—I fear the appeal of its, and all, narrative. How easily I might overlook mess when it is arranged into the neat shape of a story! For instance this tree, which is rooted in a very specific narrative language: *journey, future, forests, Heritage*. The nationalized heroics of space exploration and the "final frontier," plus E.T.'s benign botany . . . .
. . . .
. . . .
. . . .
. . . . . When E.T. is afraid, his heartlight flashes, though his heart's mechanism is not fear-specific; it lights in response to any extreme emotion. In some fear-based scenes, E.T. screams, a sound intranscribable, almost robotic. After the movie was released, it is rumored that NASA offered Spielberg a research payload slot aboard a shuttle. He donated it to a university (allegedly) which sent up radish seeds in his stead . . . .
. . . .
. . . . The other story is that in springtime I collect as treasure the moon tree's fallen seed pods, that I sometimes dream about what it must be like on the moon . . . .
. . . .
. . . .
. . . .
. . . . . . though in fact the moon tree's seeds never actually touched down on the moon's surface at all, but merely orbited around the moon in the command module, in Astronaut Stuart Roosa's pocket. I suppose it isn't lying to say these seeds *journeyed to the moon and back,* but it does seem to imply a different image . . . .
. . . .
. . . .

. . . .
. . . .
. . . When Laika, the space dog, was afraid post-launch, her heart rate doubled, and her breath rate quadrupled. No one was with her to observe this response, but the monitors caught it; fear is so physical. This famous dog, whose name in Russian means *barker*, has become a famous (-ly edited) narrative: she was the the first animal to orbit the Earth . . . .
. . . .
. . . . But her ending was revised so her narrative would satisfy, so she could be retold as our valiant pet. The Soviet broadcasts reported that she lived in orbit for nine days when in fact the monitors showed she died from excessive heat in the capsule a few hours post-launch. The dead dog's encirclement of Earth lasted five months before Sputnik 2 reentered, and burned in, our atmosphere. The nine-day narrative stuck around much longer, until a scientist came clean about the matter, thirty-six years later . . . .
. . . .
. . . .
. . . .
. . . .
. . A sampling of other moon tree signage and commemorative plaques: . . . .
. . . .
. . . .
. . . . "This tree is a living symbol of our spectacular human and scientific achievements. May this young tree renew our deep-rooted faith in the ideals of our founding fathers. May it inspire us to strive for the kind of growth that benefits our own citizens and all mankind. –Gerald Ford" (Oregon State University) . . . .
. . . .

. . . .
. . . . *"This tree was grown from a seed that journeyed to the moon and back aboard Apollo 14 1971 planted here on Arbor Day March 15 Bicentennial Year 1976"* (Sebastian County Courthouse) . . . .
. . . .
. . . . *"...planted here by Governor Bob Straub on Arbor Day, April 30, 1976 to celebrate America's bicentennial."* (Oregon State Capital) . . . .
. . . .
. . . . *"Forests greeted the first explorers to these Florida shores. They provided the material for the pioneer's meager existence, and are part of the bold, rich heritage that led man across the threshold of space."* (Kennedy Space Center) . . . .
. . . .
. . . .
. . . .
. . . . What I mean is I can start to panic picturing the slow yearly accumulation of orbiting space junk around us, these new constellations. It does not matter that the likelihood of falling debris causing me personal injury is infinitesimal, nor that scientists say the burn of debris when it reenters our atmosphere has a negligible impact on climate change (comparatively), nor that the Kessler Syndrome Theory—that an overcrowded orbit could produce such significant and cascading debris collisions, collision after collision, like dominoes, that the belt would become littered with nearly infinite pieces of continuously proliferating space junk, and impassable for spacecraft—is for now still just a theory . . . .
. . . .
. . . . though certainly this theory does heighten my fears . . . .
. . . .

. . . .
. . . . . what scares me most is how relentless and silent accumulation is. Our material infestation has moved, preceding most of us, into space, this problem so terrifying and alien, hard to see. 30,810 debris objects orbiting us as we speak, and those are just the ones being tracked. In actuality there's too much to track: half a million pieces of space debris larger than marbles, one hundred million pieces of debris larger than a millimeter each, paint flecks travelling at fifteen thousand miles per hour, dead satellites, rocket and payload fragments, no plan for how to get any of it down . . . .
. . . .
. . . .
. . . . . "So that Earth may live." (Topton Mini-Museum, Pennsylvania) . . . .
. . . .
. . . . "Honoring Earth's Green World of Trees." (Washington Square, Philadelphia) . . . .
. . . .
. . . .
. . . .
. . . . I was raised, as I suspect many in my generation were, to think environmentalism meant Earth Day in April, the whole elementary school ushered outside with small spades to help plant a new tree in the schoolyard. It is hard to divest oneself of this appealing romance, its ease; the idea that replanting is sufficient care, not a symbol but an end itself. It's a behavioral platitude that segues neatly into the small self-righteousness of an aluminum straw sticking out of a disposable cup. And of course I too am guilty of this type of limited thinking, inventing my own arbitrary rules and exceptions for how to ethically navigate the compromising world . . . .

. . . .
. . . (without substantial harm to comfort or convenience?)
. . . . (with a Diet Coke can still in hand?) . . . . .
. . . .
. . . .
. . . . *Wall-E* is like *E.T.*'s
reversal. It tells the story of a trash robot (a *Waste Allocation Load Lifter Earth-Class*) tasked with cleaning up our ruined planet while earthlings orbit thoughtlessly above on a pleasure-filled space station. The movie ends after Wall-E successfully delivers a small seedling to the space station's pilot, proving growth on Earth is once again possible, and the humans head back home . . . . . .
. . . .
. . . .
. . . .
. . . . My favorite YouTube therapist counsels me that obsessing over one's anxiety, how to avoid it, only increases the anxious feelings. And for the longest time I understood the phrase *we have nothing to fear but fear itself* to be about that intensification which results from suppression. I thought the saying meant that if we only faced up to fear, we would become fearless . . . .
. . . .
. . . .
. . . . Now I understand this saying differently. There is so much here that genuinely ought to provoke fear, including but not limited to the nature of fear itself. If we faced up to the feeling of fear and saw just how wholly it nurses inaction, our willful delusions, increasing itself dot by dot, line by line, we would be not fearless but terrified . . . .
. . . . (and, potentially, still unmoved?)
. . . .
. . . .

. . . .
. . . .
. . . . Really, what troubles me most about the moon tree is my attraction to it—my sinister, easy gardener's delight standing before the tree of a seed that was once shot up into space. I'm so easily distracted. . . . .
. . . .
. . . . and the proliferation of trash has already overtaken our planet so fully I hardly notice— less mourn—its presence (ours) on the sidewalks, the shorelines, the water, in the air I breathe. Even now, trying to look directly into the face of our problem of proliferation, trying to direct my gaze away from the neatening narrative, I'm still inclined to send my worries up and away, out into (outer) space . . . .
. . . .
. . . .
. . . .
. . . . Fear makes us balk: fight, flight, or freeze. When Wall-E was scared, he made this sound: *WAOOOOUUUUUUUGHHHH!* And drove in circles. . . .
. . . .
. . . .
. . . .
. . . . What's being covered up in most narratives— especially in the narratives we tell ourselves about who we are—is anti-narrative: that we are telling ourselves a story with such a satisfying build that arrival at a good ending is increasingly impossible, that for the pleasures of our narrative climax, we've agreed not to think much about the ending at all. The hidden disorder is composed of endings, and in each one, we have left nothing untouched . . . .
. . . .
. . . .

. . . .
. . . .
. . . . . .A count can creep up silently, line by line, page by page. You'd have to read this essay through 4.5 times to arrive at 30,810 dots, a number still increasing, day by day, and now hidden . . . .
. . . .
. . . . (how many reads are we at now?)
. . . . (and now?). . .
. . . .
. . . .
. . . .
. . . . What I mean is our bites are much worse than our barks. Like fleas drawn to blood, we crave the solace of empty space, but we can never leave what we long for untouched. . . . .
. . . . We'll bite and bite, in the ending, until the emptiness

empties

and still our teeth will click . . . .
. . . .
. . . .
. . . .
. . . .
. . . .
. . . .
. . . .
. . . .
. . . .
. . . .
. . . .
. . . .
. . . .
. . . .
. . . .
. . . .
. . . .
. . . .
. . . .

TO TELL STORIES
HENRI BENSUSSEN

"To tell stories is to attend directly to the dead."
— Martin Shaw, *Scatterlings*

When the parks re-opened, I re-found myself alone trudging up a new trail after a wrong turn, surprised by a glade almost pastoral. The trail divided recovering victims of recent fires rising through a carpet of grass— young oaks and maples with their charred trunks—from the gleaming foliage of older survivors.

Vibrant maples, massive with age, sent forth great arms held aloft by trunks born before humans took flight. The mid-section of the largest had in some bygone era been eaten away by an earlier fire or struck by lightning. Missing viscera left a space I imagined my body could fold into, this cavity where other animals had nested, listening for a history sung to all those who understood tree language: how its inner tissues continued to feed and minister to every root, limb, stem, leaf, flower.

Like a man I knew without the use of one leg, barely able to speak, retaining only enough control for his fingers to communicate through a piano. Between six and seven each night, he practiced his own compositions. We listened in hallways, behind walls, allowing ourselves to be carried forth to other dimensions of a history we had yet to bear.

APPLE TREE
EMMA WILLIAMS

There are too many apples to pick and not enough time
to save them all, so sometimes the fruit rots and falls with
a thud and squish onto the earth. Cloying sweetness
turns sour as flies hover. The apples we pluck from
the branches are green, and they don't taste like those
shiny, waxed red things piled high in the grocery store.
They crunch hard and tart and pucker your lips tight.
There's cyanide in the apple seeds, but *it won't hurt you,
no, it won't hurt you*, but I'm careful and spit them out
anyways. Grandpa's vegetable garden sits close by, and
a slice of kohlrabi tastes like the soft turned soil next to
raspberry bushes, earthy and wormy and warm. Thick
leafy greens hide squashes, and sometimes small apples
roll over to the edge of the garden where dirt meets grass
and, if you look close enough, small bugs crawl over
green blades to blend in with thick clumps of brown.
Grandpa kicks the rotted apples into the compost pile,
and their scent mixes with coffee grounds and vegetable
peels, but the flies still hover. Inside, Grandma carefully
peels the ripe apples, green skin against sharp knife,
too close to flesh but never drawing blood, deft fingers
and the sound of apple skin hitting stainless steel and
sometimes falling onto yellowed linoleum. When I
climb the apple tree, my hands scrape into calluses that
carry me farther than I've ever been, until the branches
are too thin and I still can't see over the top. Maybe I
can reach the apples up here, save them before it's
too late. *Be careful, don't fall.* Sometimes a spider lurks
between the leaves, but I turn my head and pretend not
to see it because up here I can be brave.

OAK TREE ON ELM STREET
ERICA TRABOLD

I don't need a sixth sense or sixth floor to see *history happens beside trees.*

When the motorcade left Main Street for Houston and turned onto Elm, triangling its way through Dealey Plaza, the crowd knew where it was headed—lunch. The dignitaries in cars and sunglasses paraded toward a meal, toward their expected future. They smiled and waved, parting a crowd of horn rims who had never seen a president so hungry in the flesh, so human and in color. The motorcade passed the site of a future memorial and an oblong fountain pool. The motorcade turned and passed, on its right, a particular oak tree.

When the shots rang out—from somewhere, *where?*—they moved faster than the speed of sound. Before the crowd could hear what happened, they saw it: both hands reaching for the throat. They witnessed the next tragic blow, the one everybody knew was fatal before anybody had to say. The limo sped off down the highway.

When the noise caught up to the bullets, it sounded like four doors slamming in different corners of the room. *What happened?* Testimonies conflicted, echoed. One man recorded a tape. *What happened?* The question rooted itself in American imagination, reverberating for half a century, as if on a loop, but any way you arrange the facts—inevitable tragedy.

Today, a man who has lived in Dallas for a lifetime, eleven years old and stunned beside his auntie when he finally heard what he had seen, paces among visitors on the grassy knoll. He gestures toward a window. He points at the pavement. He repeats his testimony into a microphone, but I am distracted—looking at the oak tree, that tangle of branches between six floors of red brick and the white X painted in Elm's middle lane. I suppose I like the problem it presents.

I want an oak tree on Elm Street—gnarled roots, dense branches, a thing between threat and consequence that could have (should have) stopped the blow.

At 10 a.m., a line of hungry visitors spills out the side of the former Texas Schoolbook Depository. I am hardly the first to arrive with a ticket and curiosity, a hunger to see the place for myself. Inside, roped pathways will sweep us up to the sixth floor and into the sniper's nest, above Elm Street and backward through time.

I had just left a cab. I had just left a plane. I had just been driving in my car down a highway, imagining a death scene. And then, I was seeing it.

•

Logging trucks thundered all night from forest to coast. For the first few months my husband and I lived on the edge of Highway 20, I didn't sleep. Diesel-charged cargo and my own imposterous dreams awoke me on the hour, every hour, when we first moved to Oregon.

It was hard to get anything done on so little fuel, and in the little logging town, I remember thinking, *They cut down so many trees.* And wondering, *Won't they ever stop?*

The first winter seemed mild, milder than any we could remember. We had lived our whole lives somewhere else. On a day too warm for November, we visited a farm, arguing next to the gingerbread house. *Who would hold the saw and who the tree?* It seemed an arduous task, one worsened by indecision. Eventually, exhausted, we chose. I held the fir steady as he severed it from itself, and we lugged the thing home in my Jeep, barely speaking.

Other things we weren't used to: this distance. Back home in Nebraska, we had watched our parents pull Christmas trees from the basement, packed away in boxes that resembled caskets, artificial and plastic and perfect. But we wanted something alive—*a real tree*—every year since we married. We wanted to ride the hayrack and sip cocoa from Styrofoam cups, things we had never done as children, feeling too chitter-chattery to be out, but doing it anyway. We wanted our own experience.

A couple like us had to drive over 30 miles to find a farm like that, but even in Nebraska, there had been places. We would drive the tree home, unload it into the living room of a similarly rented space, nearly the same floor plan we will find ourselves inhabiting halfway across the country. Our choices made the unfamiliar feel like tradition.

But in Oregon, I was becoming new. We had moved across the country because I wanted to write, and moving toward that goal, finding my way into a community of graduate students striving toward something similar, felt like an achievement in itself. Then, the days cooled into a rainy gray. My anxiety about surviving in an academic community felt like twisting my branches toward the sun, looking for a little patch of light. I felt contorted. I never unwound. At the end of that first year, it was as if my husband and I had grown apart, that I had created a huge distance out of sleepless nights on the edge of the highway, days dazed in front of the keyboard.

We couldn't stop arguing about the rest of our lives. *I never want to go back*, I said, and he winced. *I hate my job,* he said, and I frowned. When he couldn't find his passport days before the vacation I'd planned to Canada, it was the kind of metaphor I felt compelled to deconstruct. *You're holding me back from the things I want to do,* I said one hundred times in my head.

And then, I said it out loud.

I swam alone in the apartment pool and, downstairs in the kitchen, tried to find words for the place we had left, the rivers, the trees, the particular paths and roads and highways I had grown used to driving but could no longer access. I liked viewing my life from a distance, but sometimes the distance between myself and the person I loved the most seemed too great to bridge.

When I wasn't silent and angry, I was loud and angry. I ate my lunch in the parking lot just to avoid the tension the move had created in our home. Between bites of peanut butter and jelly, I called a friend back in Omaha to complain. She listened, hung up, and called her mother to say she thought we were on the verge of divorce.

•

I imagined it bigger.

On the podcast that punctuates my commute, a guest introduced me to *the oak tree on Elm Street.* He presented it as a concept, a problem. A practical gunman would have taken a different shot, he reasoned. A practical gunman wouldn't have waited for the president's limo to round the corner—blocked by the tree—to fire. Either the shot came from somewhere else, or the man we have always blamed didn't actually pull the trigger. Because *he* was a practical gunman, trained and steady. The fact of the tree gets us closer to the truth.

On the podcast, the guest called it *massive*. My thoughts were often leaping to other big things—the distance between our apartment and the hospital, the operating table on which I was asked to place my body like a sacrifice—and the doorways that separated these moments from the rest of my life, sealed and sterile. Our second November in Oregon, I was hurting, angry. Every obstacle felt so real. In my car and on the other side of that experience, I found myself snared in the same question. *What happened?*

The tree, however, seems unmonumental. More teenager than sage. But even the voice on The Sixth Floor Museum's audio tour feels compelled to acknowledge it: *Remember, the trees were much smaller then. The shooter would have had a direct line of sight.* My wishful thinking becomes evident. Looking at the intersection from the sniper's nest, so far above what happened, I am believing my own eyes.

Through the branches that have surely grown and changed in the last 55 years, I can see a bullet (or three, or four) slicing their way through the gaps. They will reach the motorcade faster than the sound of a Carcano rifle firing. And in two minutes, the gunman who did the damage will have passed through the stairwell and the lunchroom, passed through the building's front doors, and out onto Elm.

•

In Oregon, in so many ways, I was getting my life right. I wrote my way into a new shape. On the page, I shared the parts of my life I wanted to share, and through daily practice, tried to uncover more. In every sense, I was determined to become a better steward of self. I saw the doctor about the things I'd been meaning to. I saw

217

a therapist for the first time. I had the mole on my face checked for cancer the dermatologist did not find and renewed my acne prescription. I saw a gynecologist about the odd bleeding, the pain during my period, enough to wake me up in the middle of the night when the logging trucks didn't. Every doctor I'd seen in Nebraska told me I was just unlucky. *Sorry, pumpkin,* they said.

From the clinic I was referred to a specialist, on the road to somewhere like *better* or *improving.* All summer, as the arguments about our relationship tangled and elongated, I took breaks from the writing and the swimming to drive to the hospital for appointment after appointment, monitoring the growth of something strange.

•

When Jack took the podium, he wasn't wearing a coat, not even in the January cold. Other men wore scarves and hats. Breath left his body as steam. On Inauguration Day, 1961, the youngest President of the United States wanted to appear healthy, fit, and strong—because he had never been those things.

Jackie sat behind him on the stage, understanding the truth was a different matter, sheltering her experience in fifty-cent-piece buttons and a high collar. As a senator, soldier, student, and child, her husband had suffered. More than once, illness kept him from the things he wanted to do: near death in childhood twice, scarlet fever, colitis, appendicitis, spinal injuries, spinal repairs, surgery after surgery, adrenal disease, chronic pain, alleged addiction. More than once, a priest had administered his last rites. And yet, that November he won.

Among the elms that line the National Mall, he asked the people to begin anew.

Here at the pinnacle of his achievements, a charming man stood, giving Americans courage in the face of almost certain thermonuclear annihilation, what he called mankind's final war. His body (that didn't shake), his teeth (that didn't chatter), his words (that called for peace), communicated effortless strength. The story he told was about surviving. His story, the nation believed.

History revealed more of the truth only after it was over; Jack was tragedy before myth, weak well before a bullet to the brain. And yet, Inauguration Day still felt like a beginning. A strong man took the podium, asking us to do something difficult: believe our entwined futures could be changed for the better. And for a moment, we wanted to do just that.

•

What happened? The pain, psychic and physical, was hard to untangle. The doctor said she didn't know what was growing on my ovary. We would have to take it out and see. To resist a true crisis, I did what I'd been practicing, embodied what I'd been becoming—I told myself a story. I repeated the sentences over and over to my parents, to myself, to a handful of friends. I couldn't stop the surgery from happening, but I could downplay its significance with language, make it seem like no big deal. *No big deal.* Those were the words I used to describe the *minor incisions* and *outpatient procedure.* The three-syllable chant kept the fear somewhere to the side of the room, behind a closed door.

My doctor and I laid a strategic plan. If we scheduled the surgery over Thanksgiving break, with only a few weeks of classes left, I could heal a bit and hide the rest. And so, I continued to weave the narrative. The fewer people that knew, I reasoned, the smaller the impact on my life would be. A pinprick on the map of my body instead of a larger, deeper wound.

Feelings I chose not to acknowledge: rage, fear, loneliness. I isolated myself in their invisible grip. If the surgery revealed cancer, I knew my doctor might encourage a hysterectomy. At twenty-five, I was far from prepared to confront the possibility of losing my fertility, while struggling to understand the barest facts of my life, the larger story about myself I wanted to find, and to tell. *What happened?* I downplayed my anxieties until I almost didn't think about the surgery anymore. Because thinking about it would mean facing the obstacles and all that could be wrong—truths, when spoken, that could change a marriage completely.

•

The *oak tree on Elm Street* took root in my mind because in it, I heard a story I knew—a November that echoed a November half a century ago. Because after Thanksgiving is the perfect time to decorate an apartment for Christmas. Drive out to the forest. Pick out a tree.

That was our plan two days after the fact, and though my body begged me not to stand, a plan is a plan is a plan. I put weight on both feet—the ache of bending at the middle—pulled on my most comfortable clothes, and zipped up my old coat. I made my way down the stairs for the first time in days.

We would venture out to the same farm, visit the same gingerbread house, and sip the too-sweet cocoa—our oldest tradition. He drove, while I steadied myself with deep breaths, wincing each time the car bounced over a rock or pothole. But when we arrived, the parking lot was already full, cars and trucks spilling out onto adjacent gravel roads. I imagined how far I'd have to walk. Not a single movement seemed worth the additional pain.

I can't do it, I said, shaking my head.

Then quiet, an understanding.

We drove back toward our apartment, barely speaking.

Inside the cage of myself, I reeled in familiar indecision. The task was cold, so troubling and so bright. Though my body insisted it was impossible, I still wanted a tree. If I had made this much of an effort to leave home, *How could I go back with nothing?*

The results of my surgery had been inconclusive. A borderline tumor, the doctor called it, neither totally malignant, nor totally benign. Another tumor might reappear in five, ten, even twenty years down the road. There was no way to predict when. And though this surgery had been fertility sparing, when that inevitability arose, true healing would demand more.

We were retracing our path, about to cross the intersection of two highways, one we'd crossed hundreds of times. Only now, in late November, someone had brought the trees close, arranged them on the pavement beneath strands of twinkling lights. *Why don't we stop here?* I said, and he changed course, pulling into the lot. He opened his door. Pain pinned me to my seat. He pointed at the trees, and I waved him on.

I trust you, I mouthed through the glass.

•

Trees have names like poetry. I can't hear *California*

and *great sequoia* in the same sentence without feeling something for the rhyme, the memory of drives I like most—windows down on the Pacific Coast Highway. Instead of Canada, we drove south the summer he lost his passport, all the way to L.A.

Our newest tradition was this: buy a Kit Kat, split it in two, and eat the chocolate before it melted in our hands. Every day, another gas station and another candy bar. Every day, another podcast about things unexplained—flying saucers, bigfoot, JFK—we marveled at the big, strange world. The road and the car and the two of us inside felt like the answer to any question.

I was behind the wheel. All morning I had been saying I wanted to camp in a redwood forest, but then the sun set fast. We panicked on the streets of a little Califonia town, trading our tent for a room at a budget motel. I joked about the novelties: a bottle opener attached to the sink, an indoor swimming pool, cable TV we didn't even want to watch. But in the morning, it didn't take long to regret my decision. Less than a mile down the road, we would have found the campgrounds I imagined. Outside the city limits, the forests began.

The next night, we tried our luck in Big Sur. A wooden sign spelled *vacancy* at the park entrance, but I let the first campground pass, not wanting to repeat the mistake, stop driving too soon and miss the thing I wanted. I passed a second campground in pursuit of perfection, drove and drove, drove for nearly a hundred miles. Much like it had the day before, much like it always will, the sun slipped easily behind the horizon.

The moon was a ghost's reflection on the surface of the ocean. With every zigzag of the dark mountain road, its pale, pock-marked face peeked around the side of a cliff, hid, showed itself, hid. We never found a place to rest.

I drove us through the night, until the cliffs and moon and trees deposited us somewhere in a dark desert. When the campground I eventually found existed on the edge of a dusty city with no running water, he gave me a look that said *come back from wherever you are*.

By lantern light, we stuck our tent poles into the dirt.

•

On my flight from Dallas to Portland, I watch Natalie Portman play *Jackie*. From this small window into her world, I see a woman fall into union, ruin, despair, and mourn the thing she'd known as her life. She had been in Dallas, too, holding roses. The place she sat and the things she held are facts she calls attention to over and over in her telling. I notice how closely I am listening. I am a woman who recognizes her own game—distracting myself, distracting everyone else, from my grief with an image.

The revelation happens at the end of the film, when I am almost home and we begin our descent into Oregon's forested Cascade Range. One week after the parade, Jackie sits for an interview at the family home in Hyannis Port. She smokes a cigarette and serves the journalist tea. She strings together the moments of her marriage, crafting the story the world will hear. To do it, she takes us backward through time.

She had just left a cemetery. She had just left a parade. She had just left the home she had shared with him for the last time. And now, she is editing the reporter's notes from her kitchen—determined to write a history more beautiful than the one she has lived.

•

What happened? I must have said, *I'm sorry.* We slept all night in a tent, and in the morning, shared breakfast in a garden. Under a canopy of unfamiliar trees, our conversation loosened. He laughed at something I said, and a local, a table over, asked us where we were from, how we had ended up here. Our story was long and winding. *And now we really need to shower,* I said, at the end of it.

He offered a suggestion, a place to go from here. It came with a story of its own. The man had been very sick once, and while he was recovering from cancer treatments, found the perfect place to rest. Every day, he wrapped a towel around his shoulders and drove to the Masterpiece Hotel. *It's beautiful,* he said, describing a jacuzzi surrounded by Grecian columns and faux frescoes, waterfall showerheads and an oversized tub. *Go, and tell them I sent you.*

We could feel it, a plan beginning to unfold. The instructions were vague, but they had something to do with cleansing, a matter both practical and spiritual. Together, we needed to wash it all away. After breakfast, we parked the car, snuck into that hotel, and felt like thieves. Our moods improved alongside our conspiracy. It was morning and it was summertime, and we just had to keep moving.

Of course, the winters we'd weathered had been another matter. November after November, I had murked them, muddled them, played the record, as if on a loop—and then, I recast it all. From someplace higher, far enough way. On a day that was warm and movement felt easy. I thought then to kiss him hard.

We were making our way out of the woods, but I don't yet think we'd reached the end. Anyway, I decided a long time ago to keep driving.

TO GROW IN SPITE OF POISON
KELSEY FRANCIS

Nanny called the black walnut tree El Capitan. "Let them dry on window sills," she said. "The sun will do half the work for you." And once the sun had done its work, with an old hammer in her right hand and a cast iron clothes iron squeezed between her aproned knees, Nanny smashed open the walnuts on the flat side of the iron and let the pulverized bits of shell fall to the floor. She repeated the violence over and over again until she was surrounded by a field of brittle carnage. The small nuts, hardly worth the effort with their oily bitter taste, would then sit on window sills to dry again. Once dry and chopped, she baked black walnut pound cake from scratch, scooping flour and sugar from dented metal tins in the cupboard.

•

In seventh grade, while your mother tried to recreate this cake with a Betty Crocker mix and some stale store-bought nuts, she told you the story of your great-grandmother, Nanny. A woman with hands so thick and skin so hard she was as impenetrable as her iron, her hammer, and her giant El Capitan walnut tree. Your mother's loaf came out of the oven flavorless and dry, but you ate it anyway, imagining the earthy sweet flavor of Nanny's cake. You choked down the bites with a large glass of milk.

•

While on a trip many years later, your mother discovered

225

a black walnut tree and collected a giant bag of unshelled nuts, packed them into her suitcase, and flew them home. In your linoleum-floored kitchen, she attempted to crack them open just as Nanny had done, pulling an old iron used as a bookend off a shelf and fishing a hammer out from underneath the sink. The shells, still fresh and damp, not ready for cracking, smashed into a mealy green paste.

•

In middle school science class, you learned the black walnut tree is a killer. An *allelopathic* tree. A tree that poisons other plants. Its roots contain a toxin, juglone, that can kill sensitive plants: tomatoes, azaleas, peppers, apples, cabbage, lilacs, and chrysanthemums. You knew girls whose tongues dripped *juglone* in middle school. The ones whose toxic roots reached far and wide. Who told you your ass was too big and your boobs were too small. They made fun of your Kmart clothes, so you snuck your older brother's rugby shirts out of his closet and pretended they were yours. They told you your bangs were thin and flat, so you bought more hairspray.

•

In science class you also learned there are some plants that tolerate and even thrive on juglone: birch, maple, ferns, carrots, and beans. Even certain tulips. You want to be one of those tolerant plants—less sensitive, thicker skin, hardier. To grow in spite of poison. You want to hold a hammer in your hand and squeeze an old iron between your knees. You want to hear the satisfying crack of shells and deeply inhale the earthy smell of black walnuts drying on a sunlit windowsill.

FELLED
SOPHIE HALL

> Then he lay down to sleep like a snow-covered
> road
> — Li-Young Lee, *Eating Together*

I tattooed a piece of Li-Young Lee's Eating Together on my forearm two days before the end of 2019. I could call this an impulse, or I could tell you how the syllables of that snow-covered road have returned of their own volition since their first roll over my tongue in the spring.

A small pine tree lies in the backyard of a green house in Mount Storm, West Virginia, framed perfectly by the kitchen window. You would never see it from the dinner table because the window requires a standing view if you want anything except the slightest glimmer of light (slight because even the sun is blocked by the cluttered back porch). Not that anyone is struggling to crane their neck for a view—we do not eat at this table, opting instead for its use as a dish rack while we take our meals alone.

This tree, the young pine, is clearly not full-grown. Between the kitchen window and the tree, a clothesline stretches with the translucence of a stray spider web. Most of the time, the clothesline maintains that translucence without definition, typically unused, no drying t-shirts to tell its purpose. But around my tenth birthday, my father reworks it: attaches a wire and rope to the line for easy use as a leash for the dog.

Cooper is only a puppy. He wakes the house with intermittent barks through the night, followed by choking sounds, canine coughs from a habit of chewing on stones in daylight. Dad is always the first shaken from his slumber on the couch. I can picture his sluggish journey to the back door, his smoker's cough with a similar undertone like gravel. He clips Cooper into his collar, the buckle overlapping matted fur. And then he lets go, Cooper's paws flying through the dewy grass along the length of his rope.

Gravel scatters while my father lights a cigarette. Often, he loses track of the reason for his midnight stroll, snuffing out the cigarette and returning inside so that we find the dog shivering outside with the rising sun. Once, we find only the collar lying still in backyard snow, wet blades peeking through and stuck like pilling. I spend the following weeks mistaking bunnies and old rags for his gray coat. My father's reassurance lasts years. "Cooper's just livin it up with the neighbor! Listen, that old lady back there took him in." I have my doubts. All I know of the neighbor is the chain-link fence between our yards with single holes the size that three should be; the upper edges of the fence dip, as if someone has made a habit of sitting in the wire, their company hard to forget.

One day, the young pine will stand tall all year, but for now, it stands upright only for most of the year. In my head, it's always winter, and the dense snowfalls of this season are hard on its backbone. The tree bends to the ground in an arch: trunk thin as branch, branches stubby and awkward, reaching with spirit more than limb. In negative temperatures, the pine begins and ends in feet of snow, root extending to body extending back to earth where the ice tries to make a beginning happen again.

> What is left of the day flames
> in the maples at the corner of my eye.
> — Li-Young Lee, *Eating Alone*

•

Some kind of tattoo was my only New Year's resolution. Possibilities were drafted for months: watercolor stems, the bend of that young pine in graphite, digital camera reference photos unearthed from untouched folders, all to culminate, instead, in last-minute Times New Roman.

•

On the other side of the green house is a red maple. This tree signifies all sense of direction in relation to the outside world. We live five houses down from the Liberty gas station: green house, brown garage door, red maple in the front yard. My parents repeat these words enough to have them drilled in my head in preparation for visitors, even though I have never stopped to check the accuracy of the number of houses between our driveway and the gas station. I don't have to look that close to find my way home.

This red maple carries two swings of different proportions, fashioned by my father. On some golden day, he tightens the coarse strands with knuckles that threaten to bleed, a *harrrrumph* the only sound I can hear as I stare at the back of his head. With a turn and dusted hands, the planks float, sturdy. "Give 'em a try."

A shorter olive-painted board rests to his left, perfectly fitted for my younger sister, Clara. On the right side of the tree, mine sits slightly crooked; the right branch is level for only an instant and then stretches upward. I embark, first tryout, to find that kicking my legs, moving air, carries the sense of simultaneously moving sideways and uphill. My legs seem to be pointed in the direction of something that is not there, airflow magnetized instead to what is, eyes searching and wet,

Clara's sneakers lighting up in the wind where we come so close to meeting in the middle. Dad's guffaw is the *whiz* of the swing coming a little too close to the trunk for comfort.

Though both my sister and I will grow too old for the swing set, we will still squeeze our legs between the ropes for years to come.

> It is my father's
> nap-hour. Outside, one dove tunnels the
> corridor of maples.
> — Li-Young Lee, *My Sleeping Loved Ones*

Something about the "r" in road and movement of wrist deforming my still skin has people asking, "Have you seen many snow-covered toads?" I considered boldly defining the letter with a pen until I learned how the words for path and toad are the same in Dutch. My own homonym.

•

Fifteen feet away from the red maple lies another pine tree. This one, the older pine, is nearly hidden from view of the road by a wooden fence. This tree is alien in comparison to the other trunks. In relation to the rest of the yard, the old pine is too far away from anything else to ever spend time in its presence: it lies just outside the pond but is still distant enough that its branches get little spotlight as a part of this home.

The red maple is close to the pond, too, enough that when peering into its water you are thinking, always, of the maple. Water pools, crimson, a thickness to it from fallen leaves—if you dip your fingers in it, they might web. Miniature frogs hop from overflowing cattails. In my family's return from evening grocery shopping, my siblings and I tagging along to spend food stamps after dark, my father sends stones flying towards the slick skin of frogs and other pond residents with the Honda's not-so-gentle sidle up to the front porch.

We weight our arms with groceries: I send six handles down to my elbows like the world's clunkiest bangles, except the only noise is the whisper of plastic, muffled clash of soup cans. I hear these sounds intermittently, notes in the larger hum of West Virginia insects and my father's voice with the laugh underneath: "I see bigfoot over there! He's right there by the woods!" I don't exactly quicken my pace, but I won't look in that direction. The last haul is accompanied by slow creaking as my father pulls the car into the gravel extension of the already massive expanse of asphalt driveway. In the aftermath of our interruption, quiet submerges the maple, a ripple left only for the long *rrrrrribbbiit* of a toad's mating call.

I pull the shades down
so the sun isn't in their eyes,
or arrange flowers over their heads.
— Li-Young Lee, *My Sleeping Loved Ones*

Dad always hated tattoos. Some appeared on my mother's arms shortly before they divorced. He always said the ink would go to her brain, the same idea he had that the metal jewelry she made would leave copper rings in her eyes. Sometimes his voice was enough to conjure up a fleck.

•

In the sun, that gravel extension is an ordinary piece of yard. In any kind of precipitation, it becomes a land of its own: tire tracks five feet deep, mud enough to last days past a storm. Even days of sun have the mark of past rains, streams running faces from asphalt to grass, foggy pools full enough to act as birdbaths.

In the loss of definition between yard and parked car, an assortment of stones belongs to the red maple's base, some the rough gravel of pavement, and others carefully placed, upright, with even spacing. Alongside roots protruding from dust are tiny headstones. They range at any time between five and fifteen, depending on the weather's toll on the cemetery and a person's ability to tell grave from naturally resting rock. Beneath each stone, in the barest sweep of dirt (you can count the granules), lie the sun-dried bodies of salamanders.

They always die this way.

We collect them from the woods beyond the backyard in a process we call "hunting," me and my sister. Dad leads us past Big Rock at the entrance to the trees. His walking stick scrapes the familiar rocky path, echoing like the sound of the lawnmower blades he carves the trails with on his own. He passes this carved stick over logs with the kind of laziness that looks like intention to a child. Pushed aside, the mossed insides of the logs fray, centipedes breaking from earthy threads.

Bricks of anthills become stray loam. My father's boots toss inner fungi to the side and spits with gravel tones: "There's a big guy down there! It's Godzilla!" Clara and I cross our hands over one another, turning sediment in gardening gloves (socks, when we can't find a match), until a small wet body is in her grasp or mine (sometimes both, if the salamander tries to trick us predators by detaching its tail and each of us ends up with a piece). We then secure our catch in a hole-punched plastic container that still smells of Dad's coffee grounds where soft amphibian skin will ricochet on the walk back.

We keep these animals in dollar-store terrariums, fascinated for the first twenty minutes after the catch until we abandon them to the porch. Dad sometimes watches the ones we release in the pond but doesn't pay much attention to those we decide to keep. We take the sun-magnifying glass to them in a divorced way. There is always remorse, as comes with unintentional recklessness, but the headstones—pillowed with dandelions and moss—always crowd one another.

> The ground is cold,
> brown and old.
> — Li-Young Lee, *Eating Alone*

I waved away his words on my mother, his concrete belief in bigfoot, the conspiracy videos that auto-played beside his pillow all night. But I always had the rest in my head. His directions to our home: five houses down the road from the Liberty station, green house, brown garage door.

•

The red maple only holds the second such pet cemetery. The original rests a short distance away from that determined young pine. It lies behind the old boat—something untouched except by saplings bursting through emerald upholstery, a gold-dipped spider in her web, moss.

This machinery lives for years without a breath. Dad tells us the story: around the time he and my mother move to the house, he buys a boat from a friend. The friend disappears before my father receives the keys. The boat lies in wait. I do not know if it has ever been where it was made to go. We are not supposed to climb inside, ever, but even in my youngest years I traverse tires and spilling foam, choosing to crouch in my exploration. The seats are overtaken by ferns long before I get there.

Behind the boat, salamander graves stretch over the base of another unnamed evergreen where lower branches tangle with the neighbor's chain-link. Jagger bushes shoot their fingers through the fence and grasp ours as we reach for berries, the red on our skin sometimes ours, sometimes not. Beside the graves are larger memorials: a cross made of baseball bats for the cat, Fastball, name courtesy of Dad's backyard pastime. Each burial is carried out by my father's peeling knuckles. I hear the soft dirt, collision of cough with ground turned, a sound he makes alone but I still understand when looking at the cross for the dog that ran out in the road during one of his fights with my mother. Smaller, unidentifying stones mark the deaths of stillborn kittens and mice, red-bellied snakes taken in from the weeds and briefly homed in terrariums before passing on at the top of our television stand.

When my sister and I play house, I choose this area as my home.

> winding through pines older than him,
> without any travelers, and lonely for no one.
> — Li-Young Lee, *Eating Together*

I saw my father often from the back of his head, tires of our Honda padding over snow-covered road in the quiet ride up the mountain, windshield blanketed white. His cough fizzled in an afterthought of cigarette smoke and put me to sleep in the same way it kept me up at night.

•

I wonder if it would have been more appropriate to situate the cemetery beneath the limbs of that other, older pine, free from outdoor recreation, close only to the roar of the road and far from neighbors—dirt underneath with no one to shift it, no knees scraped on roots. I wonder if some collective subconscious force had insisted we all stay away from its alien trunk. The hush. My father told me once, that beneath the bark, years before I set foot in its circle of solitude, a rope had been tied by a previous owner of our home and then cut, but just before the knot—so that the tree would forever live inside a collar, every trip around the sun adding a ring, every ring bulging until forced to wrap around that coarse hold, swallowing in time the fraying strands that might have freed it if only sawed from the outside.

MEMORY VAULT
LYNETTE VIALET

1

I collect dead trees. Not exactly. I collect photos of wind- and snow-weathered branches, gnarled tree trunks, roots wrenched from the forest floor, hillsides of beetle kill pines. I have a varied collection of photographs— friends, travels, art—begun when my father gave me a Polaroid camera in high school. I begged for it. Back then, the idea of seeing pictures instantly was the future. A click, ejected photo paper, the chemical smell of developer, waiting patiently for ninety-seconds before peeling off the covering, then watching the black and white image sharpen into focus. I've saved those old photos, curled edges, piled up in boxes, fading backward in sepia tones. The instant digital world usurped that magic, my expanding collections now stored as .png. jpeg—viewed anywhere on my phone. I can swipe through recent images of a rotted, hollowed out tree stump furred with moss, or wet branches clustered in a hodgepodge that only determined beavers could build.

2

My deadwood collection, the most recent, began on a trip to Fort Warden on the Olympic Peninsula, overlooking Puget Sound. I wandered the hillside of bunkers and gun batteries constructed by the Army Corps of Engineers from 1898 to 1907 and used for protection from invasion during WWI. In the quiet, the hundred-year-old battlements are reminders of man's ability to leave marks in this grand rainforest of Douglas fir, hemlocks, and big leaf rhododendrons. Of my many photos, I capture a tree, tilted awkwardly, exposed to too much sea spray, a disrupted trunk of dried bark and browning needles leaning toward oblivion. I focus in. Are those cormorants in the distance, pointed beaks peaking above the water line? No, just jagged edges of more dead wood, and there, broken branches bleached by sun resemble old, discarded bones. And there, at the edge of the parade grounds, a cemetery for WWI veterans, clean lines of white tombstones aligned in formation, emerald grass mown to sober perfection, a miniature version of Calverton, *aide-memoire.*

3

Calverton is the largest veteran's cemetery in land area in the United States: 275,000 veterans laid to rest, and over 3000 more graves added each day. The recorded sound of taps blares hour after hour as another soldier receives a final honor. Located in eastern Long Island, the smooth paved roads wind between one thousand acres of plush green lawn. White marble headstones stand at attention in geometric precision. I've saved a recording of the man playing the bugle at my father's burial there, and though it is not a photograph, it remains so in my mind whenever I listen to it. My collection only added one image that day—one dried branch, perhaps blown by the wind—that marred the immaculate intimacy.

4

At Fort Warden, at the top of the bluffs, I stumbled upon Memory's Vault, a sculptural installation created by artist Richard Turner. As I meandered between the ten-foot concrete, rectangular pillars, deliberately placed yet randomly spaced, I discovered that a side of each monolith bears a bronze plaque engraved with a fragment of a poem by Sam Hamill: The shadows of moments mean everything and nothing. Richard Turner called Memory Vault, "a place of contemplation-of nature, of man and his intentions."

5

So began my collection. I kept taking photographs. An alpine hillside, once a forest before a massive wildfire transformed it into giant black matchsticks, a holocaust of burnt-out trees. A towering pine before beetle infestation. A decrepit oak, scrambled upon and climbed by children, shading an old cabin, supporting a makeshift swing. A wayward branch belonging to a tree transplanted from the far reaches of Asia, perhaps Okinawa, where my father worked after the war, helping to rebuild the island. He said only bare trees, bits of bone and skulls, bleached and polished by the weather, remained, a picture too far in my past, too far from my own existence to imagine.

6

I keep saving photos—a faded photograph of my father, age twenty, in his crisp new army uniform, standing on the tarmac about to board a plane out of the US Virgin Islands, leaving home for the first time, about to become a veteran of WWII. It is black and white, fitting for a man who will join a segregated army, blacks separated from whites, except for the white officer in charge of their unit.

Another saved photo, in my horde of dead trees, a favorite—in the upturned weathered roots, I see a face, one hollowed out eye, another smaller, orbital disc gazing directly at me. Below a rotted nose, a lipless dark space for a mouth appears, as if a leper has come into my vision. Its unlit hollows, like wood caves a finger could fit through. Bits of pine needles, broken cones, silver splinters, a sliver of dried branch become a tortured expression sucked into the bowl of the tree.

7

Below its manicured grass, Calverton is a city of underground bones. The roots of blossoming trees and shrubs are the roots of my family, so many families' bones, decayed but safe from weather and wind. There are no photographs under there.

8

Photography can shade, shadow, crop, magnify, or refocus any image, distort, or sharpen it so that the eye sees something else. Perhaps the jagged edges of rotting roots, the curved, worn stumps, a decaying tree's rings resemble a topographic map, curving lines that trace history backwards in time. These relics share their secrets, gifting memories. I search each time for the stories in them, capture images as I walk a trail, climb along a cliff, or wander barren beaches. Even a tree trunk, with its gnarled, thick burl that roots down deep into the repository of the forest floor contains fragments of memory, incorporating air from the breath of a soldier who says, here I am, capture me in time, record my decay, until I am gone.

THE FRUIT WILL COME
JENNIFER MAXON

Before the quiet cancer slinked its way down my spine, I was focused on developing my residential Landscape Architecture business. From my first plant identification course, I became spellbound by florae and the natural world. In one year, a single tree can flash fire-red leaves, reveal its silhouette of flaking bark, and produce brazen inflorescence announcing its revival. After years of sifting through tiresome jobs, I found my treasured career designing with this living art form. With control and restraint, I arrange plants to complement and contrast enduring materials, giving light and movement to a lifeless space. Until the diagnosis, I spent 12 years dedicated to achieving my professional goal, designing stunning sensible gardens for families in Northern California, where most of life is lived outdoors.

To become a Landscape Architect, I drove from Mill Valley to downtown San Francisco three nights a week for four and half years of school. I put in my time working stressful, late-night, greasy-pizza-fueled deadlines at design studios for less pay than I had made as a college kid sweeping tennis courts. After tucking in my two little girls, for my demanding licensing exams, I stayed up late to memorize wetland restoration guidelines, ADA requirements, lumber sizing charts, stormwater management practices, and large-scale development grading plans. At 40 with metastatic breast cancer, my dream job was wiped away with one bold YES checked on a long-term disability form for the question, "Will you die from your medical condition?"

I panicked when I realized that I may not have time to leave my mark. I spoke with palliative care doctors, priests, Zen meditation masters, and holistic cancer specialists. Finally, I found my footing from a good friend who had open-heart surgery at 38 with three little children, one a newborn. I asked him how to contend with the possibility of death with young children.

"Write to your girls," he said. "And plant your dream garden. That is something more visual for them to remember you by. It will continue to grow even if you are not here."

For my clients, I select plants based on light exposure, soil conditions, microclimates, function, form, and seasonal interest. Then, I layer in the subtle cues of budget and desired maintenance. My younger clients, often on a tighter budget, are willing to install smaller sizes as they have years to nurture them to maturity. My older clients talk about general style and then wave me off. "Do whatever you need to do to make this vision happen," they tell me. "I'll write the check." When I asked a client in her mid-80s what size tree she preferred, she guffawed: "Crane in a big one, Jennie. Let's see her beauty now!"

How do I design my own garden? Am I young or old? Living or dying? If I have hope, do I start from seeds and cuttings? If my medications stop working, do I bring out the crane?

One half of me screams, *I do not have time to wait!* I drive two hours to a South Bay fruit tree farm and select nearly twenty 45-gallon fruit trees. I need to see my girls' hands reach to pick a mandarin, claw away at its peel, and let the juice drip down their sun-kissed cheeks.

The other half of me buys hundreds of small pots. I may not be here to tend to them, but I can imagine my garden in its prime, each plant sited to reach its potential. That is, after all, what I am trained to do.

I think of my front garden, the head of a firebreak road and hiking trails, as a gift to passersby. I install Australian, New Zealand, and California natives: spikey succulents, ornamental grasses, and bright flowering perennials that attract hummingbirds and bees. I position fast-growing flowering trees and shrubs to screen our cabin. Drought-tolerant, my selections will not deplete our water supply. More importantly, easy to prune and maintain, they will not use up my precious energy.

Behind the fence and gate, I sculpt a terraced fruit and vegetable garden. I shape dry-stacked stone walls for the heat-lovers: tomatoes, cucumbers, melons, and peppers. Along the paths, I add sturdy wire trellises to train raspberries and thornless blackberries. On a hillside, I transplant rows of everbearing strawberries that do not need my attention and will produce yields throughout the year.

My husband, handy with wood, builds a redwood treehouse on our girls' favorite tree they have named "Arthur." He adds a detailed railing and a shingled roof to match the craftsman style of the main cabin. Next to the primary gravel pathways, he constructs large vegetable boxes that make it easier to rotate the quick growers: lettuce, spinach, and kale.

I assemble a greenhouse on a deck that hides an enormous, unattractive tree stump. I run an electrical cord to grow lights and heat mats to germinate vegetable seeds. I attach shelves for the transplants to mature ample time before hardening them off in the shade. To balance the height of the greenhouse, I set a lofty pomegranate tree, prolific with fruit so hefty the branches droop like limbs of a Christmas tree with ornaments placed too close to the periphery. I position a donut peach, a nectaplum, and some plum trees, so I can take in the flowers and bright colors from the window above.

For the girls, I lay out paths that lead to an assortment of swings that hang from the sturdy branches of old live oaks. Beneath the swings, I create a gentle meadow of native grasses to abate the occasional fall. A resting place from the summer heat, I form a gravel patio with seating and a hammock. A mix of ferns, chartreuse perennials, and variegated foliage brighten the shady understory.

As a destination, a focal point, and a soft landing for my girls to play tee ball and practice cartwheels, I level a grass lawn. Along its lower edge, I set most of the evergreen citrus trees. I hope to prune them into a dense hedge to stop any balls or visiting toddlers from rolling downhill. I envision our neighborhood children picking the Lisbon lemons to sell at a lemonade stand as the grown-ups juice Bearss limes for the observation deck Margaritas.

When I see the garden take shape, I catch my breath. In my panic, I was only thinking about the finale. As I dig between scans, I observe my girls inventing dinosaur nests with Manzanita branches, hunting for worms and roly-polies, and reading books in the hammock, bare toes touching bare toes. Between biopsies and surgeries, I teach my girls how to start seedlings and transplant to larger containers. After long hospital visits, I see them pointing at Red-tailed hawks while dancing in squishy soil as they help prep the boxes. Waiting for news on treatments, I hear the thumping wings of hummingbirds when I spray the hose, holding steady to sip water on a dry day. Soaking in the sun on my skin, I watch as early spring bees swarm the bright pink flowers of the nectaplum, purple buds rising like frogs' tongues ready to snap at flies. Even if I do not witness, I know the fruit will come.

LAYING THE WILLOW'S GHOST
LAURIE KLEIN

I blame the lightning. But at the time I also wondered, had I somehow offended the God of my parents? The year I turned twelve, a single earthbound jolt felled the backyard willow tree. My willow.

She was not the weeping kind. Yet how wetly her leaves now mingled with grass. Her body lay parallel to the banks of the lake, the root ball a thicket, upended.

No more shinny-and-clamber, from ground to crown. No more fitting my spine between outstretched arms, to savor the exploits of Nancy Drew. Where would I conjure daydreams now, soothed by a rustling lullaby? O tender solitude. O green sleeves of spangled light. A kid's eyes could brim with no warning there, because solace beckoned. I would slip my thumb into a pocket, stroke the deckled, metallic edge of my flattened penny for luck. And a reminder: *In God We Trust.*

Who made the lightning? Who unravels the wind like lace from a cloud?

Kneeling beside my tree in the westerly light, I stroked splintered bark. What drove me to tear off that first shred? The exposed heartwood felt root-cellar-cool, virginal, palest green to milky-white.

I ripped again. Soon, dark scrolls littered the lawn. The trunk seeped.

After dinner I peeled an entire limb, then stood back. I felt fierce, methodical as a coroner. How striking, at twilight, her stark beauty. I'd strip the whole tree, ask my friends to help. What kid doesn't relish making an epic mess?

Strangely, as the days passed, my parents neither scolded nor marveled nor moved to stop our endeavor.

My father mowed around us.

At night, Sister Willow looked almost spectral, ghostly as bones.

·

Is this how doubt sets in? The turncoat winds of late August arrived to quarrel among the boughs. No longer lissome, now they clattered. Leaves turned in on themselves, the undersides ashen. Force open a seam and a smell dankly bitter as used tea bags tainted the air. I kept expecting groans.

People once chewed willow bark to relieve pain.

·

Day by day, I kept after the bark. Was I angry? The willow was more than a personal hideout. It had sheltered woodpeckers, tree frogs and squirrels, and once, a porcupine. An inscrutable muskrat had burrowed among the roots. Where were they now?

When my father came out to watch me work, I asked did he know the exact tree name.

"Too many possibilities," he said. "Someone before our time probably planted it here for erosion control."

Now, our shoreline was vulnerable.

The next day, I stood tongue-tied alongside the lifeguard who lived next door. He'd sauntered over to see my project. He trailed his fingertips along the raw wood.

"Think we can count the rings?" I asked, hoping he'd stay.

He didn't reply. Red-faced, I turned away, and a branch hooked my sleeveless top at the armhole. I pulled free but the motion split the fabric across my front and those torn edges gaped open until he could see past my tan line and *right inside*—at my nothingness—and I whirled around, thinking, *What if he tells his friends* and then . . . *Faint, just fall down* and *do not move,* and *after a while he'll go away.*

But who can be nimble when shame suffuses the body? I fled to my bedroom.

•

After that, I skinned my willow alone, slowly earning the silent permissions of grain. I relished revealing the knots. It was tricky work, like worrying the knobbly edge of a scab.

But *why* uncover the tender places? Compulsions are so confusing. I'd work on a smaller scale I decided, and turned to the twigs. Where the younger bark clung, tight and smooth, my Girl Scout jackknife chipped off confetti.

And the willow accepted it all.

•

Now, decades later, I ponder harm. I loved that tree. Did I ravage a fallen companion? Or was I given a revelation of inmost beauty, a tree's most intimate gifts? I tend to assign the worst motives to my actions, often creating misplaced guilt. Had helpless rage provoked flaying the willow? Hindsight suggests it was never about shame. Or blame. Lightning is lightning: stark, mercurial, and impersonal.

So, I ask myself: What lasts? Do those we love who leave us somehow free us for a later wholeness we dare not imagine?

Who decides? The Japanese say a ghost appears where a willow grows. I feel haunted, perhaps by a God-given ghost. Will I trust those sent my way—especially those who can help me shed *my* protective layers?

One more thing needs telling. After my parents divorced, our house changed hands several times. Married by then, with a child of my own, I dropped by. Could I visit the backyard?

"Take all the time you need," the owners said.

Close by, a woodpecker's rattlepate energy distracted me as I followed a stony path, new to my feet. It wound downhill toward the shore. I stumbled, then straightened, slowly. And stood, amazed. A lofty willow tree shaded the lawn. A squirrel chirked. The canopy rustled. I laid a hand on her warm bark. Gazed upward. Turns out that, even belatedly, a lingering root will respond.

BRANCHES
EMILY DONALDSON

The year before I miscarried on a small island in Maine,
I was living on another small island a half-world away,
with a Marquesan family I'd known for most of my adult
life. The Timaus had adopted me as their "American
sister" in the easy way Marquesan families often
absorb children in need. They welcomed me "home,"
as they had for decades, to their three-bedroom pre-fab
perched high over the bay. My project that year was to
understand the ancient ruins littering the forest floor of
those lush, mountainous French Polynesian islands, and
I figured I'd be learning a lot about coconuts, bananas
and breadfruit.

But the Marquesans didn't just talk about
cultivating the forest. They spoke of mysterious
illnesses, hauntings and misfortune. Of vengeful spirits
that caused miscarriage and death. As a native New
Englander raised Unitarian, these stories splintered
my vague, idealistic notions of "Mother Earth." In the
months after my miscarriage, back home in Vermont,
they hovered at the messy edges of my pain. Gazing out
past winking late summer oak and maple leaves to the
distant blue-black of Lake Champlain, doubt crept in
like a soft and unexpected fog.

The doctors had reassured me that some spotting
and dark, clumpy clots were normal. But when I lost the
baby, they couldn't explain why. So I kept returning to
this question, and to the Marquesas, again and again.

Some days at the Timaus began with a dog's
shrill bark in the grey hours before dawn, when a
friend would pick up my adoptive father to go fishing.
Others rolled lazily into focus as roosters crowed and

animé blared on the family television, sunlight flashing through the curtains. I tromped through clinging, prickly weeds, across massive stone platforms furry with moss and ferns. I repeatedly tried, and failed, to remember Marquesan words whose vowels crowded around the same ten consonants, plus a glottal stop. I bobbed on the ocean, out fishing past midnight and shivering from cold beneath a sparkling expanse of stars. I perched on rocks, stone walls and rickety chairs listening to men and women talk about planting trees, chopping coconuts, and harvesting fruits and seeds. I sat quietly through Catholic mass bathed in the heady scents of coconut oil and Tahitian gardenia, surrounded by restless children and ladies in lace-fringed floral dresses. I tried in vain to block out the whine of mosquitoes, sweat dripping into my eyes, as I used an old machete blade to pry stiff chunks of coconut meat from its shell. I tiptoed around countless stone ruins, their half-buried silhouettes whispering of thriving settlements inhabited by chiefs, princesses, priests, warriors and craftsmen.

The more time I spent there, the more I came to understand that in the Marquesas, the land is more than a backdrop. It breathes, and it connects. Marquesans believe in spirits and *mana,* the spiritual power of their ancestors. They tie little Catholic crosses in *noni,* a squat tree with healing fruit and leaves that protect against angry spirits. Their stories of the forest describe places feared and avoided, where dangerous spirits play sinister tricks. They tell of women who miscarried or bled to death after walking on the wrong ruin, and others who fell ill after peeing next to a banyan tree where bones were buried.

"But you should be fine," they assured me. "You're an American!"

For the most part, I believed them. But in a

way I had to, since my research brought me so close to so many ruins. Living descendants always gave me permission to visit and, in some cases, take photos, and I was almost never alone. Yet still there were times when the forest enveloped me like a fragrant green cloak, shutting out everything but the chatter of birds and the gentle murmur of the trees.

•

Moiti and I walk along a narrow path littered with fallen mango leaves. Our feet crunch with each step, nearly drowning out the distant trill of a Marquesan warbler. The air is sweet with the tang of earth and rotting mangos. Beneath the leaves, barely visible but for its lower edge, a straight line of stones leads us on, down an ancient road.

When we reach the ancient settlement, I wander up a gradual slope, through a dense array of old stone structures and foundations. The forest hums with the rush of a nearby stream. Chestnut, mango, and breadfruit leaves rasp in the breeze, flashing silver in the sun. My curiosity pulls me on through the spindly spread of mango saplings, across terraces and over walls crumbling with age.

Moiti takes a different route through the site, and our paths diverge. I duck through some branches and step carefully over a rotting log, wary of giant centipedes. Then I stop, suddenly realizing I am standing at the edge of a stone enclosure. Most of its walls are crumbling. Those that remain stand a few feet high in spots. And there in the center, surrounded by terraces of stone, looms a massive banyan tree. A tree whose branches reach deep into Marquesan life and spirituality. The aerial roots of banyans are medicine; their bark, cloth;

their layered trunks hallowed receptacles for the bones of Marquesan ancestors. Still considered sacred by many Marquesans, old banyans are alive with *mana*. Inhabited by spirits.

Standing at the break in the wall, I look around for Moiti. She's nowhere in sight. In most cases I divert my steps around such places. But today I pause to listen and feel. I've been told that if I am unwelcome, my skin will prickle with goosebumps. I might feel a weight pressing on my shoulders, or my head might suddenly seem to balloon. I might hear strange animal sounds or laughter.

I wait, and none of the usual signs appear. So I take a deep breath and step inside the enclosure.

Beneath my feet are the smooth, flattened stones of an ancient pavement. I approach the banyan slowly, still half expecting to hear or feel something. But the forest is peaceful, the warblers trilling overhead. About fifteen feet from the trunk, I stop and look up. And as my eyes reach into that vast, vibrant canopy, everything else fades.

I remember feeling something similar staring up into the soaring, layered domes of Hagia Sophia. Only this is even better. A lightness of being. A joy so sudden and complete, it makes me laugh. I am standing in a cathedral, beneath a blanket of leafy buttresses and graceful black columns of roots. The roof sparkles and glows a brilliant green, backlit by the sun. High overhead, tiny in the distance, the banyan's leaves tap faintly, like pattering raindrops.

For an instant I feel myself rise up out of my body, straight into the arms of that ancient tree.

•

I lost the baby a year later; an unusual, surprising miscarriage that pounced upon us at sixteen weeks. And still today, I worry about all the things I can never know. I think about the spirits and about all the times Marquesans have volunteered to show me human remains or spirit places. About the few days I ventured into the forest solo and wandered in ways I hoped, but couldn't know, were respectful. About the women whose miscarriages were warnings.

In these moments I try to focus on the science, the wisdom of my body, and the statistical facts. No one likes to talk about it, but as many as one in five pregnancies end in miscarriage. So the sharing of my story brought out countless others from family and friends, like so many birds waiting to be released into the sky. Yet the question of "why" lingers on, faded and worn. I wonder whether it was a kind of fate, or just bad luck. Or were the spirits angry with me, after all?

Then I remember the feeling I had, standing under that banyan tree. The power and absolute peace of that moment. And the urgent need to know seeps away, through the canopy's sun-lit filaments, into acceptance.

LAST ONE STANDING
FELICITY FENTON

When I moved in, I was a stranger. The rhododendrons and cedars weren't used to my knotted hoses and rusted shears. Instead of overalls, I wore a sunburn and stained underwear. In droopy garden gloves, I battled grass, slugs, brambles, and ivy. I was mostly angry, but instead of yelling, I pitched rotting apples from an aging Granny Smith across the yard, over the fence, and found satisfaction when they thud-splatted the side of my neighbor's abandoned shed. I had just signed up to own the land I live on, land to nurture and maintain, land with names I needed to learn. But all of this seemed impossible with two hands and one human brain.

On the south side of the lot, there was a bedraggled shack with a corrugated roof, dirt floor, and rat shit. *Is anyone in here*, I whispered, hoping someone would reveal themselves, someone from older days, a ghost farmer with deeper land wisdom and sharper tools than mine.

Elderly at 90, the Granny Smith had lived on the land much longer than I had, one of the last remaining trees of its kind in a neighborhood that used to be all orchard. Teetering far to the left, it stood 25 feet high with a fungus-covered trunk. Its limbs cracked and snapped off in mild gusts. On the ground below, its twigs and branches scattered in piles.

There are people who are paid to remove dangerous trees that pose a risk of falling onto houses, cats, and children. Some call them arborists. Others call them overzealous.

Skeptical of the arborist who insisted I remove the tree, I asked around for other advice. What does a human do with a sickly tree? One friend suggested I simmer its remaining apples with ginger, turmeric, and honey. Another friend told me it would be best to lop it down and use its wood for piggy smoking. Others said that once the trunk is no longer living, once it's hacked into nubs then dried for several months, it will create a sweet-smelling fire, a blended smolder of fossilized syrup and excavated earth. Its wood could generate abundant heat with good coaling qualities. And also, cooking utensils are best when made from apple wood because it's lower in toxins than other wood, and maybe the sweetness of its trunk would somehow bleed into soups or slaws or shakshukas.

They all told me the Granny Smith tree might be better off dead, but I didn't believe them. Because every year, it's thicker, loftier, with new leaves and fat apples. And despite their dry, mealy crunch, I eat them. But more importantly, the insects eat them, the soil eats them, making space for a new tree, one that grows there now, looking rather confident, ready to climb.

TRANSLATING TREES
COURTNEY AMBER KILIAN

Tonight, as I put my one-something-year-old to sleep by nursing I start to "write." Words spill into my thoughts that I can't wait to capture, inking them indelibly across thick journal paper. Once written, perhaps I'll return to them, or more importantly, they'll live outside of me, a therapy unto itself, for me, the highest act of self-care. I haven't had this feeling in a long time—that writerly misty magic, gotta-capture-this-now type of energy rising in my chest and goose pimpling my arms.

It all stemmed from a line I'd read in a book that afternoon; not the author's words but my own: a notation in the marginalia I'd made years earlier as an undergrad—that pre-mother person almost someone entirely different than the one who lays here nursing her son—and it twisted and twirled in my mind all afternoon.

Now, in complete darkness, it's materialized into something more. Alive, and throbbing out of the ether, a constellation of creative impulse ebbing like a nebula, a bioluminescent jelly fish, sometimes vanishing, sometimes too quick, sometimes a dull, distant memory of creative ability, sometimes just within reach, like tonight. So, I tug on the thread of this ethereal muse, and it unravels before me like starlight or fairy dust to become the first line of a story I've been aching to tell but didn't know yet: *I've been interviewing our trees.*

And then the next line(s) come as I tug a little further, allow myself to be the receptive vessel of creative thought whirling around me in the dark quiet of our bedroom, my son's blonde hair indiscernible in the darkness, its fine softness a memory disappearing beneath my fingers even as I play with it, baby fading into toddler within my grasp.

I watch the story play out before me behind closed eyes: I'll sit for a month at a time next to each kind of tree in our yard to see what they tell me. Then I'll sit by the same species, but different specimens to see if they are different from each other—their tenor, their creaks and tones, the way they lean, what is similar for their species, what is unique to each one. I feel my breastbone alight with a pressing, fluttering question: *Do trees have different personalities?*

I'll start with the oak that holds my children's swings. Sit on the rock wall my husband and father built with stones unearthed under the sweltering, dry sun on our property to give us a single shaded patio. I'll listen with my eyes closed. Play a game of translation, pretend if I observe long enough, I'll learn a new language, will be able to interpret something beyond myself. I'll enter another world, a portal in the universe, much like I was thrust into while giving birth to each of my two children.

Can you tell which tree is speaking in the wind? The palms are easy, their *tick tick tick* is recognizable. Instead of bird calls, I recognize the voices of our trees. The swish of the pepper tree, the raspy crunch of the oak, how the leaves let out a soft sigh when the wind travels through our sumac, like they are sharing some ancestral secret just beyond my grasp.

•

We're planning on moving, listing this home, our first. The home where both of my children were born. Births in early morning dark hours, the midwives and my newborns here to greet sunrise with us each time. The trees I walked under and sat next to pregnant, carrying lives I had yet to meet or know. Most of all, it's these trees I feel rooted to, anxious about leaving; they hold parts of me and me parts of them.

There's a grouping of oak trees on our street that I've walked beneath on as many mornings as I could in the six years we've lived here. I've gotten to know them, and they've gotten to know me. Subtract migraine days, the occasional rain, mornings I had to stay in bed because I was up all night breastfeeding a particularly fussy newborn or teether, and the mornings my daughter caught me just before I could step out into inky before-dawn darkness and was too distraught at the thought of me leaving, having my own time, and that's at least 300 days a year. 1800 mornings I've walked under those oaks, beside them, with them. It's not a friendship; they are part of me.

Is it too cliché to say they make me feel grounded, rooted? It's their very nature. I'm steadied by them, anchored when I've swayed unbuoyed in postpartum haze, the ups and downs of emotion, in migraine fog, and the type of unraveling exhaustion that is perhaps a hallmark of early motherhood.

They've inspired a practice of sorts, just like I would arrive on my yoga mat ready to begin, I arrive beneath them. I stand still, rooting myself to the rough earth below me and begin to move my arms through the morning air—sometimes cool, sometimes already stifling—tracing their limbs. I've grown attached to their bodies, know each of their curves as I follow their silhouettes with my fingers. I scan them with my eyes, sketch their bodies into space with my arms. My neck and shoulders open, I find freedom in my lower back and hips. I wonder for a moment if our older bachelor neighbor can see me in the dimly lit morning hours, but I don't care: this is my time, my space, and I move within my own body, feel myself as separate from my children for a few moments.

•

I study the juvenile oak that grows from a thin crevice in a boulder outside our bathroom window. My eyes are drawn to it as I sit in the tub with my baby boy and small daughter splashing around me. My son stands up and clings to the tub's edge for support, looking out the window.

See the oak, I say pointing. *I'm watching it.* His eyes light up, and we watch it together: late afternoon sun turning the wind rattle of leaves into a profusion of gold glitter, splintering, undulating light that we drink in.

When I was pregnant with him, I saw an image over and over when I put my hands to my belly: green moss, stones, the dark brown of damp wood, massive bases of hundreds of trees, and then a flash of one cut open to reveal rings: thousands of them. I'd return to this image and breathe, as if to breathe in the dampness, the greenness, the freshness of it, a forest bath of my dreams, to nurture myself in the ancient forest my son was growing in.

A week after he was born, I held him close to me and whispered, *I know about the ancient forest you come from.* He turned his head and looked at me with an alertness I hadn't seen in him yet as if startled, surprised, as if saying with his eyes: *You know about that?* And I tell him, *I want to know more about it.* I want him to hold onto that wisdom of cells dividing at an exponential rate, of life unfurling, of what it was like to just be. *Teach me,* I say. *Before you lose it.*

•

I realize that besides my family with me, the one thing I need when I move is trees. It helps make the idea of uprooting us and going into the unknown easier. There will be more trees to rest near, to listen to, to know, to hear, to empty and fill me, to become part of me. It's a song, a softness, a calling I feel through my body. When I am with them, I am part of them.

I interview our trees. The trees in my yard and on my street because I want to spend time with them. I want to hear their stories before we leave. But how can I translate something that doesn't have words even though they're speaking? Those thousand pins across my chest, the bumps rising along my arms, the whisperings at my collarbones. No matter how much I try to capture it in words, it's this:

Just space. Openness. Extension. Expansion. Emptiness—not in them but within me, an emptying so I can find space again. I become the vessel so they can refill me. So I can return to being a mother again. Come back inside after the sun has risen and the oaks' bodies are no longer just outlines, to the click of the side door opening and scraping across Saltillo tile, to arms and hands and squishy warm bodies racing toward me and swallowing me into their delightful, all-encompassing world.

STAYING WITH THE DESTRUCTION
LAURA M. COTTERMAN

There is no way to recount or even remember all the springs I have lived. This one, though, is unforgettable: while my wild neighborhood was transforming, the rest of the world was in chaos due to a virus.

It was early April and nights remained cold, with full and gibbous moons pinned between bare branches. Winter had been snowless and now—*too soon*, I thought—leaves were ready to unfold, and vines had picked up where they'd left off last fall. Wrens, as usual, were building nests in odd places; blue jays hollered at everything.

It had started back in February. Bulldozer drone accompanied by counterpoint whine of feller-bunchers. The polyphonic racket from neighboring wooded acres ripped into my pandemic-limited days. There was a crazy irrationality to it: *Why cut them now?* I tried to cope by un-hearing the sounds, by willing them to end. The property is 200 acres, give or take. *Maybe it's just another minor timber cut?*

But the awful symphony played on, and now, two months later, I heard it every waking weekday-hour: a tree-fall fugue.

Most of my adult seasons were mapped on this forest, which, by the way, was never "mine." Since before I arrived, at age thirty, it had been a tree farm. Trees (primarily loblolly pines) were periodically removed in small batches—what you might call a sensible rotation. But most seasons, nothing happened. Trees grew, birds sang, I wandered. I trespassed because no one lived there anymore, and besides: these acres and mine conjoin, adhere. They are not separate. Ask the mycelia:

they can explain how all of the forest on this Carolina upland is one living thing.

Year after year, I walked. I am of these trees, and they are of me.

To be sure, the orchestrators of destruction did not know what was being erased. They never saw daffodils yellow the ground where abandoned cabin and barn once stood, nor a walnut tree's crimped shadow cross the leather boot that sank deeper into duff each year. Distant business owners, they hadn't walked winding paths through pines or noticed eerie architecture of hardwood stump sprouts that arose in the wake of each of many minor fellings.

Yes it was April, and close as the crow flies, machine clamor tortured my root and marrow. One day I finally told myself to welcome the evicted birds and others who would drift and scrabble toward my own wooded acres. That was the least I could do.

•

Next came May. Under the warmth of a post-equinox sun, and dazzled by honeysuckle, iris, and peonies, I began to roam local roads rather than the forest, hoping to outpace the killing cacophony. By now I knew it wouldn't end for months, and roaming in the opposite direction seemed a sanity-saving strategy. After all, chances are always good that I'll encounter something on my wandering way. My steps may make a scuffing disturbance, and unseen lives are crushed by my blind feet, but that is the way of it.

One particular late-spring day I encounter a tortoise on asphalt, head raised the better to see me. Her patterned shell gleams with yellow highlights, and I pause to watch her do that thing reptiles do—throat moving like a bellows to sample air. She hopes to discern whether I am friend or foe. I hope she understands I mean no harm.

A voice in my head says *Move Her! One less death disrupts the murderous rhythm of a road.*

I pick her up and on my palm she clamps shut with a hiss. Now she resembles river-worn stone. In just one more moment I will leave the road. I will step into nearby woods to place this tortoise on last year's brown leaves. Once there, I will look up and realize I have entered a kind of brush arbor: a mercifully green place where, once upon a time, people would have gathered under the shadowing boughs of trees to pray and sing. There, in the silence, I will realize it makes sense to stay a while. It makes sense to stay.

THE POWER OF PLACEMENT
SUSAN CHARKES

I stand listening to the forest. No sound. No whisper, no rustle, no call. Nothing moves.

I tug back the starter cord. My chainsaw rips the air into shards, unleashing a primal scream into the quiet of the forest. I touch the saw to the top of the log in front of me. The running chain catches ragged bark in its jaws, spits it aside, and with a heartbeat's hesitation, slices into sapwood. Sawdust spews onto the forest floor like snow.

Once, this log was a living tree. Now it bridges the trail: one of its ends is resting on the ground, a tangled wall of newly exposed roots; the other end, suspended waist-high, is cradled in the V of a still-standing tree. I'm excising a four-foot section from the log, beginning at its perched end.

The rotating chain wants to drive me into the log with the sawteeth; it's reeling me in as if I'm a caught fish, and my back muscles are twisting and straining with the effort of resistance. So I relax, give myself up, and let gravity draw the saw down, until the moment when the kerf—the opening in the log—suddenly, swiftly, begins to close. I whisk the saw up and out, stepping back as I do.

Sliced half-through, the log sags. I reach underneath it and pull the whirring saw up from the bottom. Now I'm simultaneously working against the gravitational force that resists the saw's ascent and using it to do my work: the weight pressing down on the saw pops the fibers on the underside of the log that are being stretched taut by the wood at the apex of the bend. As the margin shrinks between the top and bottom cuts, I ready myself, primed to escape.

The log waits, too. Waits until the instant the cuts merge, space to space, to become a separation that sunders the continuity into pieces. Almost with a shrug, not so much cracking in two as shifting its weight groundward, the log splits. I flick my left wrist forward against the chainbrake to stop the rotating teeth and quickly step back. The portion of the log that blocks the trail drops with a thud, just the way a seesaw crashes when one rider bails.

The cradled end is now a stub stuck in the tree like the last of a cigar. It's long enough, balanced against the portion on the other side, that it should drop too—but if I've miscalculated it could knock me out with an uppercut. Slowly, gently, as if it's on a puppeteer's string, the freed end sinks, touches the ground, and stops. I switch off the saw to plan my next cut.

Quiet returns to the forest. Quiet—but not quiescence.

Forest trees, living and dead, relate to each other within a complex system of physical forces. A tranquil woods is at equilibrium. But it's full of pent-up potential energy, expressed in relationships defined by leaning angles, sprung arcs, arrested falls.

As a trail maintainer, I've learned to read these relationships. I must—for I must change them.

A trail represents more than a path through a woods. To bushwhack through a forest—ducking under branches, stepping around tree trunks and over logs, hopping boulder to boulder, leaping over streams—is to discover a path that works one time. Establishing a trail, though, says: this will be repeated. I will walk this way, again and again. A trail carves a course through space that attempts to freeze time in its tracks.

But of course, time refuses to cooperate. Trees

grow, water flows, wind blows; rocks slide downhill and leaves decay into soil. Left alone, the trail will be absorbed into the forest.

To keep the trail functioning as a time machine, it must continually be re-carved through space. The footpath must be cleared of obstructions or else re-located to accommodate them. To maintain a trail is to add a new force to the forest system: the maintainer.

Forest forces are balanced against and within each other. Change one value—as when I cut one end of a log—and I compel the system to recalculate. Energy is conserved; it doesn't go away but merely shifts elsewhere. That breeze that elicits a creak from an orphaned limb caught up in the swaying treetops operates within the range of the system's tolerances. A stronger wind may bring down the branch. A fierce wind from a storm, perhaps.

Or the breeze from a falling tree. That one, the one that had been pinned in place by the hanging deadfall I've just finished removing. *Whoooshhh.*

They call those branches widowmakers.

A log lying on a downslope, however slight, is in the grip of gravity that wants to slide in a vector along the log down the hill. Stand below it at your peril.

Even within a log, forces are at work. Seemingly inert, the log bends, just as a bridge cable does, wherever it is suspended between two points—rocks, or roots, or undulations in the terrain. Along the bottom of the curve, fibers stretch in tension, while along the top of it they are being compressed. Imagine holding a thick twisted rope, one end in each hand, and let it drop into a U: the fibers at the top crumple, while those below become taut. A log cantilevered from a single point has the forces on opposite sides: let go of one side of your rope and see the crumpled fibers tighten, while those underneath slump.

The living tree is displacing air that would have occupied the space that life has made for it. At the moment the tree falls, equipoise is broken. As the tree falls it creates a wedge of low pressure. Something must fill that space. Another tree—an older one, say, one that is hollow and lightning-scarred and ready to lie down and die—feels the tug of differential pressure like a noose tightening and pulling it down. *Shhhhhhoooomp.*

When it falls, the old tree doesn't just fall to the ground. It falls through a space filled with the limbs and branches and trunks of its fellows. The oldest trees may lose limbs or tops, yet survive; the youngest ones, those at the bottom of the heap, are more likely to be crushed, their thin trunks snapped off or bent double.

Even bowed down to the ground, the young tree may still live, if its cambium layer can still transport nutrients. Dead or alive, though, it's a trap: a springpole waiting to be sprung at the least disturbance, ready to snap back and decapitate the unwary hiker. This force must be neutralized.

By drawing imaginary tangents on either side of the springpole's arc, then bisecting the angle where they meet, I identify the point of greatest stress. At a 45-degree angle from this point, I shave the inside of the tree, reducing the tension on the outside by breaking the compressed fibers on the opposite, inner side of the curve. As I shave down the tree, it relaxes, the arc widening degree by degree until with a snap, the curve is transformed into a right angle. I turn off the saw.

I stand listening to the quiet. It is the sound of forces not immediately comprehensible by any of our senses, of relationships forged out of the temporary holding-off of chaos, of power gained in death that life never afforded. This is the system that creates the four-dimensional structure of the forest: what is standing, sitting, lying, leaning, bending, or hanging at any one point in time. To chainsaw is to enter into this system, to work with it, and, in the end, to alter it.

Every trail that traverses a forest by its very purpose gives sensate access to the natural systems at work within the woods: those systems we can see and hear, feel and smell. These impinge on our senses by kinetic forces that create movement, at the macro, the micro, or the molecular level.

But the trail itself is the artifact of a process that gives access to the forces that create stasis. Each cut log is the remnant of a release of tension and a discharge of pressure. Every sawed-off limb is the stub left over from a shift in the fulcrum of a lever; every stump, the base of a re-located column of air. All the piles of sawdust are the atomized remains of fibrous chains that bear the weight of the earth back to itself.

I stand and listen. The forest is quiet. Nothing moves. I am held in place by its power.

BENADRYL DAYS
RUTH JOFFRE

Eastern red cedars and box elders shed pollen from March to May. Elms bloom as early as January and continue into March, with southern species flowering again in summer and as late as November. White pine are monoecious, producing two sexes of cone, one of which releases pollen by lifting up its overlapping scales and letting its granules fall out into the wind. I make this list in winter, when pollen is at a minimum, preparing myself for what's to come. My allergist has given me a list of what vexes me: all the trees, all the grasses, half the weeds in the state of Missouri. His assistant checked the boxes for him, brought out a kind of ruler with a series of half-moon notches, each bigger than the last, to measure the hives induced by the scratch test—the *first* half of the test, I should say. My body was too reactive to continue safely. My heart beat faster. Temperature rose. Blood pressure spiked to more than 190/90, which, I learned later, qualifies as hypertensive crisis. In the photos from that day, my forearms are dotted with angry pink bumps, as if I had been stung by dozens of bees, one after the other, until the lines of the stings blurred into one large hive. Only this reaction was caused by needles, not stingers. Each one coated in a known allergen. Birch. Ash. Bermuda grass. The list goes on.

•

Prior to moving to Missouri, I would have said I wasn't allergic to plants. Tarragon, maybe. Some seasonal plants, sure—but nothing more than a passing sneeze, the occasional itchy eye. Not something that could spike my heart rate. Definitely not something that could kill me. I lived then in Seattle, which I now know is one of the best cities for people with allergies. On the Asthma and Allergy Foundation of America's list of 2022 Allergy Capitals, it's #100, the least challenging city listed. "It must be all the firs," I told my partner. "All the evergreens." I had only just learned how to love and appreciate them. How to walk through the forest and listen to the quiet majesty of trees. On hikes, I sometimes placed a hand on a tree trunk and thanked it for helping me find my balance again. That was something I never had as a child. Awareness of a tree as a site of life, of abundance, of care, as opposed to a piece of the background, another part of the landscape.

When did that change?

As a child, the only tree I thought of as distinct was the weeping willow off the asphalt trail to the old elementary school. Every summer, it filled with caterpillars I never learned the name of, their fuzzy little bodies pinching into the shape of the omega (Ω) as they inched across a branch. I tried not to step on them if I walked past, but inevitably the onslaught of boots and bicycles, sandals and strollers, would turn that path into a graveyard.

Few trees have been as memorable: the burr oak right outside the Dey House in Iowa City; the famous cherry blossoms of the University of Washington flowering on the main quad; the giant chinquapin oak across the street from our apartment in Seattle—its leaves turning green, then gold, then red, cycling through the seasons for two years of the pandemic before we moved to Missouri. When we first drove up to the house, we saw the sycamore towering over it from the backyard, the pin oaks lining the fence, the sweetgum with its spiky pods. Our house was built in 1963, and from their size I would guess the yard trees are at least as old as that, if not more so.

•

As far as I know, the oldest tree I've ever seen is the near-850-year-old Douglas fir on West Beach in Deception Pass State Park, Whidbey Island. It's like no fir you've seen: short and twisted, battered by the wind. Its gnarled branches recalled a bonsai tree in its tortured pose. When I paused before it, sap was leaking from a fresh wound, and parents were warning their children to be gentle and not to climb onto its low-slung branches. *This tree is older than we'll ever be,* I told my partner. No doubt it will outlive everyone we've ever loved.

•

Pollen is just one of many methods of survival trees have evolved over the millennia. Seeds might be more tolerant of shade, drought, lack of nutrients, or the presence of pollutants, depending on how a given species has adapted to a local ecosystem in the long term or human industrialization in the relative short term. Last December, while arctic conditions across the Midwest caused temps to dip to a maximum of 4° for several consecutive days here in central Missouri, all the trees in the backyard were already prepared. Newly pliable cell membranes expelled water into the pockets of space between cells, while converted starches mixed sugar into the tree's remaining liquid, thereby lowering its freezing point. It could survive outside, naked but for its bark, all winter, every winter, weathering harsh conditions only to bloom again in spring or fall or those unseasonably warm days in January when plants get confused and release their pollen early. On Benadryl days, I call them. Maybe two if we take the dog on a long walk. I'm not sure yet how many pills spring will require.

THE BLACK SPRUCE
CORINNA COOK

To understand the black spruce, remember it grows from a fist-sized root ball as grey and compact and crucial as a brain. Each black spruce spindles itself straight up into the crack of the cold, stout branches making a skyward scrub from base to apex all winter night. And below that brain of roots lies permafrost, even in summer. This, then, is a tree that keeps ice in mind.

I remember meeting black spruce during my move from southeast Alaska to the interior. I was ill at the time, a fjordlands creature with an immune system gone haywire, taking temporary leave from the rainforest and a sabbatical from the whole glaciated coast against which my fevers flared. I went inland, aiming for semi-arid, boreal-forested Fairbanks, where I hoped to find a kind of medicine.

It was end-summer when I went, fall-not-winter. The road north took me through Tok. Here is what I remember: I rolled down the highway, and the spruce flanking the road shot me an uncanny glance. Thus arrested, I glanced back.

Hello, said the black spruce. *We are the toughest things you have ever met.*

Those black spruce on the road to Tok, they told me something about where I was going and what kind of cure I might find. They said it straight—with their tight skyward shape, their dark color, their dry firm trunk-stems as spindly as old canes, their flaking skin bark and waxy stout needles, that fierce clod of roots that looks like a dry brain—they said just what it means to live outside. In winter. And to do it well.

As if falling into step with a tree might heal my ailment.

I reeled a little bit. I was still sick, see—strong enough to drive, but not strong enough to open my car door in a crosswind.

Yet I heard them clearly.

Hello, said the black spruce. *We are the toughest things you have ever met.*

I learned something about myself then: if the trees will talk, I will listen.

What did I hear? For starters, those trees' toughness so far exceeded mine I laughed out loud.

We are the toughest things you have ever met, they repeated, *except maybe for chickadees.*

Deadpan truth-humor: the black spruce appreciated my laughter. That is how I became friends with a kind of a tree.

I thought of Emily Dickinson, of course—

I'm Nobody! Who are you?

Are you — Nobody — too?

So it went that on land that loves to be frozen— that lives for it, really—I sidled up to a kind of tree, the black spruce, the tree that keeps ice in mind. I paused in Fairbanks for a few years to consider this. A pair of nobodies before those all-important chickadees, the black spruce and I leaned in shoulder to shoulder; we went on arm in arm.

•

Some years later and many miles south, my mother gives me the gift of a painting. An artist from Juneau, Constance Baltuk, has returned from a residency with the Parks Service. A crew of some sort brought her into the backcountry of the Kobuk valley for a few weeks.

The crew did their science—counting caribou?—while Constance set up her easel every day. Made sketches. Then she returned home, some eight hundred miles southeast of the Kobuk, completed a series of paintings, and had a show. My mother picked a painting from this show.

It's the trees, my mother explains. *It's not the flashiest painting of Constance's Kobuk series,* but there is *something about the trees.* The trees remind her of when I took my leave of our rainforested island and passed those seasons in Fairbanks. She figures the painting will remind me, too.

It's an arctic summer landscape. The greenery in the foreground is lush and streaked with yellows and dotted with pinks and oranges; an urgent bloom. There is one cluster of five black spruce standing together; otherwise they are in twos and ones—this is not a forest landscape, but perhaps the northernmost reach of black spruce habitat. The far plane of hills is abstracted to dusk colors, grey lavender mauves, and the sky behind is clouded, pale grey-blues shaded in the shape of cumulous billows. High clouds, puffy, but dense. Summer sky bearing down hard on land that just holds its breath, waiting for a good hard frost to clear the air.

•

In the Goldstream Valley, where I first got to know the boreal forest, the black spruce grow in the low places, wetlands or bogs, while birch trees grow on hills where the ground is drier. But soil type is only one of the differences between birch and spruce habitat. There are also inversions: during winter's coldest spells, an inversion sends the most bitter air downhill into the bogs while a fluff of warmer air sits on top. Above the inversion among the birches, it may be twenty below—but forty below beneath the inversion among the black spruce.

I wintered both ways. And as it had by the side of the sea, my immune system kept its own counsel: persistent reactions came and went. Sometimes they swelled, ruptured the skin, and became the site of strange infections. For one winter I nursed these while living in a cabin among the birch trees above the inversion. And for two winters I pondered these flare-ups from a home below the inversion, alongside the black spruce.

Have it either way on the question of "warm" and "cold." Two Rivers poet Derrick Burleson cuts to the chase by gauging not winter's cold, but winter's color. He arrives at an understanding of blue, sees that in the winter night the birch trees glow blue, that their shadows cast dense blues on the paler blues of the snowpack. Derrick sees even the blue shadow of his breath. But that breath itself—this makes a cloud of white rolling out into the air over blue snow, against blue tree trunks in a birch stand. I re-read his book *Melt* to verify all this: indeed, the moon, the snow, the birch—all the hues of winter are blue save one: there is white in the poet's exhaled breath alone.

I was grateful to Derrick for teaching my eye to see how shades of blue bind the snow and the moon and the birch trees and everyone's nightshadows to winter, to cold.

And so imagine my surprise when one night, I perceived red.

It was there among the black spruce, down in the deepest nightcold. Unmistakable. A one-color aphorism inscribed in the trees. I adjusted, centered my attention, and proceeded to study those trees long and hard for many months, for many looping miles. I studied that red by touch and by tongue. I studied by sorrow, by insistence. I found heat. And I didn't know what to make of it, for with the ebb and flow of my own fevers this much was clear: my illness was at its core also a kind of heat. Yet the black spruce, spindling their heat up into the crack of winter cold, were fine.

•

About the black spruce in Constance's painting: they are flecked with red. They are flecked with flaming red paint.

I am awash when I see the painting and tell my mother over and over to look at the red. *Those trees are full of red!* I say. *They are!*

Are they? she asks me, pleased, an interested gardener. She hasn't spotted any red in real spruce herself; then again, she hasn't lived in the boreal forest. But like many mothers, she knows me better than should be possible. She picked me a painting, and she picked this one because she thought it might touch on my life in the interior, hook something, reel it forth.

Are black spruce really full of red? she still asks now and again, pleased, not particularly concerned about how literally or metaphorically I mean it.

Yes! I say.

Yes: I say it over, and over.

•

I don't know that I found a kind of medicine during those subarctic winters. I do know that I grew quite close to a kind of tree, the black spruce, and that I missed them when I returned to the rainforest. I also know the experience feels unfinished (imbalanced), as if they gave me a gift of something elegant that I am too clumsy to properly wear. I try, though, to consider red as a serious proposition, though it is not clear what this really demands.

•

And so I turn to memory and think back to those winters. How the snow came each October and I skied through the frozen bogs every day to the end of April. I skied by headlamp, by moonlight, by the scrape of sun sending its brief, midday lance across the earth. Especially during an inversion. If it was too cold to breathe or blink or budge, I skied. I think now that I did it specifically to be with the black spruce, over and over, three years in a row. To hear them thinking through the coldest of it, to gather what I could of how well they fared.

That is probably how I began to see beneath the surface of things. Through all the blue of snow and shadows, I saw in the black spruce something redhot, something I might now describe as redhot ease with winter, redhot ease with lunar cold, its airless clamp.

What I'm saying is: it is easy to be a black spruce out in forty below. They really are flecked with red.

Though memory reminds me that when I first perceived their ease, again I just laughed. Copying them would be impossible. In my sick strong fragile eager confused animal body, it would be impossible to live as perfectly as a tree. This was as freeing a realization as any other, an echo of Franz Kafka: *there is hope but not for us.*

•

Still, I think of red.

Red, the heat of fire.

In the body heat can occur at a cellular level. In excess, it is inflammation.

Medical science ties inflammation to aging. We might infer that aging (cellularly understood) is a condition of increasing inflammation.

But remember: Elders carry knowledge the young cannot fathom.

This strikes me as significant. Thus, what links inflammation to wisdom? What do I mean if I say, "the red heat of the wise"?

•

I see Constance at a dinner party somewhere in south Douglas. West Juneau maybe. I am so eager to talk to her about the red in those black spruce. I am brimming.

That red, that red—I don't know exactly what I say. Surely worry breaks the surface of me, and I have to ask, *do you remember you did that, you put red paint in with the black spruce?* Of course she does. Of course she remembers flecking those trees with red.

Perhaps we talk about her seeing what I see and the happy convergence of our seeings. Perhaps we talk about thinking in colors, joining concept to sight, question to hue. Or about perceiving truths just below the skin of the day. I'm not sure anymore. I do not really remember the conversation. Constance has curly grey hair and a splashing smile. Her voice is very small, and we both let things like the exuberance of dinner parties wash our words out to sea.

•

Those flecks of red? I'll tell you what they are. Those

flecks of red are a method. It is how a black spruce handles its heat, using it to live well winter upon winter upon winter. It is how a black spruce looks a person in the eye in order to say, *this is how to live in step with good, hard cold.*

Can a human body mimic the thinking of a tree? I try, I try.

•

The chickadees, though—they're something else. Singing this and that at the birdfeeder in forty below. Somehow this is possible: with their teeny black stick-legs and their teeny feathered bodies, somehow it is not only possible for chickadees to live through the winter night; it is also possible for them to chitter and flit, gamble and grouse, wheel and bicker and proclaim sudden notions. The black spruce and I, we watch in wonder, but have yet to find medicine in verbs like these. So we follow no chickadee's line of flight. We simply hold our admiration close where it grows, one neuron at a time, until we can make an idea of it, an idea with a mind of its own, which we quickly knob into the earth and guard until it grows thick as blood, bright as conviction, healthy as nightfall.

INTO THE LIGHT
K ANAND GALL

The day is unseasonably warm for January, a good day for pruning fruit trees.

If you have never pruned fruit trees before, there are several ways to learn. You can get yourself an arborist mentor, someone to walk you through the steps. We sort of had one of these, someone we met at a holiday gathering, who talked us through the key steps.

In lieu of a mentor, there is always the internet, the pages of YouTube instructional videos. You can sit at your porch office desk overlooking the chicken run and take notes like you are a student. Note the key principles: creating air movement between branches, pruning back any branches that might rub and chafe against each other, and encouraging lateral growth (and discouraging skyward shoots in places other than the canopy). I learn there are all kinds of pruners: loppers, anvil, bypass, straight blade. Ratchet shears are designed with an extra mechanism that allows you to cut in stages, good for hands weak with arthritis and other conditions. We have everything but ratchet shears in our garden shed, which means my wrists will ache at the end of the day. Who am I kidding? My wrists will ache within the hour.

A third way to glean the insights of pruning is to read poems about pruning, which are surprisingly encoded with these same principles (though with fewer references to shear design). In her poem "Pruning," Johanna Herrick writes "I know the cutting will make / the tree stronger, more beautiful." Frankly, the line chafes. It's that old trope: what doesn't kill you makes you stronger. Is my heart stronger for the arrhythmias?

For the congenital heart disease? Hardly. And yet, the poem dispenses solid horticultural advice. Here I am in our yard doing it to these trees. I am cutting back limbs, surprised by how the guiding triad—air movement, lateral movement, free movement—leads me to a meditative state. I think of David Wagoner's poem "The Cherry Tree," how it "suffered the pruning of its quirks and clutters, its self-indulgent thrusts / and the infighting of stems at cross purposes." I am not willing to admit that living with a heart condition makes me stronger, but I might concede that it has pruned my quirks and clutters, my self-indulgent thrusts.

Our makeshift arborist mentor told us that it's nearly impossible to prune a fruit tree back too far, and yet the slice of my pruners feels violent. I am intentionally wounding the trees, as my cardiologist did to me as he pruned back the misfires in my heart. No loppers but a blade of heat, burning rogue electrical branches down to the root. Tell me you can't prune a heart back too far. Tell me.

We did not plant these trees. They were here when we moved in. They were at most ten years old, likely no more than eight. The first summer, the peach tree was laden—laden in the way that I really understood the essence of the word laden, a weight that could drag you down, crush you—with hard fuzzy peaches, no larger than plums. One morning we woke to find not a single peach left on the tree. Instead, we found broken limbs dangling at strange angles, and a carpet of peach pits circling the base of the tree. In his first and only novel, *The Notebooks of Malte Laurids Brigge*, Rainer Maria Rilke writes, "In those days people knew (or suspected) that they had death inside them like the stone inside a fruit." We could not be sure who our reaper was—raccoon, possum, maybe even the groundhog burrowing beneath the barn could have been the culprit—but we were shocked at the volume, speed, and totality of their thievery.

We would not have chosen this part of the yard to plant the fruit trees. They stand, the five of them—two apple, two pear, one peach—not even ten feet from our farmer neighbor's field. Herbicide drift from his early summer spraying curls the leaves. But the trees are already here. This, too, is a metaphor, a lesson. Is not this body a fruit tree, inherited in a particular place under these particular conditions with particular unavoidable poisons? This body is what I have.

Despite the violence, pruning creates a strange intimacy with the trees. I notice that pear branches have a greater tendency to grow upright than the apple and peach. They are already too tall for me to safely reach the crown. I do what I can in the lower branches. I notice where the trees are strong and where their architecture might predispose them, like a septal aneurysm, to structural weakness.

I read another David Wagoner poem, his "Elegy while Pruning Roses." Theoretically, he says, "It has to be done, or they spend their blooming season / In a tangle of flowerless, overambitious arms." Here too, a lesson: my propensity to say yes to too many things. Only the many-armed gods can achieve the kind of ambitions I undertake daily, disappoint myself daily for not achieving. Pruning reminds me that I am not a god.

It isn't just that pruning makes the trees stronger. It is also meant to produce larger more delectable fruit. We've been plagued with so many tiny apples. We are told that pruning will create fewer, but larger, fruits. I keep trying to do this in my life. Simplify. Put my energy into a few, fleshy fruits instead of spreading myself thin into hundreds of tiny hard apples (See: propensity to say yes to too many things, above).

Wagoner's "Elegy" is a lament for the dead, the *flourishing* dead. I can't get the phrase out of my mind. It should be second nature to me as a Druid, the interconnectedness of life and death. All life comes from death, all death feeds life. I've seen it in the leaf litter on the forest floor. I practice it when I take food scraps to the compost bin, when I scoop the cats' daily rodent offerings from the back porch and bury them beneath the Norway maple. I begrudgingly acknowledge it when the red-shouldered hawk plucks our chicken Hollandaisy from behind the beehive. All beings need to eat. I just wish they wouldn't eat *my* chickens. Even as I say such a thing, a Costco chicken breast burbles for hours in the slow cooker, waiting to be shredded for tonight's chicken noodle soup.

If I am already marked for death, then should I not find a way to be the *flourishing* dead?

Or am I, like Wagoner says of the oldest branches, a survivor carved "by knife blades, rain, and wind"? Am I not sending shoots straight up to heaven, every time I chant? Am I not always aiming this blood red heart straight into the light?

MAPPING THE UNDERSTORY
KIMBERLY WILLARDSON

Late December, Predawn

I woke to the sounds of humming engines and grinding tires and went outside to see the house across the street crawling away. A week ago, hard-hatted men used jacks, steel beams, and dollies to lift the house from its foundation, then lashed and secured the house on a wide trailer. Yesterday, they raked leaves off its roof. I'm not sure how old the house is, but I do know that just five years ago, this area was considered deep woods, off the beaten path. And just a few months ago, the outer perimeter of the forest surrounding the house was wrapped in orange-netted fencing dotted with red-lettered signs reading, TREE PROTECTION AREA.

At one point, the house got stuck in the middle of the road, and the men whooped orders, crawled under the house to tighten the four-foot-wide straps, and burned rubber off the tow truck and trailer tires trying to get the house moving again. The trailer creaked and moaned. I could swear I heard the bones of the house snap, and its dimmed windows became the gray-veiled eyes of a mortally wounded animal.

Police officers blocking traffic from the house-moving operation waved me away from getting too close with my camera. There was no sudden lurching, no great rending or collapse. The house inched away until I could glimpse only its roof peak descending down the road. And then, it was gone.

The trees were next.

Carolina North Forest, Early Winter

I go to the forest because it's like walking through a

storybook. I go there because Josie, my 100-pound German Shepherd dog, requires daily long walks, or she becomes unreasonable and does Bad-Dog things like knocking over lamps or galumphing after our cats.

Fifteen minutes from our front door to the head of my favorite trail, there's a commanding silence that demands an attitude adjustment. We live in an area transitioning between a 750-acre woodlands and new housing developments, at a heavily trafficked crossroads traversed by minivans, bicyclists, school buses, runners, tractors, hikers, and industrial earthmovers.

I prefer to walk alone with Josie, while she thinks dog thoughts and I puzzle out writing challenges, trying to think complete thoughts in complete sentences. And then, trying to connect them in sequence. It's harder than one imagines. Often on these walks, I think nothing at all. The forest doesn't require conversation from you; it asks only that you listen.

Hovering around winter solstice, the days are shorter. Night often falls before I can take time for walks, so sometimes my husband, Roger, or our son, Tommy, or one of our exchange students joins Josie and me.

You learn a lot about a person while walking through the woods at night together. Roger walks silently, listening for owls or the chuffing of deer. Tommy, a laconic, baffling teenager, is chattiest while walking through the forest at night: which Carolina teams, he wonders aloud, do I think will go to the Final Four this year? What actions would we have to do to survive a Zombie Apocalypse? I'm stumped, although flattered he thinks I know the answer to either question.

I'm pretty sure Tommy thinks it's badass that I will walk the forest at night, even with Josie. He should. Because I am actually afraid to walk "alone," even with Josie, in the forest at night, and every single time I make it through, I'm not just proud, but relieved.

One January night, circumstances dictated that I had to walk alone with Josie. And, after a long day at the computer, I welcomed the bracing cold air on my face.

In winter, the forest floor is layered with copper-colored pine needles, which are, technically speaking, the *leaves* of these trees. It's as though the bronze waters of a massive river have flooded their banks and flowed between the trees. Floating above the copper floor, the grays, duns, and browns of trunks and bare branches blur to a smoky haze, especially during drizzly twilight. This haze lends a dreamlike air to the forest in the half hour before sunset, my favorite time there.

It was probably the beguiling fog that made me completely lose myself, causing me to slip and fall while striding too fast over the slick leaves covering the footpath. My legs flew up in front of my face, and I crashed hard. My tailbone slammed into one of the knotty tree roots studding the trail along with sharp rocks and rills carved out by fast-moving streams resulting from intermittent heavy rainfalls.

Regaining my breath after the painful impact, I gathered my senses, bolstered by Josie's concern, her wet nose and hot breath in my face, her whining in my ear. I did a quick inventory, noticing how quickly darkness had gathered in the forest, how much harder the rain was falling, and two other particulars: I'd lost my jacket somewhere along the way, and I'd forgotten to replace my flashlight and headlamp in my walking bag after taking them out.

I laid my head back down and sighed.

•

The Ritual, Summer Mornings, Ohio

The important thing was to climb up and get settled into the treetop before dark had completely vanished. The magic spell required night still suspended above the roofs and murky shadows still draped in the corners of my neighborhood. This *After-Hours* air fueled the illusion that I was the only one up watching. The world belonged to me for those moments before the blaring morning sun, chittering birds, and alarm of responsibility woke up the others and cogs began moving.

I'd balance myself on the highest horizontal branch of the Manchurian chokecherry, pull a mini Steno pad and pencil stub from my back pocket, and wait. The pencil stub was one of several that I routinely stole from Downview Putt-Putt Golf course three blocks from our house. I whittled the miniature pencils, carefully, with a jackknife I had stolen from my dad. The fact that these small items were pilfered cheered me up somehow.

I breathed very slowly, in and out through my nostrils, mouth shut and eyes half open, to keep my body still, preventing the branch from bobbing up and down and rattling the leaves. I willed myself to disappear, while sharpening my senses, and practiced patience. In this silence, I watched as the smallest details gathered and pooled, becoming the legends of my old neighborhood.

•

Real. Forever.

I met my husband during a Hammer Damage concert at the Lone Star Frat House on Buchtel Avenue in Akron, Ohio, in September 1979. True story: Before it was the Lone Star House, the Byron W. Robinson Mansion served as the Florence Crittenton Maternity Home for

Unwed Mothers, where my grandparents stashed my mom after she got pregnant with me. With the assistance of the woman whose house she cleaned, my mom snuck away from this Home to elope with my dad. And twenty years after my parents launched their future from there, I stood in that grand, Beaux-Arts Home eyeing my future husband who was standing absolutely still while surrounded by dozens of drunk punks bouncing up and down to the fizzy, dizzy spindrive of "The Doitch" in the Lone Star's living room.

We both hated Akron, and detested fraternities, but, *come on*, it was Hammer Damage. I asked him, "Has anyone ever told you that you look just like Roger Daltrey?" He sneered, said "Yeah, and my name is Roger, too," and walked away.

Oh my. A distant and angry handsome young man, I thought. *What's he so pissed off about?* Later, he told me his first impression was that I was "a real person" in "that tight green sweater." The chase was on. Thirty-four years, nine months, and odd days later, we're still chasing each other.

As a writer, I'm preoccupied with juxtapositions. I've often considered the improbable placements of people and circumstances intersecting in that one house on Buchtel Avenue. At the time of the Hammer Damage party, I had no idea that that was where my mom had spent the initial weeks of her unplanned pregnancy. Once she prodded me, the day after I first met Roger, about exactly where I had been the night before, she was notably astonished by this information.

"The house on Buchtel with the stained-glass windows on the main landing?"

"Yep," I said. Keeping to myself that my friends and I had spent quite some time the previous evening trying to figure out how we could release those gorgeous colored lead-glass panels, depicting the trees and grounds surrounding the mansion, from the heavy oak frames that held them in place.

"Oh, my God, you're going to marry that man," my mom said.

"You're nuts," I told her.

And it wasn't until a year later from that, just before my wedding, that she told me about the Florence Crittenton Home for Unwed Mothers and her time there.

Years later, other stories surfaced. A friend confided to me that she had been raped on the grounds of that house, by one of the frat members she met the night I met Roger, only weeks after the Hammer Damage party. I've read excerpts from *Following the Tambourine Man,* Janet Mason Ellerby's account of her experiences leading up to, during, and after her time at that Home, in which she describes herself reading long afternoons, "secreted away in the window seat like the young Jane Eyre." The fraternity later moved from the house, though I haven't been able to confirm exactly why. One of the rumors was that they had hanged a dog from one of the stately old trees on the property. Ugly stuff. In my research on the Home, I came across this line, regarding the condition of the mansion after the fraternity left: "Boys will be boys."

But one of my dear cousins had been a Lone Star, and there were attempts to restore the Home to its old glory, including a 23-carat gilding placed on the mantle in the living room. In the 90s, the Home became a warehouse and showroom for Steinway luxury pianos, after serving as office space for copy equipment and an insurance company.

The last I checked, the 13,000-square foot home was still for sale as a commercial property. I think of decades of quiet young women gazing out at the grounds' magnificent trees, through the heavy-leaded, colored glass representation of those grounds. I wonder how many of the old trees still stand witness. *Boys will be boys.* Sometimes I daydream about buying the place and smudging its rooms with the smoke of cedar and sage. I imagine myself sitting and writing in one of its dark corners.

•

Stop Me If You've Heard This One
A middle-aged woman walks into a bar. She shakes her umbrella and squints into the dimness, looking for a place to hang her wet coat. She's uncomfortable; she's never been there before and doesn't want to be there now.

The longer she stands there, the more irritated I become. I haven't known what to do with her since she wandered through the back door of the long story I'm working on. She came in as foil to Winnie Wrenn, one of the story's main characters, but aside from the fact that she's older than Winnie and owns the Spangled Hen Hut Beauty Salon, I can't draw a bead on her.

Whenever I push her through the door of Jo-Joe's Social Club, a key location where most of the story's action takes place, she clams up, crosses her arms across her chest, and stalls the writing.

I tentatively nudge her into another hot spot in the story—the Northern Piedmont Forest—where she hunches up her shoulders and shakes her head "No." Nothing doing. She's one of the story's citizens who never enters the forest, though most others do. She has no interest in the woods, and is, in fact, quite fearful of the forest and wants nothing to do with trees, except maybe the flamboyant mimosa standing guard next to her Spangled Hen Hut.

And that was it: as soon as I connected the woman with the floofy orangish-pink mimosa tree swaying next to her shop door, the curse was broken, her face bloomed into color, and I suddenly knew her name: Patricia (nickname: "Peaches") Lee Bedford Sinclair. Shortly thereafter Peaches sharpened into focus: she was one of the original Crimsonettes, the baton-twirling auxiliary for the University of Alabama Million Dollar Band in 1976 (and she still has her white go-go boots to prove it); she refers to both her father *and* her husband as "Daddy"; she's the most cherished customer of the Modern Aesthetics (Botox®!) service room recently added to her salon; and she calls the tree outside her shop the "Persian Silk Tree," instead of simply "Mimosa" because she likes the sumptuous way it sounds. In fact, Peaches loves everything about the sound of her own voice, Bless Her Little Heart, and now it's difficult to shut her up.

•

What I Saw from the Manchurian Chokecherry
Mr. Bill Park was always the first one out of the house. A lit cigarette always dangled from his lips, and the door to his black DeSoto squawked loudly—like an exotic bird—when he jerked it open. Before the squeak of the DeSoto's tires faded up the street, Bill's wife, Mona, was out the door and on her way to the GM Plant. Mr. Stobbs, also heading for the GM plant, was third. Mrs. Stobbs blew kisses to her husband on his way to the driveway, but he never blew kisses back.

From within my own house, after the first birdcalls, Mom put the teakettle on to boil, lit a Pall Mall, and turned on the radio. Dad would call out, "Have a good day, Kimmy," toward the tree on his way to the driveway. But, he never looked into the tree.

Next came the waves of smells: coffee, cigarettes, bacon, and the delicious scent of bread, buns, and rolls baking at the Lawson's plant all the way across town that would make me start thinking about leaving the tree.

When the tree bloomed, in late May or early June—I'm not sure exactly when and I will have to Google it (again) to remember exactly when it is that those trees usually bloom in Ohio—I had to get on the Google to discover the exact name of the tree, after all these years.

The Latin name of the tree, *Prunus maackii*, comes from Richard Karlovic Maack, the Russian naturalist who discovered it while exploring the Amur River.

Summers past, I didn't know the name of the tree or the discoverer behind it, but when the tree bloomed its tiny white cylandrical flowers, I knew it smelled bad. Like old fish.

In the summer, staring from the top of the *Prunus maackii* tree, I learned heat was also scented and visible as I watched vapors rise from the sun-scorched blacktop of our street. And that acrid, burnt-rubber smell bore into my nose until I got to the Water Works Municipal Pool and dove in, replacing the piney pitch musk with heavy doses of public-pool chlorine.

•

Googling Trees
In one Google search, I found this on Wikipedia: "Young canopy trees often persist as suppressed juveniles for decades while they wait for an opening in the forest

overstory which will enable their growth into the canopy." I wonder: is this why it's necessary for many young adults to move away, sometimes very far, from their parents before they can grow up? Or, is it that all ages of humans remain caught in that middle ground between earth and sky?

I feel embarrassed confessing my Google searches. I'm old enough to remember long hours over microfiche, "the stacks," and requesting heavy books from interlibrary loans. And I'm bothered that I never went back for my botany degree and that I don't do enough to fight for the fair and just treatment of trees. I got pulled away by the study of literature and writing. These days, most scientific or academic knowledge I have of trees, forests, and photosynthetic action comes, I'm ashamed to admit, from Google.

The term *understory* resonates with me more as a literary device than a specialized area of forestry.

Was it second or third grade where we learned that most of the oxygen we breath comes from trees? That the replenishment of this vital chemical element takes place after trees, and other living plant organisms, recycle the less life-sustaining carbon elements? Didn't this knowledge about carbon and oxygen exchange further enhance your reverence for trees?

The emotional attachment comes at birth, I believe. We are born loving trees. Our apprehension or apathy toward them is handed down by a lack of knowledge. Or a malevolent intention that conjures a seemingly primal fear—manipulated by Victorian fairy tales and Hollywood movies—that we carry with us into adulthood.

•

The Understory Is Where It's At

The *understory* is where you walk if you visit the rainforest. It's where moss creeps up the ankles of pines, like socks, and where boas coil, jaguars pant, and thick liana embrace the solid, scaly barked tree trunks and swoop in loops between them.

The understory is Tommy, as a brave toddler, racing around the dark backyard, stopping to pat each of the trees, as if checking to make sure they were really there. The understory is Tommy breaking his wrist in a fall from the apple tree next door and me still making him write out his vocabulary words, not knowing it was broken. And the guilt of that episode was nothing compared to the pain of telling Tommy to say goodbye to the twenty-seven-year-old river birch tree, with its undulating slender branches and quaking leaves that seemed to sigh, on the east side of our condominium that anchored us for four summers. The tree the HOA Board cut down out of spite because we were asking too many questions about our HOA's budget, falsely claiming the river birches were damaging the foundations of the buildings.

And the morning of the scheduled tree culling, Tommy didn't know I was watching, and he went up to the river birch and literally hugged it. He stood there hugging the tree for a few minutes, and when he turned around I could see from the car that he was crying.

My heart broke and soared at the same time. My heart cried for him and for the majestic gorgeous tree that was being cut down so that people full of ill will could feel strong over other people with whom they had disagreements.

But my heart also lifted because it was obvious that Tommy had the trees in his blood, too, and he was a tree-hugging fool like his parents. This made me glad for him; people who "get" trees seem to be much smarter, kinder, and happier people. Good for him.

Sad for him because people who "get" trees also get their hearts torn out on a regular basis. These people understand why I sometimes went out and literally cursed and screamed at the men cutting down the acres and acres of trees across the street from us. The sound of grand living trees crashing to the ground is hideous and gut-wrenching; it unhinges me.

•

Ashes and Longleaf Pines
I might prefer to die in a forest when my time comes, but I'm not completely sure about this. I was positive I didn't want to die that particular January night in that particular forest, so I made myself get up and regain my footing.

And I wasn't, of course, anywhere near death— merely jolted and sore. But when I'm in the forest, especially on rainy nights, I often think broody, dramatic thoughts like, "Shiny red blooddrops trailed her, and she knew Death was close, but still she soldiered on." Or, "Every forest has the same dark heart, once you've wandered deep enough into its silence."

Days later, as Josie and I got closer to the scene of my accident, I noticed my missing jacket neatly folded and sitting atop an insect-engraved tree stump marking where the rocky single footpath breaks off from the main trail. Goosebumps shivered up from my ankles to the top of my scalp, and I stopped and peered around into the gloom of the darkening forest, expecting to catch sight of Boo Radley's pale face watching for my reaction.

And this is another reason I go to the forest. It

takes me out of my daily grind and opens all the doors and windows of my imagination. The forest is drama. The forest is a love story. The forest fires up my vision factory and tunes me into the insistent voices of friends I haven't yet met. Or, written.

The forest helps me hatch plans like this one: there are four places I've instructed Roger to scatter my ashes after dividing them into equal quarters, should I precede him: 1. East Glacier forest, where we spent our most memorable vacation, so far; 2. a forested spot of his choosing in the Carpathian Mountains (neither of us have been there, though we speak of it often, so I want to force him to go—from the grave!—if we don't get there together); 3. the wooded banks of the Cuyahoga River, behind Water Works Park, where I spent some of the happiest days of my childhood; and 4. the "spot" we both love in this forest, just past the longleaf pine grove, where it slopes down sharply, turning into the densest foliage where deer sleep and the green is so intense that I believe I hear a harp glissando, and my heart stops every time I pass through it.

This is romantic twaddle. I don't blame Roger for tuning me out when I drone on about this during our walks. I have no idea how anyone could possibly divide a person's ashes into four equal parts.

Besides, we still want to consider ourselves young, hip, and modern, though we're both closer to 60 than 50. We work computers and dream about high-tech toys, like solar-paneled rooftops, wireless streaming, and an electric car in our garage.

But the best parts of our days usually happen in the simplicity of the forest.

I fell in love with Roger in the woods, on our first official date—a walk in the Top of the World Park in Northeastern Ohio, now part of the Cuyahoga Valley

Conservation Park. Though Northeastern Ohio is part of the rustbelt, it has learned how to protect its green spaces and taken serious stewardship actions for future generations. At least more so than North Carolina, my adopted state, whose "leadership" has squandered troves of natural resources, including longleaf pines whose numbers have dwindled to thousands of acres in the Southeastern United States, where they once filled millions of acres.

On our first walk through the forest, Roger confided that he'd spent as much of his childhood as possible in the woods, just like I did, and had an obsession with climbing and sitting in trees. As I did.

He told me one of my favorite stories, later echoed by his mother a few times before she died, about how, before he was 10, when he lived in Smethport, Pennsylvania, he loved climbing into the top of a pine tree in his parents' front yard and swaying on the breeze through the highest branches. Mrs. Rose, one of their neighbors, would call his mother and complain that she was worried that Roger would fall and hurt himself. Roger's mom, rather than scolding him for being in the tree, would call Roger down and ask to move into one of the trees in the backyard so that Mrs. Rose wouldn't see him.

I love this story for a few reasons. For one: it reveals what a considerate and understanding woman Roger's mother was. And for another, I just like picturing a young Roger swaying around in the top of pine trees.

And, for all my falderal about ashes and auspicious meetings, I grow less romantic, less spiritual, the older I get. This surprises me because I always expected that people became more sentimental and swayed by the supernatural the older they get. Not so, for me, anyway.

The nearest I get to believing any theory of Destiny or Soul Mates is when I think of young Roger sitting in one of his trees, while miles away, there I am, sitting in my tree, both of us brooding, dreaming, or just listening. And there's Tommy sitting in his apple tree, without falling out of it. I imagine all the other tree sitters, energetic children and limber adults also born with the tree-climbing obsession, in different countries, in a vast diversity of trees, all across the globe, sitting in their trees, brooding, dreaming. And pretty soon, in my mind's eye, the bears, birds, panthers, and gibbons, the lions, sloths, and katydids join in, and all of us are sitting in our trees, dreaming, brooding, observing. And this image, the closest thing I have to religion, makes me want to go out and climb a tree. To take notes. To join the observant silence.

CONTRIBUTORS

Currently a student in Miami University's MFA program and Editor in Chief for *OxMag*, **K Anand Gall** also holds an MA in Creative Writing from San Francisco State University. K's work has appeared recently in *Thin Air Magazine* and *The Journal*. She is the 2023 Academy of American Poets Betty Jane Abrahams Memorial Poetry Prize winner, a 2022 finalist in The Arkansas International C.D. Wright Emerging Poet's Prize, and 2022 Midwest Writing Center's Foster-Stahl Chapbook Series finalist. A member of the Order of Bards, Ovates, and Druids, she has been known to hug, meditate on, and hold ceremonies with all manner of trees. Find her on Twitter and Instagram @kanandgall or at kanandgall. com.

From her home in the sagebrush-steppe and coniferous forest of the South Thompson Valley in southern British Columbia, **Lyn Baldwin** teaches botany at Thompson Rivers University. For more than two decades, Lyn has worked to cultivate care between the people and plants of place by sharing the stories she finds with her illustrated field journal in art galleries, in journals such as *Terrain, Camas, The Fourth River*, and *The Goose,* and in her book, *Drawing Botany Home: A Rooted Life.*

Henri Bensussen approaches and interacts with nature, wild or wild in pretense, in an attempt to make sense of her world, to communicate with its various aspects, learning what's required to live in a world like ours. She has a B.A. in Biology (UC Santa Cruz). Poems and stories have been published in various anthologies, and in *Blue Mesa Review, Common Ground Review, Sinister Wisdom*, and *Into the Teeth of the Wind*, among others. Her chapbook of poems, *Earning Colors*, was published by Finishing Line Press in 2014.

Amy Boyd is a professor of botany, ecology, and evolutionary biology at Warren Wilson College. Her writing has been published in literary journals such as *Whole Terrain, Dark Mountain, Flyway,* and *Appalachia Journal.* Scientist by training, educator by profession, and artist by nature, she lives in Swannanoa, North Carolina, nestled in the Blue Ridge Mountains

Brian Braganza had lived on three continents by the time he was four years old. He now lives on Mi'kma'ki, also known as Nova Scotia, Canada, the traditional and stolen lands of the Mi'kmaw. Brian writes creative nonfiction and was recently published in the *Fiddlehead Review*'s BIPOC Solidarities Issue, *Existere Journal of Arts and Literature,* and *The Willow Herb Review.* He is also a singer-songwriter and facilitates spaces for personal and social transformation. Brian's 87-year-old mother lived with him and his family for over a year before moving to long-term care. www.brianbraganza.ca

Joanna Brichetto is a naturalist and writer in Nashville, the Hackberry-tree capital of the world. She writes about everyday marvels amid everyday habitat loss at SidewalkNature.com and on Instagram (**@Jo_Brichetto**); her essays have appeared in *Creative Nonfiction, Brevity, Ecotone, Fourth Genre, Hippocampus, The Hopper, Flyway, The Common, The Fourth River,* and other journals. An almanac of urban nature encounters is forthcoming.

Kit Carlson is an Episcopal priest and a life-long writer with work appearing in publications as diverse as *Seventeen Magazine* and *Anglican Theological Review.* She has been a Pushcart Prize nominee, recently published in *River Teeth, Pensive: A Global Journal of Spirituality and the Arts, Bending Genres*, and *The Windhover*. She is author of *Speaking Our Faith* (Church Publishing, 2018). She lives in East Lansing, Michigan, with her husband Wendell, and Lola, a nervous rescue dog. She has loved the tamarack in this piece for more than thirty years.

Susan Charkes lives in southeast Pennsylvania amongst many companion trees. A writer and author about nature and the outdoors, she also writes poetry and fiction and has long been involved in land conservation and stewardship by vocation as well as profession. She is an active member of the Appalachian Trail volunteer community. More at susancharkes.com.

Corinna Cook is the author of *Leavetakings*, an essay collection. She is a former Fulbright Fellow, a Rasmuson Foundation awardee, and the recipient of an Alaska Literary Award. Corinna teaches in the Low-Residency MFA in Creative Writing Program at Alaska Pacific University. More at corinnacook.com.

Contemplative walker, **Laura Cotterman,** writes on her own and in the company of a small writers' group. Now retired, she worked as a botanist, editor, and publications coordinator, primarily for nonprofit organizations engaged in biodiversity conservation. She is coauthor, with colleagues at the North Carolina Botanical Garden, of a field guide titled *Wildflowers of the Atlantic Southeast* (Timber Press, 2019), which won a 2019 National Outdoor Book Award. She has also published in the online magazine *Scoundrel Time*.

Steven Church is the author of six books of nonfiction,

most recently the collection of essays, *I'm Just Getting to the Disturbing Part: On Work, Fear, and Fatherhood*. His essays have been published and anthologized widely, including in the *Best American Essays*, the *Best of Brevity*, and many others. He is a founding editor of the literary magazine, *The Normal School*, and teaches in the MFA Program at Fresno State.

Emily Donaldson is the author of *Working with the Ancestors: Mana and Place in the Marquesas Islands* (University of Washington Press, 2019) and has worked and studied in French Polynesia for over two decades. An anthropologist and writer, she also researches and writes on a range of social / science topics such as social psychology, identity, data science, career guidance, and neuroaesthetics. She lives in Vermont with her husband, two daughters, their dog, and six chickens.

Marianne Erhardt's writing appears or is forthcoming in *Orion, Oxford American, Kenyon Review, Conjunctions, River Teeth, Ruminate*, and elsewhere. She is the winner of the 2021 VanderMey Nonfiction Prize from *Ruminate*, a 2021-2022 NC Arts Council Fellowship, and a recent Pushcart nomination. She has an MFA from UW-Madison and teaches in the writing program at Wake Forest University.

Felicity Fenton's stories and essays have been featured in *Fanzine, Split Lip Press, Wigleaf, The Iowa Review, Pidgeonholes, The Denver Quarterly, The Masters Review, Passages North, X-R-A-Y, Northwest Review, New Delta Review, Pank*, and others. Her book, *User Not Found*, was published by Future Tense Books in December, 2018. *Elegy For My Art Monster / Tumors Everywhere*, co-written with Drew Burk, was published by Spork Press in the summer of 2022. She lives in Portland, Oregon.

Kelsey Francis's work has appeared in *Porcupine Literary*, *HAD*, *Twin Pies Literary*, *The Washington Post*, *Adirondack Life Magazine*, and the "Modern Love" column of *The New York Times*, among others. She lives, teaches, and writes in the Adirondack Mountains of upstate New York. She can be found on Twitter @ADK_Kelsey.

Robin Foster studied creative writing at Bennington Writing Seminars and has a Ph.D. in American Studies from Rutgers-Newark. She is the author of *Carl Van Doren: A Man Of Ideas*, National Indie Excellence Awards Finalist for 2019. "I Know a Tree" is excerpted from her forthcoming book, *Grit and Ghosts*, to be published by University of Nebraska Press Bison Books. She lives outside Portland, Maine with her husband, where she teaches history at Southern Maine Community College. www.robinkayfoster.com

Ross Gay is the author of four books of poetry: *Against Which*; *Bringing the Shovel Down*; *Be Holding*, winner of the PEN American Literary Jean Stein Award; and *Catalog of Unabashed Gratitude*, winner of the 2015 National Book Critics Circle Award and the 2016 Kingsley Tufts Poetry Award. His first collection of essays, *The Book of Delights*, was released in 2019 and was a *New York Times* bestseller. His new collection of essays, *Inciting Joy*, was released by Algonquin in October of 2022.

Laura Girardeau grew up in the Pacific Northwest and wandered the forests with a pen, translating stories the trees told her. She holds a master's in Environmental

Studies and worked as a forest biologist during the timber wars. Her essays, fiction, and poetry are published in several anthologies, including *What Wildness is This: Women Write About the Southwest*. "Hooters" previously appeared in *Deep Wild: Writing from the Backcountry*.

Lydia Gwyn is the author of the flash collections: *You'll Never Find Another* (2021, Matter Press) and *Tiny Doors* (2018, Another New Calligraphy). Her work has appeared or is forthcoming in *F(r)iction, Midway Journal, Anti-Heroin Chic, The Florida Review, New World Writing Quarterly*, and others. A selection of her stories and poems is slated to appear in Ravenna Press's Triples Series in late 2023. She lives with her family in East Tennessee, where she works as an academic librarian.

Richard Hackler lives on the east side of St Paul, Minnesota.

Sophie Hall writes about homes and fears, especially where the two overlap. Her creative nonfiction and poetry have appeared or are forthcoming in *Ruby Lit, Jeopardy Magazine, The Nasiona*, and *The Helix*, among others. Sophie was awarded a fellowship for the 2022 Bucknell Seminar for Undergraduate Poets and was a 2021 winner of the Sue C. Boynton Poetry Contest. Also a postcard collector, frog parent, and lover of orchids, these days, Sophie is most dedicated to her dream journal. You can follow her on Instagram @ sophieuhmanda.

Steven Harvey is the author of *The Beloved Republic*, the winner of the Wandering Aengus Press Award. He is also the author of *The Book of Knowledge and Wonder*, a memoir about coming to terms with the suicide of his mother published by Ovenbird Books as part of the "Judith Kitchen Select" series. He has written three collections of personal essays—*A Geometry of Lilies, Lost in Translation*, and *Bound for Shady Grove*—and *Folly Beach*, a book-length personal essay about easing fears of mortality and loss through creativity. He is a professor emeritus of English and creative writing at Young Harris College, a founding faculty member in the Ashland University MFA program in creative writing, a contributing editor for *River Teeth* magazine, and the creator of The Humble Essayist, a website designed to promote personal prose. He lives in the north Georgia mountains.

Richard Holinger's work has appeared in *Witness, Chicago Quarterly Review, Hobart, Iowa Review, Catamaran*, and garnered four Pushcart Prize nominations. Books include *North of Crivitz* (poetry) and *Kangaroo Rabbits and Galvanized Fences* (essays). "Not Everybody's Nice" won the 2012 Split Oak Press Flash Prose Contest. He lives northwest of Chicago, far enough to see fox, deer, and turkeys cross his lawn. But his forest place, the place he is most rooted to emotionally, is on a lake an hour north of Green Bay.

Ruth Joffre is the author of the story collection *Night Beast*. Her writing has appeared or is forthcoming in more than 50 publications, including *Lightspeed, Pleiades, Fantasy, khōréō, The Florida Review Online, Kenyon Review, Reckoning, Wigleaf*, and the anthologies *Best Microfiction 2021 & 2022*. A graduate of Cornell University and the Iowa Writers' Workshop, Ruth served as the 2020-2022 Prose Writer-in-Residence at Hugo House and as a Visiting Writer at the University of Washington, Bothell in 2023.

Kevin Richard Kaiser publishes fiction, nonfiction, and poetry internationally and is EIC and Fiction Editor of the multilingual online arts and literary journal *Punt Volat*. They also work in music, film, and performance, frequently in collaboration with Companyia Lake Angela. They hold a PhD from Universitat Pompeu Fabra in Barcelona and an MFA from Chatham University in Pittsburgh. Their book, *An Ethics Beyond: Posthumanist Animal Encounters and Variable Kindness in the Fiction of George Saunders*, is currently available. For more information, visit kevinrichardkaiser.com

Christina Kapp teaches at Rutgers University—Newark and The Writers Circle Workshops in New Jersey. Her writing has appeared in numerous publications including *The Forge Literary Magazine, Passages North, Hobart,* and *The MacGuffin,* and her fiction has been nominated for Best of the Net and Pushcart Prizes. She welcomes you to follow her on Twitter @ChristinaKapp and visit her website: www.christinakapp.com.

Courtney Amber Kilian is a mother/writer living in rural San Diego County. She received her MFA from UCSD and has been published in numerous anthologies including *Rooted's* first rendition. Giggling with her kids, journaling, yoga, hiking, and a good cup of tea sum up her quintessential day. You can find her sporadically at @om.and.ink.

Laurie Klein's work has appeared in *Brevity, Beautiful Things* at riverteethjournal.com, *Eco-Theo, New Letters, Cold Mountain Review, Louisiana Literature, Ars Medica, Tiferet, The Windhover,* and numerous anthologies. She is the author of a poetry collection, *Where the Sky Opens,* and a chapbook, *Bodies of Water, Bodies of Flesh.* Home is a house sheathed in cedar, tucked beneath pines valiantly battling bark beetle swarms. She blogs monthly at lauriekleinscribe.com

Andrea Lani is the author of *Uphill Both Ways: Hiking toward Happiness on the Colorado Trail*. She writes at the nexus of family and the natural world, and her work has recently been published in *Literary Mama, Deep Wild, Stonecrop Review,* and *The Art of Everyone,* among others. She is a Maine Master Naturalist and has degrees in human ecology and creative writing from College of The Atlantic and the University of Southern Maine's Stonecoast MFA program. She lives in central Maine with her husband and nearly grown sons. Find her at www.andrealani.com.

Julie Lunde has work published or forthcoming in *Fourth Genre, Seneca Review, Passages North, Cream City Review,* and elsewhere. She is the winner of Western Humanities Review's 2022 prose contest and received her MFA in creative nonfiction from the University of Arizona. She currently serves as assistant nonfiction editor at *DIAGRAM*. Her essay is a cover of Ander Monson's essay "I Have Been Thinking About Snow." See more at julielunde.com.

Jennifer Maxon is a landscape architect and a writer. Her work in landscape design uses site-specific details, materials, and plant form to compose spaces that enrich outdoor experiences by connecting play to environment. As a writer, Jennifer focuses on creative nonfiction to discover and express beauty in brief moments and simple truths.

Judy McClure is a writer, teacher, and co-owner of

Rozzie Bound Co-op, an independent bookstore. Her writing is published at *Chautauqua, WBUR's Edify, 805 Lit Mag,* and *HerStry.* She is the 2021 winner of the Friends of the Chautauqua Writers' Center prose prize and is a graduate of Grub Street's Essay Incubator. She lives in Boston with her wife.

Meg Muthupandiyan is a pilgrim, writer, and ecologically-minded public humanities artist. The founding director of Poetry in the Parks (*poetryintheparks. org*), much of her creative work explores how pilgrimage and participation in the life of public lands foster humans' ecological consciousness. Her poems, illustrations, photographs, and nature essays have appeared in thirty journals and anthologies, and her illuminated poetry volume *Forty Days in the Wilderness, Wandering* was published in 2021. Join her for a saunter at meganmuthupandiyan.com.

Mackenzie Myers Fowler is a gardener, yarn fanatic, and wordsmith (for work and sometimes for fun). She earned an MFA from Portland State University and after a couple newspaper stints in California, she now lives in northern Michigan with her husband, two cats, and too many houseplants.

Aimee Nezhukumatathil is the author of *The New York Times* best-selling illustrated collection of nature essays and Kirkus Prize finalist, *World Of Wonders: In Praise Of Fireflies, Whale Sharks, & Other Astonishments* (2020, Milkweed Editions), which was chosen as Barnes and Noble's Book of the Year. She has four previous poetry collections: *OCEANIC* (Copper Canyon Press, 2018), *Lucky Fish (2011), At The Drive-In Volcano* (2007), and *Miracle Fruit* (2003), the last three from Tupelo

Press. Her most recent chapbook is *Lace & Pyrite*, a collaboration of epistolary garden poems with the poet Ross Gay. Her writing appears twice in the *Best American Poetry Series, The New York Times Magazine, ESPN, Ploughshares, American Poetry Review,* and *Tin House*.

Scott Oglesby began as a reader for *Bellevue Literary Review* (*BLR*) before becoming assistant nonfiction editor in 2018. An NYC transplant from Louisiana, his varied history included stints as a disability analyst, actor, singer, photographer, teacher, homemaker, and café-owner, along with other sketchy side-gigs, before publishing his first novel, *Riding High* (Scott@ridinghigh. net). He also writes nonfiction and humor columns for Manhattan weeklies: *the Villager,* and *Village Sun*. The literary review, *Gravel,* published his story, *Divorcing Rhonda,* and his (*BLR*) essay, *The Best That Love Could,* was also produced as a podcast. His critique of David Amram's book, *Upbeat,* was in *American Book Review.* Currently, like every other guy he knows with white hair, he's writing a memoir.

Alexandria Peary serves as Poet Laureate of New Hampshire. She is the author of nine books, most recently, *Battle of Silicon Valley at Daybreak.* Her work has received a 2020 Academy of American Poets Laureate Fellowship, the Iowa Poetry Prize, and Notable Essay for 2021 Best American Nonfiction. Her writing has appeared in the *Yale Review, North American Review, Southern Humanities Review, The New York Times, New American Writing,* and the *Gettysburg Review.* She specializes in mindful writing, the subject of her TEDx talk, "How Mindfulness Can Transform the Way You Write," and is editor-in-chief at *Under the Madness*

Magazine, a magazine publishing teens from around the globe.

Daniel A. Rabuzzi (he/his) has had two novels, five short stories, 30 poems, and nearly 50 essays/articles published (www.danielarabuzzi.com). A life-long birdwatcher and "tree enthusiast," he was influenced by his great-aunt, who was a research scientist at the Arnold Arboretum and then the New York Botanical Garden. He met the Wye Oak in the 1990s. He lives in New York City with his artistic partner & spouse, the woodcarver Deborah A. Mills (www.deborahmillswoodcarving.com), and the requisite cat.

Eric Sandy is a Northeast Ohio-based journalist and editor. He is a graduate of the Northeast Ohio Master of Fine Arts program with a focus in creative nonfiction.

Angela Sucich holds a Ph.D. in Medieval Literature from the University of Washington. Her poems and prose have appeared in *Nimrod International Journal, Cave Wall, River Teeth/Beautiful Things, Whale Road Review*, and elsewhere. Her chapbook, *Illuminated Creatures* (Finishing Line Press) won the 2022 New Women's Voices Chapbook Competition.

Erica Trabold is the author of *Five Plots* (Seneca Review Books, 2018), winner of the inaugural Deborah Tall Lyric Essay Book Prize and a 2019 Nebraska Book Award, and co-editor of the anthology *The Lyric Essay as Resistance* (Wayne State University Press, 2023). Her nonfiction appears in *Literary Hub, The Rumpus, Passages North, Essay Daily,* and elsewhere. She writes and teaches in central Virginia, where she is an Assistant Professor at Sweet Briar College.

A native New Yorker of Caribbean descent and recent graduate of the RWW MFA in Creative Writing, **Lynette Vialet's** writing melds medicine with cultural identity, race, gender, class, and the ineffable. Her work has appeared in *Balance, The Permanente Journal,* and was longlisted for the 2021 Fish Short Memoir Prize, alongside fellowships at Vermont Studio Center, Breadloaf Writers Conference, and completion of the Book Project at Lighthouse Writers in Denver, Colorado.

Kimberly Willardson's work has appeared in *American Short Fiction, Robert Olen Butler Prize Stories, Rosebud, The Dayton Daily News, North Carolina Folklore Journal, Nexus,* and *Ohioana Quarterly,* among other journals. She's currently at work on an essay collection about the adventures she has with Teddy, the Pet Therapy Dog. Under her other hat, she serves as editor-in-chief for *The Vincent Brothers Review* literary magazine.

Emma Williams is a writer based out of Spokane, Washington. She holds her MFA from Eastern Washington University and currently teaches English at North Idaho College.

Carolyn Williams-Noren's poems have been in *AGNI, Boxcar Poetry Review, Gigantic Sequins,* and *Sugar House Review.* Her lyric essays have been in *Willow Springs, Hobart, Water~Stone Review,* and *Tahoma Literary Review.* Past awards include a McKnight Artist Fellowship (2014) and two Minnesota State Arts Board grants. Carolyn's poems are also compiled in two chapbooks: *F L I G H T S* (2020, Ethel Zine & Press) and *Small Like a Tooth* (2015, Dancing Girl Press).

ACKNOWLEDGEMENTS

As always, a special thanks to Matthew Grewe for his keen editorial eye and invaluable judgement, and to my son, Levin, who was instrumental in getting out the word for *Rooted 2* at every literary journal we could gather.

"Pawpaw Grove" is from *The Book of Delights* by Ross Gay, copyright © 2019. Reprinted by permission of Algonquin Books, an imprint of Hachette Book Group, Inc.

"Catalpa Tree - *Catalpa Speciosa*" is from *World of Wonders: In Praise of Fireflies, Whale Sharks, And Other Astonishments*, copyright © 2020. Reprinted by permission of Milkweed Editions.

"To Grow in Spite of Poison" was originally published in *HAD* in January 2022. *https://www.havehashad.com/hadposts/to-grow-in-spite-of-poison.*

"Wild Apple," was previously published (2021) at *Terrain.org.*

"Apple Tree" was previously published in the Fall 2021 issue of *Whale Road Review (www.whaleroadreview.com).*

"The Black Spruce" originally appeared in *Alaska Magazine*'s winter 2020 special creative writing issue, and a short excerpt appeared later in *Plant Human Quarterly* (2021).

"Last One Standing" was originally published in *Plant-Human Quarterly* (2022).

"Branches" was previously published in the *Plant-Human Quarterly* Issue 4, in 2022.

"The Bees" was published in *Blue Earth Review* in Fall 2021.

"At the Edge of Her Grasp" was published in the BIPOC Solidarities Issue of the *Fiddlehead* No.290 Winter 2022.

"Comfort on the Death of the Ancient Oak" was first published in 2017 in *Willow Springs,* and it was listed in the "notables" section in *Best American Essays* in 2018.

"Hooters" was previously published in the 2022 issue of *Deep Wild Journal.*

"Faith in a Seed" was previously published by *Spire: The Maine Journal of Conservation and Sustainability,* in April 2020.

"Copper Beech" was originally published in June 2021 at *805 Lit+Art.*

"Blue Atlas" was first published in issue 5 of *Sepia,* a literary and arts journal.

Josh MacIvor-Andersen is the author of the critically acclaimed memoir *On Heights & Hunger* and editor of the anthologies *Rooted* and *Rooted 2, The Best New Arboreal Nonfiction*. His essays, reviews and reportage have won numerous national awards and nominations for the Pushcart Prize, and can be found in journals and magazines such as *The Guardian, Normal School, Gulf Coast, Paris Review Daily, Fourth Genre, Arts & Letters, Sycamore Review, Sojourners, Geez, Ruminate, Rock and Sling, National Geographic/Glimpse, Diagram, The Collagist, New Millennium Writings*, and *The Northwest Review*, among others. He lives in Marquette, MI with his family.